Java Professional Interview Guide

Master the Java skills to crack Java interviews using the latest Java features

2nd Edition

Tejaswini Mandar Jog

Mandar Maheshwar Jog

www.bpbonline.com

Second Revised and Updated Edition 2026

First Edition 2022

ISBN: 978-93-67080-929

www.bpbonline.com

Dedicated to

All aspiring Java developers striving to turn interviews into opportunities.

About the Authors

- **Tejaswini Mandar Jog** is an accomplished Java consultant and corporate trainer with nearly 15 years of experience in delivering advanced technical training. She specializes in Spring and microservices architecture, with a strong focus on building scalable, resilient, and cloud-ready enterprise applications. Over the years, she has successfully trained a wide range of professionals, from fresh graduates to experienced engineers, enabling them to adapt to modern development practices and frameworks.

  She has extensive experience working with leading global organizations, including Wipro, Accenture, and Citibank, where she has delivered customized training programs tailored to real-world business needs. Her training approach emphasizes a balance between strong fundamentals and hands-on implementation, ensuring practical applicability in enterprise environments. Currently, she is expanding her horizons in the GenAI field, where she facilitates the team to upgrade themselves on the cutting-edge AI tools and adapt them in day-to-day work.

  In addition to her training contributions, Tejaswini is a prolific author and has written several well-regarded books, including *Java 9.0 to 17.0 Cookbook*, among others. Her work reflects deep technical expertise and a commitment to simplifying complex concepts for learners and practitioners alike.

- **Mandar Maheshwar Jog** is a seasoned Java trainer with over two decades of experience in delivering high-quality technical training. His core expertise lies in Java and J2EE technologies, including Spring, Spring Boot, and Hibernate. He had consistently empowered both fresh graduates and experienced professionals with strong conceptual understanding and practical skills aligned with industry demands.

  In addition to his training engagements, Mandar is a freelance author and has authored numerous books like *Java 9.0 to 13.0 New Features* and *Java 9.0 to 17.0 Cookbook*. He also contributes as a technical reviewer for various Java-based books, ensuring accuracy, clarity, and industry relevance.

  Mandar actively participates as a key panelist in technical interview processes across multiple organizations, assessing candidates for both entry-level and experienced Java roles. Furthermore, he collaborates with academic institutions and organizations to design and enhance the computer engineering curriculum, ensuring alignment with evolving technology trends.

About the Reviewer

Abhijeet Rathod is working in the software industry since 2006, and now working as a hands-on Software Development Manager-Architect involved in the architecture, design, and implementation of microservice architecture, distributed systems, and deployment over different clouds. In his career, he has successfully delivered several projects for various product-based organizations using Agile methodology, code reviews, DevOps, and CI-CD.

Also, he is actively involved in hiring team members with different skillsets and grooming them as part of proudly leading successful teams.

To the challenges of budget, incomplete requirements, he kept focusing on having clarity on the basics of every language or technology that is required in the project.

For delivering big value in small packages, he believes to have good knowledge of OOPS, SOLID principles, and design patterns.

In addition, Abhijeet thinks one should develop an X-Ray vision to understand – *How data is flowing through various layers of application from UI to the database?*

Acknowledgements

This book is the result of a creative and collaborative journey. This would not have been accomplished without support, guidance, and inspiration from people around us. During this wonderful journey, right from thinking of the idea of writing a second edition of a book and publishing it, we were fortunate to receive support from many such individuals.

To begin with, we are thankful to the entire team of BPB Publications for their continuous support, valuable guidance, and showing the trust in our work. We would like to thank our students and friends who constantly kept us motivated by suggesting that this book is needed for everyone.

We would also like to thank our parents for their blessing, and of course, last but not least, to our lovely son Ojas, for his patience during this wonderful journey.

Preface

Similar to the earlier edition, this book is a complete digest about how you can crack a Java interview to get placed in your dream company. We strongly believe that getting successful in an interview is a result of structured and systematic preparation. Not only should you have the knowledge, but you should also know how to represent your knowledge in the interview. You need a mentor who can guide you on how to prepare for the interview. Understanding the mindset of the interviewer is the key aspect of getting successful in any interview. You should know what type of questions would be asked and how to answer them precisely. This book covers all the aspects of Java interviews that you may face in top IT companies.

The book provides you with information about the entire interview process, right from how your profile is shortlisted and how you should prepare for a non-technical interview round. Though this book does not focus much on hands-on, you will get enough interview questions on Java, J2EE, and so on. In an actual interview, the interviewer is interested in knowing whether you have sound conceptual knowledge of Java or not. This book is designed in such a way that you will get an overview of the concept, which is followed by probable interview questions on that concept.

The attempt has been made so as to cover almost all the concepts of Java till the recent version of Java, which are important for the interview. To achieve this, the book is split up into 14 different chapters. The chapters cover Java architecture, OOP, exception handling, concurrency, and important features like functional programming, design patterns, Spring Boot, and microservices as well.

Chapter 1: Preparation Beyond Technology — No matter which interview you are appearing for in terms of technology stack, representing yourself in the interview is a skill. There are definite patterns the interviewer is looking for in the personality before hiring you. This chapter explores all such areas of HR interviews. In this chapter, we have covered how to prepare yourself for the interview before the actual interview, how to analyze your interview, and some common mistakes that you should avoid in the interview. The chapter also talks about the mindset of the interviewer while conducting the interview.

Chapter 2: Architecture of Java — This chapter is dedicated to the internals of Java. Through this chapter, you will gather sound knowledge about the typical Java program execution. Moreover, this chapter covers the concepts of JRE, JDK, JVM, and JVM memory management. We have also discussed the most probable interview questions on each of these concepts of Java.

Chapter 3: Object Orientation — Understanding the object-oriented programming concept is vital to getting placed in any of the top MNCs. Object orientation is a vast topic to explain, but this chapter covers almost all the important concepts like abstraction, encapsulation, polymorphism, and inheritance. Additionally, the chapter covers the advanced concepts like record classes and sealed classes, which were launched in Java 16 and 17, respectively.

Chapter 4: Handling Exceptions — This chapter is focused on how to handle exceptions in Java. Throughout this chapter, you will learn about try, catch, finally, throw, and throws keywords along with the interview questions associated with them. The chapter also covers how to work with user-defined exceptions and updates in exception handling, which were introduced in later versions of Java.

Chapter 5: I/O and File Handling— Dealing with file handling is one of the important concepts when you deal with data. There are certain operations, like serialization and deserialization, that the developers can perform only with the help of the File I/O API. This chapter starts with the basic operations on a file, like reading and writing to the file. Gradually, the chapter discusses in detail the process of serialization and de-serialization, and also it explores all the interview questions associated with these concepts.

Chapter 6: Concurrency — The chapter covers the basics of threads to the advanced concepts like the new concurrency API of Java. In the modern era, every application needs the support of multithreading. As a result of this, multithreading forms a very important part of the interview process. This chapter explores how to work with traditional threading, which is then followed by advanced topics of multithreading. The chapter talks about the concepts and interview questions on the important topics like CompletableFuture, Flow API, virtual threads, and structured concurrency.

Chapter 7: Java Database Connectivity — This chapter is all about understanding how to persist data in the database. In this chapter, you will learn about how to connect with the underlying database and how to perform different CRUD operations in the database via a Java application. The chapter also covers the important concept of transaction management and the interview questions based on it.

Chapter 8: Collections — This chapter starts the discussion with an overview of the Collection Framework. This is followed by an in-depth discussion of the concepts like List, Set, Queue, and Map interface, along with the most probable interview questions associated with each one of these. The chapter also talks about different updates that have been launched as part of the recent versions of Java.

Chapter 9: Miscellaneous — This chapter includes a discussion on interview questions based on miscellaneous topics of Java, such as String API, Reflection API, Optional class, inner class, unit testing, etc. Additionally, the chapter also explores advanced concepts like the var keyword, Compact Number Formatting, random number generator interface, hidden class, etc.

Chapter 10: Functional Interfaces, Lambda Expressions, and Streams — Functional programming is one of the useful or complex topics of a Java interview. Understanding the functional interfaces in depth provides a solid background to work with lambdas and the stream API. This chapter provides detailed information about different types of functional interfaces and how to utilize them using lambda expressions. The chapter also covers the stream API and interview questions based on the stream API.

Chapter 11: Design Patterns — The software architectural design requires strong knowledge of design patterns. You may be tested sometimes on your skills in designing the software architecture. This chapter covers almost all the design patterns that can be considered while we design the software. The chapter explores different design pattern categories such as Creational design patterns, Structural design patterns, Behavioral design patterns, and J2EE design patterns.

Chapter 12: Spring and Spring Boot — The introduction of frameworks has made the life of the developer easy. Spring is one of those frameworks that is very famous for its flexibility. The chapter talks about the Spring Framework in detail. It covers how the Spring Framework facilitates Dependency Injection and inversion of control to ease application development. Later, the chapter also covers the Spring Boot Framework, which extends from the Spring Framework, along with the different probable interview questions.

Chapter 13: Hibernate — Hibernate is another framework that eases the database operations we execute from any application. This chapter explores the architecture of the Hibernate framework, ORM, and HQL, along with the interview questions and answers.

Chapter 14: Microservices Architecture — This chapter covers the microservices architecture concepts, which are nowadays used at large scale in the IT industry. The chapter covers concepts such as Cloud Config Server, inter-service communication, discovery servers, Load Balancers, resiliency and distributed request tracing.

Code Bundle and Coloured Images

Please follow the link to download the
Code Bundle and the ***Coloured Images*** of the book:

https://rebrand.ly/djxhnst

The code bundle for the book is also hosted on GitHub at **https://github.com/bpbpublications/Java-Professional-Interview-Guide-2nd-Edition.** In case there's an update to the code, it will be updated on the existing GitHub repository.

We have code bundles from our rich catalogue of books and videos available at **https://github.com/bpbpublications**. Check them out!

Errata

We take immense pride in our work at BPB Publications and follow best practices to ensure the accuracy of our content to provide an indulging reading experience to our subscribers. Our readers are our mirrors, and we use their inputs to reflect and improve upon human errors, if any, that may have occurred during the publishing processes involved. To let us maintain the quality and help us reach out to any readers who might be having difficulties due to any unforeseen errors, please write to us at: **errata@bpbonline.com**

Your support, suggestions and feedback are highly appreciated by the BPB Publications' Family.

Piracy

If you come across any illegal copies of our works in any form on the internet, we would be grateful if you would provide us with the location address or website name. Please contact us at business@bpbonline.com with a link to the material.

If you are interested in becoming an author

If there is a topic that you have expertise in, and you are interested in either writing or contributing to a book, please visit www.bpbonline.com. We have worked with thousands of developers and tech professionals, just like you, to help them share their insights with the global tech community. You can make a general application, apply for a specific hot topic that we are recruiting an author for, or submit your own idea.

Reviews

Please leave a review. Once you have read and used this book, why not leave a review on the site that you purchased it from? Potential readers can then see and use your unbiased opinion to make purchase decisions. We at BPB can understand what you think about our products, and our authors can see your feedback on their book. Thank you!

For more information about BPB, please visit www.bpbonline.com.

Join our Discord space

Join our Discord workspace for latest updates, offers, tech happenings around the world, new releases, and sessions with the authors:

https://discord.bpbonline.com

Table of Contents

Chapter 1
Preparation Beyond Technology

Introduction

We are pleased to inform you that you have been selected for the position of Java developer. This sentence represents the aspiration of every job seeker. Being selected by a reputed organization is one of the most rewarding outcomes of years of education and continuous learning. Most candidates set clear goals regarding the organization they wish to join and the role they aim to secure. Of course, to get selected in any company and to be part of that company, one needs to go through a rigorous interview process. The interview is not only about evaluating the technical abilities, but also about testing how the candidate responds in pressure situations. Equally important is the evaluation of interpersonal skills and the ability to collaborate as a team player, as organizations seek individuals who can contribute positively to the work environment.

This book is specifically designed to help you navigate technical interviews effectively. In the era of tools like *ChatGPT, Gemini, GitHub Copilot*, and *Claude*, expectations from job seekers have evolved significantly. Interviewers now look beyond generic or tool-generated responses; they expect precision, clarity, and depth in your answers. More importantly, you must demonstrate your own unique approach to problem-solving and decision-making while addressing technical questions. Throughout this book, we will discuss different questions on different concepts, but this chapter is something that goes beyond that. Rather, this chapter focuses on the prequel or the first round of your selection process. In this chapter, we will discuss how you can represent yourself better at interviews. By representation, the focus is not on teaching what to wear and what not to, but on sharing insight into different psychological aspects that can help to achieve success in interviews. To reiterate, technical knowledge is the top priority. After all, the role is in the psychological clinic, but in the software development company. If you know the mindset of the interviewer and if you also know what mindset you should have during the interview, that will increase your chances of getting selected for the position you are applying for.

Structure

This chapter covers the following topics:

- Types of recruitment
- Java career opportunities
- Selection process pipeline
- Choosing a career or role
- Interview readiness
- Practicing for interviews
- Interview mistakes to avoid
- Key areas interviewers evaluate
- Mantras to succeed in an interview

Objectives

By the end of this chapter, readers will gain a clear understanding of how to prepare for interviews from a non-technical perspective. The chapter explores various types of recruitment, outlines Java-related career opportunities, and explains the end-to-end selection pipeline. It also helps readers evaluate and choose the right career path or role, assess their current level of preparedness, and adopt effective interview practice strategies. In addition, the chapter highlights common interview mistakes to avoid and provides insight into the criteria and analysis interviewers typically use when evaluating candidates.

Types of recruitment

It is important for a job seeker to understand the sources from which companies conduct recruitment. Organizations follow specific recruitment channels to identify and hire the best talent they require. Recruitment may take place during college or university programs, or after the completion of graduation. In general, two major types of recruitment processes are commonly followed. Depending on this, you have to prepare yourself for the interviews, as different preparation might be required for different types of recruitment.

On-campus recruitment

This is the easiest way to get selected in an organization. Normally, company representatives visit some good colleges and conduct the interview when you are in your final year of graduation. Such interviews are typically based on your aptitude and knowledge of C and C++ programming skills. Typically, these tests are based on data structure-related questions. Today, such questions are language-independent. This means you can choose any programming language to solve the problem statement given to you. To get shortlisted in an on-campus recruitment process, you need to maintain a good track record in your curriculum. Furthermore, your performance in the aptitude and technical tests is ranked, which will be followed by a personal interview.

Off-campus recruitment

If you are not selected via the on-campus recruitment process, it is not the end of the world. You still have many options available through the off-campus recruitment process. Here, companies will publish advertisements in the newspapers or job portals like *naukri.com*, *indeed.com*, or sometimes on their websites. You can apply as per the company norms, and if your profile fits the criteria, you will be invited for the interview process. Sometimes, there will also be walk-ins where you can see thousands of job seekers waiting in a queue for their turn. Off-campus recruitment will also have similar rounds like on-campus interviews, but often, it is observed that off-campus recruitment is technically tougher than an on-campus interview.

Java career opportunities

The IT world is huge. What we see from the outside is just the tip of the iceberg. If we need to discuss the different career opportunities in IT, then probably, one needs to write a separate blog or book to cover it thoroughly. The jobs are categorized according to domain, language, and many other factors. In this chapter, we will concentrate only on the job roles that are aligned with Java technology. In the following sections, we will be discussing the different job roles one can expect as a Java developer.

Java full-stack developer

This might be one of the most challenging job roles you will come across in the IT industry in the present day. A full-stack developer is a developer who not only develops applications but also designs the **user interface** (**UI**) and tests it. This means that you should have knowledge of programming, UI designing, like HTML, CSS, jQuery, Bootstrap, or any of the JavaScript frameworks like Angular, React, Vue, and NextJS, and testing to apply for this position.

Java web developer

To become a Java web developer, you should know the overall architecture of the web application. Your job would mostly consist of generating the responses for the requests that are generated from the UI. You must have some knowledge of HTML, and along with that, you should know Servlet and **Java Server Pages** (**JSP**). You should also have a detailed knowledge of how the HTTP protocol works internally. Though the technology of the web has evolved beyond Servlet and JSP, unless you know these two technologies, you will find yourself in a difficult position to learn other technologies.

Java mobile app developer

This is one of the most rapidly growing fields nowadays. You talk about any business, and then you immediately think about the mobile app for that business. There are different frameworks for mobile application development, but, as far as Java is concerned, you should learn Android if you would like to make a career as an app developer.

Java EE developer

Enterprise developers take care of large-scale application development. Unlike normal web applications, these applications have a lot of features like logging, messaging, and web services. These applications may be web applications or normal applications, but they need to be more scalable, maintainable, and flexible. The technologies that form such applications are **Enterprise Java Beans** (**EJB**), Spring, Hibernate, **Representational State Transfer** (**REST**), etc.

Java API developer

The evolution of REST has really made a shift in the way applications are created. Instead of creating everything as an application developer, you can now just utilize the services created by an **application programming interface** (**API**) developer. As an API developer, you can create an API to update the database, respond to a request, consume data, etc. The major technology you can use as part of API development is Spring Boot. Spring Boot is built on top of the Spring Framework, which is completely written in Java. This framework is constantly updating its services with updates in Java.

Selection process pipeline

The selection process in IT companies is often rigorous, requiring candidates to clear several rounds before being selected for a vacant position. The stakeholders are always focused on ensuring that the right person is selected for the right role. During the selection process, candidates typically go through several evaluation stages. Each round is designed to assess different skills and competencies. These may include technical expertise, problem-solving ability, and communication skills. Together, these rounds help organizations identify the most suitable candidate for the role.

Telephonic interview

Good morning!! This is Stella from Google Incorporated. Am I talking with George? This is what you can expect on early morning weekdays if you have applied for a position at Google Inc. Telephonic interviews are one of the most elementary interview rounds that follow after you apply for a particular position. If your educational qualifications, skill sets, and experience (if you are applying for higher positions) match organizational expectations, someone from the HR team will connect with you. Sometimes, the interview will be a surprise interview, which is very rare, though. Many times, the HR team member will block your calendar for a telephonic interview round.

Telephonic interviews are best suited for the interviewee because they give you the flexibility to attend the call from anywhere. However, you have to ensure that the place you choose is free of any disturbance and does not have any network issues. A telephonic interview is almost similar to a face-to-face interview; the only difference is that you are not sitting in front of the panel physically. That does not mean there is no panel at the other end, virtually. Sometimes, you might expect that a project manager is going to call you for an interview, and during the process, there are some other people also getting involved in the call. This is now an era of technology. Thus, be wise enough to use different tools available, like *Skype, Zoom, Google Meet,* and *Teams,* which are now preferred ways to conduct interviews rather than normal conference calls.

Technical tests

If you are through with the phone screening, the next round of the interview will be a technical test. Technical tests can be of two types:

- **Multiple-choice question** (MCQ) test
- Algorithm-based test

It is not always the case that both these tests are conducted. Mostly, MCQ tests are conducted when you are applying for an on-campus recruitment process, that is, when you are applying from your college or university. When companies are scrutinizing thousands of candidates, they want to be absolutely sure that only the eligible candidates will advance to the personal interview round. This filtering process is very important because the senior persons conducting the interviews should not waste their valuable time interviewing candidates who are not up to the mark. Ultimately, these seniors are key persons in the projects, and they need to invest their time in more productive work.

Normally, an MCQ test is divided into two segments, an aptitude test and a technical test. The aptitude test segment is based on mathematical skills. The technical segment will consist of questions based on C, C++, SQL, and sometimes even on Java. Our focus in this book is not C or C++. We will be concentrating more on the interview questions based on Java. As this round is one of the selection parameters for getting selected for a personal or face-to-face interview, it is better that you practice these tests. Remember that aptitude is not an overnight success; you need to live with it. You need to make it a daily practice to be an expert in solving the questions. As a computer engineering student, your core strength is probably in programming and not in aptitude. This might be one of the bottlenecks in your selection process. A common question raised by students is the relevance of aptitude in a programming role and why proficiency in Java alone is not considered sufficient when applying for a Java programmer position. Is it only the process of rejection as companies want to reduce the numbers for actual interviews?

If you observe this from 15,000 feet above the ground, you may be correct, but in truth, your aptitude skill is mapped with your problem-solving abilities. It is an indication of how your brain quickly reacts to different scenarios of business in day-to-day life.

Solving technical MCQs will be a little bit simpler as it is based on something that you have been doing for years; after all, you have invested a few years of your graduation to learn the programming languages. This should be your home ground where you can score freely. However, sometimes, designing the problem solutions through code and solving MCQs could be a different perspective. Thus, the more concepts you read and the more programs you practice, the better position you will be in to solve such MCQs.

Face-to-face interview

Congratulations!! You have cleared your technical test, and we are glad to invite you for a face-to-face interview on <date> at <time> IST. You should be proud of yourself if you get this email from the employer. Sometimes, it may happen that the technical test and the **face-to-face (F2F)** interview happen on the same day. In the morning slot before lunch break, you might need to take up your technical test, and followed by that, post-lunch, you might get your chance to appear in front of a panel for an F2F round.

F2F is the most difficult aspect of your selection. You will not only be scrutinized for your technical knowledge, but there will also be some questions that will be mapped with your behavioral skills. Most of the time, an interview will be conducted by a panel, which will comprise technical evaluators as well as some HR representatives. The technical person could be your next manager with whom you will be working. He will be testing you on how good you technically are to be part of the upcoming or ongoing project under his leadership, and the HR person will be monitoring your behavioral skills, which consist of your communication skills.

Though the views of the HR representative are important, it is more crucial to ensure that you address the technical manager's questions thoroughly and satisfactorily. Ultimately, it will be their decision that will carry more weight when it comes to a selection or rejection. They will be responsible for the successful delivery of a project, and have full authority to choose the right person to perform the job effectively. Throughout this book, you will encounter a variety of questions that may be asked in a technical interview. It is very important to know what kind of questions will be asked during this round. Of course, there is no thumb rule about it; however, based on the author's experience, there are a few points that could be noted. One of the possibilities is that the interview will start on the basis of your performance on technical tests. If the technical test that you just cleared was about some algorithm implementation, then the interviewer will be interested in understanding the logic behind it. At times, the interviewer will ask you to change the algorithm on the fly to check how flexible you are and how quickly you can take up the challenge. Remember, it is not important at this point whether you complete the entire algorithm, but what is more important is your approach towards problem-solving. Interviewers are always masters in technology, even if you climb the first few steps of the ladder, they can assess how quickly and effectively you will reach the top using the same approach. Therefore, do not worry about that end result, and try to emphasize the process of solving the problem statement, if asked. Such solutions are always expected to be produced on white paper or a whiteboard. Writing on paper can be troublesome sometimes if you do not have practice. These days, we are so fond of systems that we tend to forget the use of paper and pencil. Think back to the last time you wrote a program on paper, and you will realize that it might have been a long time ago. So, make a practice of writing clean and tidy code snippets on paper.

The next few questions will be based on the different concepts that the interviewer is interested in. You need to apply a thought process to guess which topics would be more important for which organizations or projects. For instance, if you are applying for a position in an organization that works in stock trading, then concurrency becomes the most important concept. If you are applying to an organization that works predominantly in online shopping, then database transactions could be more important. Of course, all these are wild guesses. You might expect a few shocks from the interviewer in an actual interview, but then, you do not prepare for every shock in advance, as there is no concrete way to do so. What you can do is anticipate them and be mentally prepared to handle them.

Another important point to understand is that it is not a mistake if you do not know a particular concept or answer. However, it becomes a concern if you consistently lack fundamental knowledge. Of course, this is said in a light sense. A candidate is expected to possess at least the basic competence and preparation before appearing for an interview. Often, an interviewee panics about what will happen if they do not know something, and if it is okay to say, *I do not know this*. It is absolutely fine. You may not be an expert in everything. Ultimately, it is teamwork, where collective intelligence will matter significantly. Therefore, if you are an expert in something, another team member may be an expert in something else. Collectively, as a team, you will be able to solve a problem. So if you do not know something, accept it with grace and convey it politely to the interviewer.

This is likely the last hurdle before you are selected for the role you have applied for. The word *likely* was used because sometimes the interview process could be so stiff that even if you cleared all three rounds, that is, the telephonic round, technical tests, and F2F interview, there could still be another round where you might need to deal with the HR manager. The round with the HR manager is normally to discuss your salary scale and other terms and conditions. Typically, this happens immediately after your technical round, provided you have cleared it.

Choosing a career or role

Passion drives success. If you are passionate about something, you naturally find ways to succeed in it. Your career is not a short-term game; it is something you will live with throughout your life. If you calculate the number of productive hours in a day that you invest in your job, it turns out to be almost two-thirds of your entire day's time. Someone might argue by claiming that sleep is the most productive work because that is where the dreams are generated from.

Let us talk about a time span when you are awake., Now, I am sure that most of you will agree about the fact that most of the time you have will be investing in your job. So, before you apply for a job, make sure that it aligns with your passion. Otherwise, you may find yourself feeling resentful after a few years. It will be difficult for you to shift the job role after 4–5 years. So, before you apply, check if the job description suits you. For example, if you are fascinated about how the UI is developed for an application, you are likely someone who loves to do the UI designing job; but if you are keen to know how the dashboard is filled with different posts on *Twitter*, you are a developer who loves coding. Sometimes, you might be more inclined toward the database designing approach. Thus, knowing yourself is one of the most critical parts of the interview process.

Interview readiness

Whether you are a fresh graduate from a reputed university or an experienced professional seeking a change, thorough preparation is essential. Preparing well must be organized and should cover everything that is going to be a part of the interview, right from applying for the job. The first action you should take once you come across the advertisement in a local newspaper or website that suits your qualifications is to send your resume or CV to the concerned HR representative. Hold on there, is it a resume or a CV?

One of the important things to understand when you apply to any of the positions is what documents you need to submit: should it be a CV or a resume? Most interviewees do not know the actual difference between these two, so let us get this clear first. CV is *Curriculum Vitae*. It is a representation of your journey as part of your graduation. Such a document contains information that is more focused on your achievements in universities, your final year projects, and any publications, etc., you have achieved during your graduation. On the other hand, a resume is a document about how you have resumed your career to date. A resume normally describes your experience, your roles, and achievements during your earlier job, and if you have done any professional certification during this period. Therefore, if you are applying as a fresher, you will be sharing your CV, whereas if you are an experienced professional, you would submit a resume.

Once you share your resume or CV, you can expect an interview call or an online test according to the policy of the HR department. You will get this intimation via a phone call or an email. However, do not wait passively for a call. Think positively and assume that you will be invited for an interview for all the jobs that you have applied for. The main reason for this is that you might not get enough time for preparation after the invitation. Some companies will call you on a Tuesday evening and expect you to be in front of the interview panel on a Wednesday morning. That is when continuous preparation will help you. Always be in the first gear, so that you can drive your career forward quickly. Keep revising all the concepts regularly to stay sharp. Test your knowledge frequently, either with your friends, or through online portals. Do this consistently, even if you are not attending any interview immediately.

Practicing for interviews

Practicing for an interview is undoubtedly a challenging task, but how exactly should you go about it? Even if you are technically strong and confident, how can you be sure that you are truly ready? Are there any agencies that prepare you for interviews? There are not. Even if there are, they are in very small numbers. This makes practicing for an interview a tough job. Despite that, you can do so in three different ways:

- **By attending real interviews**: It is often said in sports that *no matter how well you practice in the nets, your real ability will be tested when you play actual match under pressure*. The same holds true in the case of the interview process as well. You may be technically sound, or feel that you will perform confidently in interviews, but reality can be different, so go and play a match to test yourself and practice in a real match. Attend more interviews. You will feel nervous in the first couple of interviews. After that, you will gain confidence and begin to understand the mindset of interviewers. You will, in fact, be able to gauge how the interview is progressing and assess your chances of selection. As a seasoned interviewee, you can then improve your strategies and increase your likelihood of success.
- **By creating mock interviews**: As a common saying goes, *a friend in need is a friend indeed*. Preparing for interviews can be made easier by creating mock interview sessions. You can form a group of friends and compile a set of hundreds of potential interview questions. Post that, you can literally attend the interview, which will be conducted by your friend (make sure that you forget that they are your friend and treat them as a *would be* manager of yours). Such practices will certainly create more comfort for you to face the actual interview.
- **By collecting feedback post-interview**: Every interview panel maintains a performance sheet of the interviewee, which they submit to the HR department. If you are notified that you are not selected for the desired position, you may politely request feedback on your interview. Many a time, this may be interpreted as rude behavior or challenging the decision, as the person at the opposite end might feel that you are asking for proof about why you are rejected. Still, if you politely relay to the HR division that such feedback will help you improve yourself in upcoming interviews, they are likely to assist you. Remember, your interactions with HR from day one of your connection matter here. If you have already created some positive relationships with HR through emails and professional communication, HR will be more inclined to help you by providing constructive feedback about your interview.

Interview mistakes to avoid

Mistakes are inevitable. After all, you are graduates in technology and not in the art of facing interviews. It is likely that after reading this book, you will master how to face an interview, but for now, you are a beginner. Mistakes do happen. You will stumble upon difficult questions, but the interviewers know that you are a fresher and take that into consideration. Even *Mike Tyson* had countless punches on his face in his early days; he fell but stood up and kept hitting back. That said, and as has already been mentioned, you should try to avoid mistakes as early as possible. Let us now list out some of the common mistakes.

Complex and confused answers

Often, when you are facing the interviewer, you are stressed. Due to this stress, you might get confused while forming the sentences. While the interviewer at times will try to understand what you want to say, there are times when they might not be in the best frame of mind to interpret your response. Therefore, keep it simple. As far as possible, form simple and short sentences to elaborate your answers.

Losing calmness

Getting stressed at the time of an interview is not uncommon. In fact, psychologists say that it is good to have some stress at interviews as it keeps you alert and focused. However, it is equally important that you learn how to manage and overcome that stress. Such stressful situations may push you to a stage where your brain feels blocked, where you will not remember what you have prepared. Make sure that you find out how to control your stress to perform better in an interview. Such a stage might put you into a situation where you might start arguing with the interviewer. This may create a negative impression. Conflicts or confrontations during an interview signal a lack of professionalism and emotional control, which significantly reduces your chances of being selected. Maintaining composure, even in challenging situations, demonstrates maturity, confidence, and ability to handle the pressure-qualities that interviewers highly value.

Giving rote-learned answers

Mugged answers can probably help you to clear the MCQ test, but they will not carry you through a face-to-face interview. Remember that the interviewers are masters of technology, and they have years of experience to bring to the table. They do not expect someone to merely recite textbook definitions, if they cannot explain what the concept truly means. Instead, try to find out different scenarios in which you can use the concept. Though the theoretical foundation remains the same, the real-time examples could be your own and make your explanation more effective.

Trying to be heroic at an interview

Never try to be overly smart at an interview. You might make an attempt in an interview by providing additional information when it is not required. Such additional information may put you in trouble if you do not have a strong understanding of what you are mentioning. Unnecessary details may invite follow-up questions that can expose gaps in your knowledge.

Moreover, this might go against you when the panel is judging you as a professional. Interviewers value clarity, honesty, and self-awareness more than showmanship. Be authentic in your responses and speak only about what you truly know. Be yourself. You must prove what you can do rather than only giving an illusion about what you can do.

Using chatbots in interview

While the evolution of chatbots makes the process of learning easier, using such chatbots in the interviews may not be the right approach. One of the challenges of using the chatbot in a live interview is the *distraction*. It may not be easier for typing or even observing the answers generated by the chatbot while the interviewer is assessing your knowledge through video conferencing. Moreover, using chatbots during technical interviews undermines the authenticity of a candidate's demonstrated skills, as interviews are meant to assess real-time problem-solving rather than assisted or pre-generated answers. Such reliance can mask gaps in fundamental concepts that are critical for on-the-job performance and prevents interviewers from accurately evaluating a candidate's depth of understanding, reasoning process, and decision-making ability. Candidates who use chatbots during technical interviews often get caught through a combination of behavioral, technical, and situational signals. Their answers may sound overly polished or generic, yet they struggle to explain *why* a solution works or to modify it when the interviewer introduces a small change or edge case. There is often a noticeable delay before responding, especially for follow-up questions, which suggests external assistance.

Key areas interviewers evaluate

As an interviewee, you know that you will be evaluated on your technical skills, communication skills, and behavioral skills. However, merely knowing this is insufficient. It is equally important to understand what exactly gets reflected in your performance sheet, which is the document based on which the final decision of selection or rejection is made. *What is the interviewer actually trying to assess through your answers?* Though there are many aspects on which an interviewer is assessing you, this section highlights some of the most basic and generic evaluation factors the interviewers commonly rely on. Understanding these will help you structure your responses more effectively, present your strengths with clarity, and significantly improve your overall interview performance.

Job readiness

This is a fundamental evaluation to be done by the interviewer. To perform this, interviewers primarily focus on the questions related to your skill sets and the depth of knowledge you possess in each of those. These questions will not only help them to understand your technical strength but also how well you understand and apply that knowledge in real-world scenarios. Your behavioral skills are always secondary requirements, so the interviewer will invest most of the time in exploring your technical competencies and problem-solving abilities. These questions typically revolve around the projects that you have worked on, the challenges that you have encountered, and the approaches that you followed to overcome them. Sometimes, the interviewer may not be keen on the end result that you achieved, or you did not achieve, but the effort that you put in and the lessons that you learned from the journey.

Maintaining professional boundaries

No organization would like to have a resource who tries to break or challenge the established boundaries of the organization. Every organization has its own set of rules and style of working. This involves following a hierarchy while escalating the issues, or knowing how to connect with immediate managers or bosses. The interviewers are normally aware of these parameters of companies, which may impact the working culture of the organization if not followed by an individual. As a result, you can expect a couple of questions designed to evaluate your adaptability, respect for organizational structure, and ability to function effectively within the defined system. These questions help interviewers determine whether you will contribute positively to the organization's culture while still maintaining professionalism and accountability.

Being highly motivated

Motivation is the key to success. A motivated person always finds a way to get the job done rather than finding reasons why it cannot be done. An interviewer is always keen to know if you are driven enough about the position you are applying for. You might get a question like *Why are you applying for this position?* or *What makes you feel this job is made for you?* Get ready to answer such questions as they are mapped to your interest in the job that you are applying.

Ability to quickly learn new tools and technologies

Sometimes, the job role that you are applying for might require additional knowledge beyond your current skill set. In such a case, ensure that your answers convey a willingness to learn new skills, even if you lack a few. This helps justify your suitability for the role you are being hired and paid for. It is not only important to have an interest in learning, but you should also emphasize that you are someone who is quick to learn. Organizations today do not have a prolonged waiting period for your progress. In fact, even though most organizations have a **learning and development** (**L&D**) department that takes care of all the training needs of their employees, the time allocated for such training is really brief. For example, in your graduation, you might have invested 100 hours in a course to learn Java, but in an organization, the same or more advanced content of Java will be taught to you in 20 to 30 hours maximum, and your manager would still expect you to be an expert in Java.

Fitting into team culture

Creating a software is inherently a team-driven activity. You will not work in isolation, sitting in a cubicle for months and building an entire system on your own. Modern software products are divided into multiple modules, each handled by different roles and individuals with varied experience.

Effective communication among team members is one of the most critical factors in delivering a high-quality product. Regular discussions, design reviews, and feedback loops help to ensure alignment and reduce errors. It is because of this that interviewers are keen to assess your interpersonal skills. They want to understand how well you communicate, collaborate, and adapt while working with others.

Additionally, conflicts are inevitable in team environments. Interviewers look for candidates who can handle disagreements professionally, resolve issues constructively, and maintain healthy working relationships with their teammates.

Mantras to succeed in an interview

To be successful in interviews, it is important to follow certain rules and guidelines. While you may be facing your first interview on a particular day, the interviewer might have been busy all day interviewing a number of interviewees. Thus, you should make every attempt to make sure that the interviewer is satisfied with your performance.

Your goal should be to ensure that the interviewer feels confident about your skills, attitude, and overall suitability for the role. Preparation, clarity of thought, and professional behavior play a crucial role in achieving this.

Outlined in this section are some of the key mantras that can help you succeed in an interview.

Answer the questions correctly and in your own words

Preparing for an interview is an art. When you get a schedule for your interview, you often choose to practice for questions that could be asked in an interview. Of course, this is not a wrong approach at all, but while doing so, there might be one threat. Many a time, when you are over-prepared for an interview, you come up with memorized answers to questions. Remember, the interviewer is an expert. They can always figure out from the answers if the answers are mugged from some books. Therefore, as you practice for the questions, try to frame the answers in your own words. Additionally, listen to the question properly. Do not create the answers even before the question is completed by the interviewer.

Body language matters

Apart from technical competence, the way you present yourself does matter. While this seems to be a secondary aspect, it often leaves a strong impression on the interviewer. The way you sit and the way you speak will have an impact on the interviewer. The interviewer might get distracted by your body gestures (nail biting, tapping, scratching, etc.) and miss some of the content of your answers, something that you should try to avoid. As far as possible, try to add a warm smile while speaking. Some candidates feel that adding a smile might give an impression of overconfidence, but it is not. Moreover, it is not entirely wrong if some nervousness shows on your face. Interviewers understand that giving an interview is not as simple as playing a game. It is sometimes interpreted as your being serious about the interview or job.

Research about the company

This may seem obvious, but it is extremely important. If you are applying to a company, then you must know what the company's working area is. Be aware of the core business areas, key products, and related services of the company. It is even better to know about the stakeholders or the board of directors of the company from the public domain. You might not get a chance to interact with them directly in your interview process, but knowing such details might help you prepare better, as in a few companies, directors have an important role to play in selecting the fresher, though from behind the scenes. Sometimes, you might get one of the panelists in the interview panel who would like to know, *What do you know about our company?* Being well-prepared for this question not only demonstrates your seriousness and interest in the role but also reflects your professionalism and readiness to join the organization.

Check your skills

Skills are one of the most important parameters for your selection. It is essential to ensure that you have the required skills for the job you are interviewing for. For example, if you are applying for the full-stack developer role, you are expected to have competencies across UI designing, database, and programming. You will be shortlisted for the interview only when these skills are mentioned in your CV or resume. A few companies have a system where they will check your skills through assignments or online tests as a preliminary round. It is always advisable to revise the required skills before attending the interview. Sometimes, it is also more beneficial to have some domain knowledge in which the company is working. For example, when applying to financial institutions such as *Citi* or *JPMorgan*, interviewers often evaluate how well your technical expertise aligns with finance, or trading-related concepts. This ability to connect technology with domain knowledge can significantly enhance your overall impression and interview performance.

Understand the job description

You probably know the famous quote, *Time is money*. When you attend the interview, you are investing not only your time but also the time of the interviewer. Thus, it is important to ensure that you know about the position, role, and responsibilities of the job for which you are giving the interview. While it is not always possible to know everything about the job role, make every attempt to understand the details as you can. You may talk to the HR or the recruiting agency about it, to get more information about the same. If you realize that the role does not align with your skills or career goals, it is better to step back rather than proceed half-prepared. This saves time for both you and the interviewer. Remember, opportunities are plenty; choose the ones that truly suit you and allow you to perform at your best.

Relationship between your personality and job role

You might wonder what your personality has to do with the job of a developer. After all, you are going to work in a system in an isolated cubicle. That is the case most of the time. However, there are some job roles where you need to be a part of a team, which requires strong collaboration. Especially in organizations that follow the Agile approach, developers are expected to be vocal and actively participate in team discussions. Having the confidence to speak up during daily stand-up meetings helps identify issues early and ultimately improves the quality of the software being developed by you and your organization. If an interviewer feels that a candidate may struggle to blend into a team or is not proactive in sharing ideas, it can reduce the chances of selection. While being highly extroverted is not a strict requirement, effective communication, collaboration, and the willingness to express one's views are critical qualities for today's software development roles.

Your expectations matter

Your expectations are closely linked with your performance. When your expectations are aligned with the policies of the organization, you are more likely to perform consistently and remain motivated. The top management is always aware of the horizontal or vertical growth in terms of the position, or even in terms of hikes in the organization. Therefore, during an interview, you might be asked, *Where would you like to see yourself down the line 5 years from now?* The answer to such a question will always make your expectations clear to employers, and they will understand whether you will be satisfied within the organization with the set policies of the organization or not.

As a fresher, dealing with this question is tricky, but the employer will always prefer someone who is going to play a vital role in the organization's growth, someone who is keen on taking ownership of the assigned task. Therefore, when framing your answer, make sure it highlights your willingness to contribute, your commitment to continuous improvement, and your intent to grow along with the organization.

You have to be flexible

Being affirmative is sometimes good. Although, in the real-time world, situations are always dynamic and unpredictable. While you may have your life principles to which you can stick, work cultures are not the same. They change drastically across organizations. An employer might expect you to be flexible in terms of working hours, technologies, or even policies that you have been using for some time. During the interview, you are likely to face questions to assess your flexibility and how open you are to shifting from traditional strategies depending on the situation. Demonstrating openness to change and the ability to adjust based on circumstances is a key trait that employers value in today's fast-evolving work environments.

You have to be proactive

Proactiveness is valuable, but it should never come at the cost of organizational policies. Managers expect team members to operate within the boundaries defined by the organization. At the same time, they value individuals who can take ownership and make decisions within their scope of responsibility. You should act proactively in situations that can be handled at your level without unnecessary escalation. Being decisive, responsible, and solution-oriented reflects maturity. Ultimately, a go-getter attitude, combined with respect for processes, helps get work done efficiently and builds trust with management.

Know your resume or CV

A resume or CV is the first impression that you create about yourself. You get shortlisted based on how effective your resume or CV is. However, that does not mean that you decorate your resume with the skills that you do not possess. While the immediate goal is to reach the interview stage, the real objective is to get selected. Ask yourself: *is merely attending an interview enough, or is securing the job what truly matters?* If you are a fresher, not only your skillset but also your hobbies and academic projects are counted in the interviews. Ensure that you know your resume. You should know what all things are mentioned in your resume. If you are unable to explain or justify the points mentioned in the resume, then the interviewer might get a feeling of cheating. No organization will be interested in hiring someone who appears to be dishonest -intentionally or otherwise. Honesty and clarity in your resume or CV build trust and significantly improve your chances of selection.

You should be trustworthy and a good team player

Once you clear the technical interview rounds, the final stage typically focuses on evaluating how well you would fit within the organization as a team member. Interviewers assess whether you can integrate smoothly with existing teams and collaborate effectively. At this stage, the emphasis shifts from technical expertise to understanding your interpersonal skills, attitude, and ability to work harmoniously with others. They want to determine how well you function as a professional and as a team player within the organizational environment.

Conclusion

In this chapter, we discussed how you should prepare for the interviews. Now, you know the key points that you should take into consideration while appearing for an interview. You also studied what the mindset of an interviewer might be, and what the interviewer wants to see in you sitting across the other side of the table. We also talked about the common mistakes that you will make and how that will affect your selection. We had a walkthrough of the different rounds that you will go through in the entire selection process. This was a relatively non-technical and behavioral study of an interview. Further chapters are more focused on technology. In the next chapter, we will be discussing in detail the architecture of Java and interview preparation that you can do for the same.

CHAPTER 2
Architecture of Java

Introduction

Developers are savants. They have a lot of knowledge about the domain, algorithms, and also how to combine them to create an efficient application. Writing code and compiling it is an idiomatic task. Once compiled, this program is executed on the underlying systems. That is where the developers get stuck. Developers are normally unaware of the internal workings of operating systems. This might not impact the way of writing a program much, but sometimes that may lead to very unpleasant surprises. These surprises often surface as performance bottlenecks, resource starvation, unexpected deadlocks, or scalability issues in production environments. A lack of understanding of concepts such as process scheduling, memory management, I/O handling, and threading models can cause applications to behave unpredictably under load. What works perfectly in a local setup may fail miserably when deployed on real systems. Hence, bridging the gap between application logic and operating system fundamentals becomes crucial for building robust, reliable, and high-performance software.

Structure

We will be covering interview questions based on the following topics in this chapter:

- Java program execution flow
- Key files in Java
- Java Runtime Environment
- Java Virtual Machine
- JIT compiler

Objectives

Compiling and executing a Java program involves a few simple commands, but the underlying process is far more intricate and deserves careful attention. This chapter adopts a gradual approach to how one writes a Java program, compiles it, and executes it. During the discussion of all these concepts, we will also discuss common interview questions related to each stage of the process that you might face while attempting your interview.

Java program execution flow

Writing a Java program, compiling, and executing it is a day-to-day task for you. However, you need to ensure that you understand every bit of it, especially from an architectural and interview perspective. Each of these concepts that appear simple on the surface often involves important internal mechanisms that are frequently explored in technical interviews. Let us discuss all these concepts in more depth, along with the interview questions.

Could you explain the execution flow of a Java program?

The most basic thing you need to understand is how a Java program gets executed. *Figure 2.1* gives a pictorial representation of how that happens:

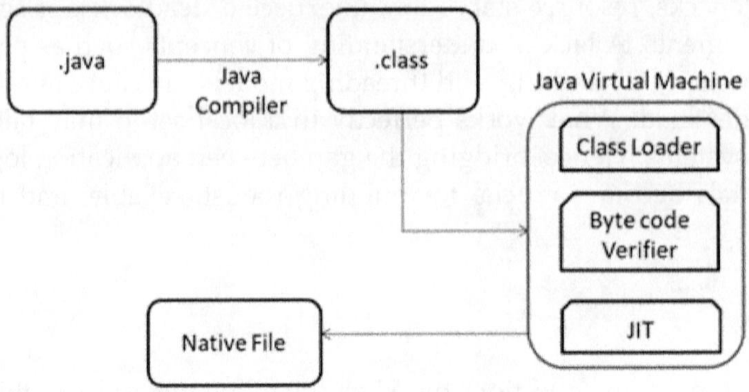

***Figure 2.1**: Java program execution flow*

As we observe, the **`.java`** file, which is a source file, is provided to a compiler. The compiler compiles the file and converts it to a bytecode file **`.class`**, which is a platform-independent file. This file is then passed to **Java Virtual Machine** (JVM), which takes the responsibility of executing it.

Key files in Java

While developing Java applications, you encounter various types of files at different stages of development. As a developer, you must be aware of all these files, understand their roles, and know how they interact within the Java ecosystem.

What are the different types of files and their significance in Java programming?

When developers write application code, they normally write code in a human-readable file, which gets transformed into a machine-compatible file that the system can execute. As a developer, it is essential to understand these key files and the transformation they undergo.

Source code file

This file is written by a Java developer with the extension **`.java`**. This is normally a program written in a high-level programming language. The following code snippet will give you an idea of what the basic structure of such files looks like:

```
class Sample{
    int x;
    //other data members
    public void method1(){
    }
    //other member functions
}
```

Bytecode file

Before Java converts the high-level code to a native compatible executable, it first compiles the code into bytecode, which is platform-independent. This file has the extension **`.class`** and is termed a class file that can be executed by JVM. Though the interviewer does not expect you to read or interpret this class file, it is beneficial to have a look at the snippet of the class file that gets created after compilation.

Why is Java termed a platform-neutral or independent language?

Traditional programming languages generate platform-dependent files after compilation to execute the program. For instance, the C programming language, if compiled on Windows, generates the **`.exe`** file, which is compatible only with the Windows platform. This means that the file is not portable. In contrast, Java generates the class file after compilation, which is platform-neutral. You can load this file on any system that has a compatible JVM, and the corresponding JVM will take care to generate the native file to execute.

Java Runtime Environment

One of the most common terminologies you come across while discussing Java is **Java Runtime Environment** (JRE). Though it is common, many of the developers are not fully aware of the internal workings of JRE. An interviewer might have some tricky questions on JRE, which you might be unaware of.

What is the role of JRE?

JRE is essentially a program that interacts with the class file provided to it. A runtime environment is typically a kind of physical operating system on which the software runs traditionally. JRE is software that runs on top of an underlying operating system. The main reason why JRE plays a vital role in the entire Java lifecycle is that it abstracts the underlying operating system from the programmer. As a result, the developers do not need to modify the code or the process of execution depending on the operating system. When you instruct Java to execute the program, the JRE accepts your code, resolves and loads the different dependencies via a Java class loader, and passes the prepared bytecode to JVM for execution.

What are the components of JRE?

JRE comprises the following three components:

- Class loader
- Bytecode verifier
- Interpreter

What role does a class loader play?

Java applications are inherently complex by design. They contain different classes, which are related to each other. Most of the classes use the services of other classes. In other words, they are dependent on some other classes. Thus, in order to make sure that a class compiles or executes, the class must find the classes on which it depends. The class loader takes the responsibility of searching and loading such classes in memory. These classes are not loaded at once in memory by the class loader; it is done on a demand basis.

What are the different types of class loaders?

There are different class loaders available in JRE, depending on where they load the classes dynamically. These are:

- **Bootstrap ClassLoader**: The monolithic version of JRE has a jar file **`rt.jar`**, which is a repository of all the system or internal classes in Java. This jar file is present in the lib directory of JRE. The **bootstrap class loader** is responsible for loading the internal classes that are present inside this jar file. Additionally, the bootstrap class loader also acts as a parent for other class loaders, and somebody needs to take responsibility to initialize them. Thus, it is also termed the **primordial class loader** of Java.
- **Extension ClassLoader**: The **extension class loader** is termed a child of the bootstrap class loader. The external classes in JRE are present in the **`jre/lib/ext`** directory. The extension class loader loads the classes from this directory if the classes are not loaded by the bootstrap class loader.

Note: **You may expect a version-specific question about the class loaders. Note that, Java9 onwards, the Extension ClassLoader is removed. With the introduction of the Java Platform Module System, the Extension ClassLoader is replaced by the Platform ClassLoader.**

What is System or Application ClassLoader?

This class loader is the child of the Extension ClassLoader. Generally, a developer sets up the class path to search the classes for an application. The **System ClassLoader** loads the classes from the class path.

If you are keen to know which class loader is utilized to load the required classes, you can use the **`getClassloader()`** method of that class as shown in the following code snippet:

```
import java.util.Date;
class CheckClassLoader{
  public static void main(String[] args){
 System.out.println(CheckClassLoader.class.getClassLoader());
 System.out.println(Date.class.getClassLoader());
  }
}
```

The following figure shows the output for the code snippet:

Figure 2.2: *Working with the class loader*

As you can observe, the `CheckClassLoader` class is loaded from `AppClassLoader`, and for the `Date` class, you are getting the output as `null`. This `null` represents that the class is loaded by the Bootstrap ClassLoader. The output `null` from the bootstrap class loader is generated because the Bootstrap ClassLoader is implemented by C or C++ libraries, which Java cannot read.

Can you select the class loader manually?

While loading the class in an application via `Class.forName()`, it is possible to specify the class loader. The `Class.forName()` method accepts a fully qualified class name as an argument in a string format, which you want to load as a resource.

What is a bytecode verifier?

As you are aware, the process for compiling and executing a Java program is quite simple and straightforward. Developers are doing chores to generate the class file and passing it to JVM for execution. Normally, this should not create a problem for JVM about inconsistency or vulnerability issues, but it may not always be the case. Sometimes, the class files supplied to JVM, may originate from untrustworthy resources. For example, the downloaded files from hot browsers often contain the class files that do not need to be compiled by JVM as they are pre-compiled within an application. Such third-party class files might have some code in them, which can exploit the Java Virtual Machine. To make sure that no intruder can enter, JVM has a gatekeeper, the bytecode verifier. As the name implies, the bytecode verifier verifies that there is no breach of constraints, which can harm JVM.

Which verification is carried out by the bytecode verifier?

The following verifications are carried out by the bytecode verifier:

- The operand stack within a frame must not overflow, and it should not underflow or be underutilized.
- The variables must be initialized before usage.
- Private data from the class is not accessed from outside of the class.
- The proper references must be used for the method invocations.
- The execution stack must not overflow.
- The final classes must not be extended, and the final methods must not be overridden.

If the bytecode verifier detects any violation from the preceding list, the code execution is blocked for that file, and the class is rejected by JVM.

A common question that may arise is: *Are these responsibilities not already handled by the compiler? What then, is the role of the bytecode verifier in this process?*

A similar question might be thrown at you by the interviewer.

Why do we need the bytecode verifier in addition to the compiler?

Though the compiler can check all the aspects discussed in an earlier question and then create a class file, the class files *can be modified*. If any pernicious person knows about assembly programming, then they can easily edit the class file and make the modifications. That is where the gatekeeper will object to such class files. This makes JVM more robust and reliable.

Java Virtual Machine

JVM is the heart of the entire Java ecosystem. Whether you are a novice or an expert Java developer, you should have enough knowledge of JVM. An interviewer expects that you know the internal workings of JVM in depth. Let us walk through some interview questions related to JVM.

What role does JVM play in the Java execution flow?

Virtual machine, that is what we refer to it as, but when one refers to a virtual machine, the perspective can vary. Often, we know that we can install virtual machines on our existing operating systems. To give an example, we can install a Linux virtual machine on our Windows system and work in Linux on top of our Windows system. Along similar lines, JVM is, in fact, an abstract machine installed on your system on which you can execute your Java programs. This approach of having a separate virtual machine on your system is to cater to the platform-independent approach of Java. Where most other high-level programming languages generate the executable file that matches the operating system, Java creates a bytecode file that can be executed on JVM. JVM has all the characteristics of a system you have with you. The hardware devices contain registers, instruction pointers, and sets. All these features are imparted in JVM because of which we can execute programs on it, which are written in Java.

Can you elaborate on memory management in JVM?

Java program contains different segments like methods, local variables, references, objects, and many more. When we execute the class, all these segments get stored temporarily as long as the program is executing. These segments do not get stored at the same location in JVM, but they get stored in different logical compartments. *Figure 2.3* shows the different memory blocks of JVM:

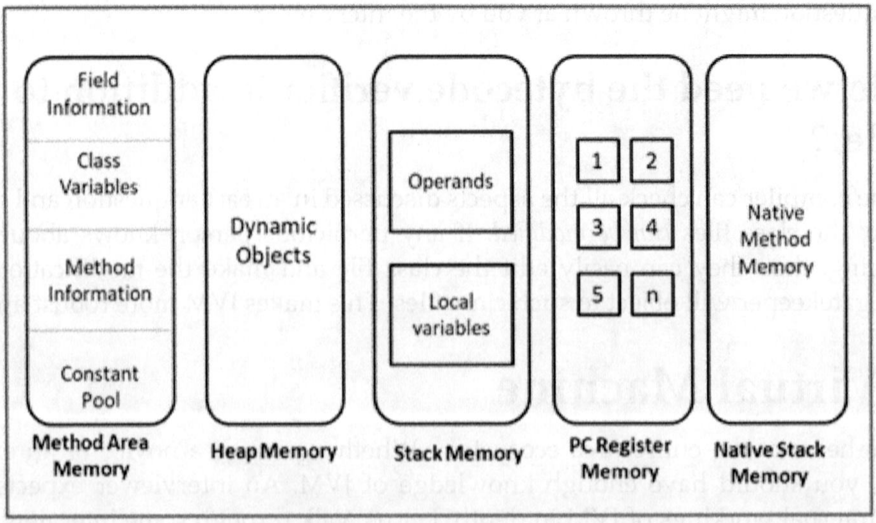

Figure 2.3: JVM memory blocks

Could you describe the different types of memory areas generated by JVM?

The following are the different types of memory regions generated by JVM:

- **Method area or class area**: This memory region stores the class information, like variables, method data, or the runtime constant pool.
- **Heap memory**: This memory is utilized by the dynamic objects and arrays created during program execution. This memory is shared across all the threads.
- **Stack memory**: The stack memory stores the frames created during execution for each thread. All the local variables and the method results are stored inside this. The frames get deleted or removed whenever the method invocation is terminated or completed.
- **PC register**: Every task that is being executed by JVM is executed within a thread. Program counter register is a memory that contains the instructions of a thread that is currently being executed by JVM.
- **Native stack memory**: Native stack memory is utilized by the native method if used in an application.

Can you increase the heap memory of JVM? or What is OutofMemoryException? How can we handle it?

This exception occurs when JVM runs out of memory. To handle this, we need to increase the heap memory allocated to JVM. We can increase the heap memory of JVM dynamically by providing additional attributes to the Java command. We can use the following attributes to modify the heap memory size:

- **-Xms**: Setting the minimal heap size
- **-Xmx**: Setting the maximum heap size

For instance, you can execute the following Java command to change the heap size:

```
java Sample -Xms512m -Xmx1024m
```

Alternatively, you can also set up the environment variable in an operating system to change the heap size every time a Java program executes, as follows:

```
_JAVA_OPTIONS = -Xms512m -Xmx1024m
```

Both these commands set the initial heap size to 512MB and the maximum heap size to 1024MB.

How can you differentiate between stack memory and heap memory?

Stack memory is a memory that is utilized to store the local variables and references to objects or arrays. This memory is expandable at runtime. The **heap memory,** on the other hand, is a fixed-size memory that is used to store objects or arrays. This memory can be configured at the JVM startup or by setting up the appropriate Java environmental variable.

How does JVM execute class?

When we load a class into JVM by using the Java command, JVM executes it. However, internally, many steps are performed before execution.

Let us consider the following command:

```
java Sample
```

As a result of this command, JVM checks if the class is loaded or not in memory. If it is not loaded, with the help of the class loader, the binary representation of this class is found; if this is not found, the JVM throws ClassNotFoundException. If the class is found, JVM does not immediately invoke the `main()` method. Prior to that, the class must be linked by the linking process. Linking typically comprises the verification, preparation, and resolution process. **Verification** is the process of verifying whether the binary representation is a well-formed class. It also checks if the class obeys the semantic requirements of Java and JVM. After the verification, JVM initiates the preparation process. In this process, JVM allocates the static storage for the class and also generates the data structure, which is internally utilized by JVM. At the end, JVM initiates the resolution process. In this process, JVM checks the symbolic references that are generated from the current class to other resources by loading those resources.

Once the linking process is completed, JVM starts the initialization process. During this process, the class variables or static initialization blocks are executed. This process, in fact, happens recursively as classes might have super-classes, and super-classes still can have a cosmic super-class. So, all these classes are initialized hierarchically before initializing the **`Sample.class`**. Once all these processes are completed, the **`main()`** method of the **`Sample`** class is invoked.

JIT compiler

JIT, a famous acronym for **just-in-time** compiler, is a special compiler present within JVM, which converts the bytecode to native code. JIT plays a major role in improving the performance of a Java application. It works in contrast to normal compilers. Normal compilers work before execution; on the other hand, JIT starts its work when the execution begins. It is dynamic in nature. Let us discuss the concept of JIT with the help of some interview questions.

What is the importance of JIT?

We all know that a Java program contains classes that need to be executed. The class is nothing but the platform-neutral bytecode. When JVM starts executing the program, it has to interpret this bytecode and translate it so as to make sure that the underlying CPU understands it. This process is time-consuming, because of which the application performance might be hampered, as every method or code invoked has to be interpreted.

Figure 2.4 shows how JIT picks up the bytecodes and converts them to native code so that JVM can execute them:

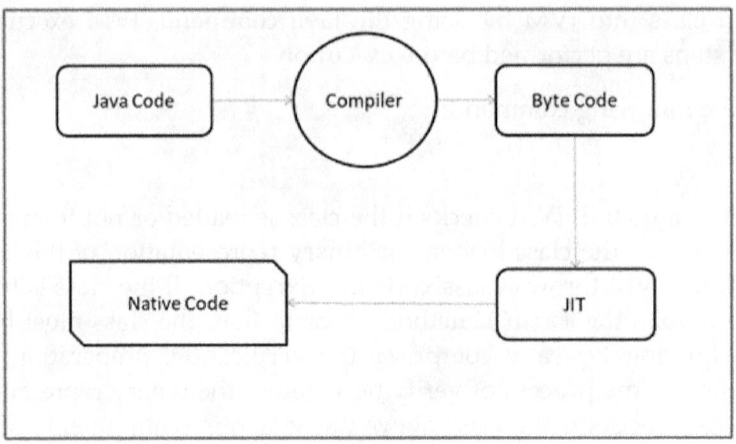

***Figure 2.4**: JIT compiler*

Of course, like normal compilers, JIT is also a bit expensive. It does require memory and other system resources. However, even if we consider this, JIT still improves the performance of an application as compared to the normal interpretation process by JVM.

How does JIT work internally to choose methods to compile?

The way JIT works is quite interesting. The JIT compiler does not immediately compile the method when it is first invoked. Instead, each method will be provided with a compilation threshold value. Each time the method is invoked, the threshold value is decremented by one, and the moment the threshold value reaches zero, JIT compiles the method to native code.

Can we have different versions of JIT than the Java version?

JIT compiler is tightly integrated with JVM. So, this option is not available where you can use different versions of JIT than JVM or Java. Normally, JIT comes bundled with JVM. Therefore, it is not possible to separate it and use it as an independent component.

Can you disable JIT?

Yes, we can disable the JIT compiler by providing the options `-Xint` or `-DJava.compiler=NONE` to the Java command.

If you disable JIT, what consequences will you face?

Disabling JIT is not recommended as this will force to interpret the entire Java program. It is because of this that the performance of the application will be hampered. Thus, normally, if you wish to diagnose an application, or debug it, or wish to analyze the JVM behavior, then only the JIT is expected to be disabled.

What is the difference between JDK, JRE, and JVM?

When working with Java, the terms JDK, JRE, and JVM are frequently used and often create confusion among learners. Although they are closely related, each serves a distinct purpose in the Java ecosystem. Understanding their roles helps clarify how Java programs are developed, executed, and managed:

- **JVM**: JVM is a runtime environment provided by Java. The primary responsibility of JVM is to execute the bytecode, which is the platform-independent file format generated by the Java compiler. Although bytecode is platform-independent, JVM is platform-dependent, so we have different JVMs for different platforms. To initiate JVM, we need to execute the Java class using the java command. Once initiated, JVM loads the required class, verifies the bytecode, manages memory, and executes the program while providing services such as garbage collection, security, etc.

- **JRE**: This is typically referred to as the implementation of the JVM. The main responsibility of JRE is to provide a runtime environment for Java. It comprises the Java libraries that will help to execute the Java files.

  JRE does not contain the development tools, such as compilers or debuggers; those are part of **Java Development Kit** (**JDK**). As a result, a mere JRE is sufficient for running Java applications, but it does not take part in the compilation of the application.

- **JDK**: JDK is an environment using which one can develop, compile, and test Java applications. It can be considered a complete developer's bundle. JRE is essentially part of JDK nowadays. Therefore, installing JDK also provides the necessary runtime environment.

In addition to JRE, the JDK includes tools like the Java compiler (javac), the debugger (jdb), the documentation generator (Javadoc), and various monitoring and diagnostic utilities.

What are the legal signatures of the main() method?

JVM expects a `main()` method in your program as a start-up method. The `main()` method must be declared as `public`, `static`, and `void`. The `main` method must have arguments of type String. The arguments cannot be a single parameter, but you can have either an array of `String` or `var` argument of `String`.

The following are the legal signatures of the `main` method:

```
public static void main(String data[])
public static void main(String[] data)
public static void main(String… data)
static void main(String[] data)
static public void main(String… data)
```

Can we overload main() method?

Yes. Technically, we can overload the `main()` method by changing the argument list. Java allows method overloading, and the `main()` method is not an exception to it.

If you answer it as yes, the next question you can expect is how the JVM decides which `main()` method to execute.

Will your program execute if you overload the main() method?

The Java compiler does not object to the overloading of the method, which means that the compilation will be successful. However, when we pass the generated class file to JVM, JVM will try to find out the signature that is known to it.

Consider the following code snippet:

```
public class TestIT{
  public static void main(int x){
     System.out.println("In overloaded main method");
  }
}
```

The following figure shows the output for the code snippet:

```
D:\>javac TestIT.java

D:\>java TestIT
Error: Main method not found in class TestIT, please define the main method as:
   public static void main(String[] args)
or a JavaFX application class must extend javafx.application.Application
```

***Figure 2.5:** Overloading of main*

Here, the **`TestIT`** class contains the overloaded main method. This class will get compiled fine, but if executed, it will throw the error as shown in the preceding output screenshot.

Can we declare the main() method as private?

Again, the answer is yes. You can declare any method as private in Java, and the compiler never complains about it. While it is permitted, you need to ensure that you are declaring it with the most restricted access specifier.

The preceding question will be followed by the next question based on the access specifier rule of the private keyword.

If we declare the main() method as private, how will JVM find it?

We can declare the **`main()`** method as private. However, if you do so, it is not visible outside of the class. Owing to this, JVM will not be able to find it and will generate an error that the **`main()`**is not found. The private **`main()`** is recommended when you are implementing the Singleton design pattern.

Can we declare the main() method as non-static?

Yes, we can **`main()`** as non-static from a language-specific perspective. The compiler does not give you any error if you do so.

Will your program execute successfully if you declare the main() method as non-static?

If we declare the **`main()`**as non-static, then somebody needs to take the responsibility to instantiate the class and then invoke the method by referring to the object of that class. If we declare **`main()`** as static, then JVM loads the **`main()`**as **`classname.main()`**.

What is single-file-source code launching? (Java 11)

Many of the programming languages provide a facility to compile and execute the program in a single step. While you can work with such an approach in IDEs like Eclipse and IntelliJ, there was no way that you could do this in the console. Java 11 launched the concept of executing the source code without compiling it.

Can you explain how the single-file-source code program concept works in Java 11?

The process is quite simple. If you have a source code **`HelloWorld.java`**, you can compile and execute **`HelloWorld.java`** using the Java command as:

```
java HelloWorld.java
```

In earlier versions of Java, the program first had to be compiled using **`javac`**, and then executed using the java command. From Java 11 onwards, both of these steps, compilation and execution, are handled internally by a single java command, simplifying the workflow and making it more convenient for quick programs and demonstrations.

What happens if the working directory already contains the class with the same filename? Does the java command replace the existing class file?

When we use the single-file-source code execution, the class is created in memory, and it is executed immediately. So, there is no physical existence of the class file. The **`java`** command used in single-file-source code execution, because of this, does not replace the already existing file with the same name.

How does the single-file-source work if multiple classes are present in the given file?

If the public class name matches the file name, then that class gets executed, but if more than one class is public, then the compiler complains.

Is it compulsory for at least one class to be public while you execute the file using single-file-source?

It is not compulsory to have any class as public in the single-file-source concept. For example, observe the given code for file **Sample.java**:

```
class First{
 public static void main(String[] args){
   System.out.println("In first");
 }
}
class Second{
 public static void main(String[] args){
   System.out.println("In second");
 }
}
```

In the code, the two classes **First** and **Second** are declared as non-public, but if you execute Sample.java, the JVM executes the **First** class as shown in *Figure 2.6*:

```
D:\>Java Sample.java
In first
```

Figure 2.6*: Single-source-file*

This behavior is based on the sequence in which the classes are defined in the source file. If the order is changed and the **Second** class is placed before **First**, the output will be **In Second**, as that class will be executed first.

What is the concept of Compact Source File and an instance main() method? (Java25)

Compact Source File is the new feature launched in Java25 through the JEP 512. This feature facilitates the simple class declaration without the decorated class structure with a mere **main()** method. It avoids the task of writing the boilerplate code of class declarations simple scripts. In this feature, the developer is required to provide only the definition of the **void main()** method. The class declaration is handled implicitly, and the JVM creates an instance of the class to invoke the **main()** method, since it is not declared as static.

Conclusion

In this chapter, we discussed the internal structure of Java. We talked about different components of Java that take an active part in the execution of a Java application. Along with this, we discussed different questions that could be asked about each of these components. We also discussed the new feature introduced in Java 11, using which we can execute the Java file without compiling it explicitly.

In the next chapter, we will cover concepts of Java surrounding object orientation. We will cover the basic to advanced features of object-oriented programming and the interview questions related to that.

Chapter 3
Object Orientation

Introduction

Object-oriented programming (**OOP**) language is a paradigm that has transformed the way software applications are designed and developed. Earlier developers were frustrated by writing boilerplate, tightly coupled code, and maintaining it. As the code base started increasing in size, such tasks turned out to be more complex. In this modern era, developers can leverage the advantages of OOP to create applications that are easily extensible and maintainable. OOP not only improved the code quality but also increased the collaboration among the developers by promoting a clear structure and separation of responsibilities. A strong understanding of object-oriented concepts is essential for any serious software developer. If you are not well-versed in object orientation, then you will certainly fail miserably while developing your applications.

Structure

We will be covering interview questions based on the following topics in this chapter:

- Class and objects
- Abstraction
- Encapsulation
- Inheritance
- Packages
- Record classes (Java 16 update)
- Sealed classes

Objectives

At the end of this chapter, you will be able to understand the core features of the OOP language and how to implement different concepts of the OOP language in Java. Furthermore, we will discuss many interview questions, as this is one of the most important segments of your interview.

Class and objects

The primary concept to understand about object orientation is classes and objects. It is kind of like the evolution of Earth, where the evolution of the planet is followed by other living organisms. Thus, one needs to understand clearly classes and objects before proceeding to other concepts of OOP. Let us discuss what type of questions you might encounter and how to answer them with a clear and effective approach.

What is a class?

A **class** can be considered a factory of objects. The properties and behavior of objects are crafted by the class definition. We can also say that it possesses the instructions about how your object will be created and how it will behave. It is a bridge between real-world entities and theoretical programming concepts. The variables declared in the class represent the physical properties of objects, and the methods of a class represent the behavior of an object. A good design of a class is always the most important part while designing the project architecture, as a poor class design can result in objects that do not behave as expected in the entire life cycle of the project.

Therefore, careful attention must be given to the class responsibilities, data encapsulation, and method design while modeling the class. Following object-oriented principles such as encapsulation, abstraction, inheritance, and polymorphism ensures that the class remains reusable, flexible, and easy to maintain.

What are the conventions of designing a class?

The following conventions should be followed while designing a class:

- Should have a capitalized name
- Should have camelCase methods
- Should be public, unless other access specifiers are explicitly needed
- Should contain private data members
- Should contain public methods

Note: **You might get a follow-up question related to what access specifiers are and their rules.**

What is an object?

While a class represents imagination or expectation, an object represents reality. An **object** is an entity created from a class definition. Every object holds the specific values for its data members, which are termed as state, and the business logic to perform the tasks allocated to it, which is termed as behavior. Objects can be logical, or they may have physical existence in the real-world.

Objects interact with each other to accomplish complex functionalities within a system. Effective object design promotes modularity and improves code reusability. It also enables the system to closely mirror real-world scenarios, making the application easier to understand and maintain.

What are the characteristics of an object?

Every object has the following properties associated with it:

- **State**: The state represents the values assigned to the properties that the object possesses at a given time. The design of an object is normally achieved by this state. For example, when a car is blue, blue is a value of the color attribute that defines the state of a car.
- **Behavior**: Behavior represents the functionality that an object can perform. This is normally defined through a method inside a class. For example, starting an engine is a behavior of a car, which might have a process written behind it inside a method such as **`startEngine()`**.
- **Identity**: Every object of a type has a uniqueness associated with it, which is termed the identity of that object. You may have any data members of the given object, which can represent its identity, or you may have the memory address of that object, considered as an identity, which is invisible to the programmer.
- **Responsibility**: It is said that there is a reason for our birth. Similarly, objects are created for a purpose; they are responsible for something. They must take part in the business logic for which they are created as a responsibility.

Detailed knowledge of an object is one of the most fundamental requirements that you must have. After all, an object is the core of OOP, and your entire development revolves around its creation and lifecycle management. You should know how to create objects, establish a meaningful relationship between different objects, and how to destroy them as well. If you fail to answer such basic questions, then you ought to fail miserably in your interviews. The answers to object-related questions are important, as the next journey of your interview depends on them.

What is a constructor? Could you explain its role?

A **constructor** is a special method defined in a class with the same name as the class. Whenever the object is created, the constructor is invoked implicitly. The main reason for a constructor is to initialize the object, or in other words, to initiate the data members of the object.

Can we have a private constructor?

Yes, we can write a private constructor. However, if we do so, there are some limitations we can observe as follows:

- You cannot create an object of this class directly from outside of the class
- You cannot subclass this class as the private constructor is not accessible to the subclass
- Normally, such practice is used in the Singleton design pattern, where the goal is to control the object creation and ensure only one instance of the class exists

Why is Java not called a 100% object-oriented programming language?

To consider any programming language as an OOP language, it should follow two principles. It must support all the pillars of the OOP language, which Java does. And second, everything in it must be an object. Unfortunately, this is where Java lacks. Java still has some features like primitives, which are not objects. Of course, Java has wrappers as counterpart objects of primitives, but the existence of primitives in an API makes it non-eligible for a complete OOP language according to many developers.

Why do all instance variables have default values in Java?

When we create an object by using the `new` keyword, the memory is reserved in the heap. To initialize this memory, JVM provides the default constructor, which takes the responsibility of initiating the instance variables to default values. This constructor is always present when we create an object. So, if you provide your own constructor, it will be invoked immediately after the constructor provided by JVM.

What are the accessor and mutator methods in Java, and what is their significance?

Every class has data members that participate in the business logic. Accessing and modifying these data members is always achieved through the use of methods rather than directly modifying them. These methods can be used to initiate the data members or set the data members. However, if we write a single method to access and modify a data member, we are violating the principle of abstraction in the OOP concept. To address this, the concept of **accessor** and **mutator** methods was introduced in Java. These methods are dedicated to individual data members. Thus, every data member will have two methods, which are **setter** and **getter**. The **setter** method is used to set or modify the value of a data member, which is called a **mutator** method. **getter** is used to retrieve the value of the data member for which it is declared, which is called the **accessor** method. In addition to this, there is one more practical advantage of the **accessor** and **mutator** methods. Many of the frameworks, like Spring and Hibernate, interact internally with the data members of objects. If the methods for accessing the data members are written by the developer, then it is not possible for the framework to search for such methods. Yet, frameworks can find the **getter** and **setter** methods internally to interact with the data members implicitly.

What are the different ways to create objects?

Take a look at the following:

- Using the **new** keyword
- Using the **newInstance()** method
- Using the **clone()** method
- Using de-serialization

The preceding answer will be followed by some more connected questions, for which you should be completely ready. Always be sure that you know the answers to those questions as well.

How to create an object using the newInstance() method?

This is termed a reflective approach to creating an object dynamically. This method is present in the **java.lang.Class**. Normally, when we use the **new** keyword, we are creating the objects of the classes that are present locally. However, when we are creating objects of the class from a remote source, it is not possible to use the **new** keyword. Or, sometimes you want a user to provide information about the class for the object you want to create. In such a case, you will need to use the **newInstance()** method. This method is used in conjunction with the **Class.forName**. **Class.forName("")** takes in argument the fully qualified name of the class; a user can provide this as an input parameter as well.

How to create a copy of an existing object?

If you want to create a copy of an existing object, you have to override the **clone()** method in your class. The **clone()** method is declared in the Object superclass. It creates and returns the physical copy of an existing object.

By default, the **clone()** method performs a shallow copy, meaning that object references within the original object are copied as references rather than creating a new object. To achieve a deep copy, additional logic must be implemented to explicitly clone the reference object.

How is the clone() method different from copying the reference of an object to another?

The **clone()** method creates a physical copy of the existing object. The objects created by this method have their own memory space and separate existence. However, if you copy the reference of one object to another, you are indicating that you have two references pointing towards the same object. Therefore, ideally, you are not creating a new object, but you are creating another reference that points to an existing object.

How to use the clone() method to create a new object?

The method **clone()** from the **Object** superclass is used to create a new object from an existing object. When we invoke **clone()**, JVM copies the entire content of an existing object into a new object. Before you use the **clone()** method, you must make your class eligible for cloning. To do that thing, your class must implement the **Cloneable** interface and override the **clone()** method, which is shown as follows:

```
public class Student implements Cloneable {
 int rollNo;
 String studName;

 Student(int rollNo, String studName) {
  this.rollNo = rollNo;
  this.studName = studName;
 }

 public Object clone() throws CloneNotSupportedException {
  return super.clone();
 }

 public String toString() {
  return this.rollNo + "," + this.studName;
 }

```

```
public static void main(String args[]) {
 try
 {
  Student s1 = new Student(101, "John Doe");
  Student s2 = (Student) s1.clone();

  System.out.println(s1);
  System.out.println(s2);
 }
 catch (CloneNotSupportedException c) {
  System.out.println("CloneNotSupportedException occurred");
 }

}
}
```

This program demonstrates the use of the **Cloneable** interface to create a copy of an object.

When will your code throw the CloneNotSupportedException?

When we attempt to clone an object that does not implement the **Cloneable** interface, JVM throws this exception. You cannot invoke the **clone()** method on any object unless its class implements the **Cloneable** interface.

The **Cloneable** interface acts as a marker, indicating to JVM that it is safe to create a field-by-field copy of the object. Without this marker, cloning is considered unsupported, as it may lead to unpredictable behavior or violate object integrity.

How to serialize an object?

When we want to serialize an object, the primary thing that we must do is to implement the marker interface **Serializable** in the class of that object. This makes the object of that class eligible for serialization.

Once this requirement is met, you can open the file in write mode and serialize your object by invoking the **serialize()** method.

During the process of serialization, the object's state is converted into a byte stream, which can later be persisted or transmitted over a network. Fields marked as **transient** are excluded from serialization, allowing sensitive data to be ignored during this process.

Note: There are a few more questions that can be asked on serialization, but we will cover those in Chapter 5, I/O and File Handling, in detail.

Abstraction

Abstraction in Java is the concept of hiding implementation details and exposing only the essential features of an object. It enables developers to focus on what an object does rather than how it does it. Abstraction is achieved primarily through **abstract classes** and **interfaces**. An abstract class can contain both abstract and concrete methods, whereas an interface defines a contract that implementing classes must follow. This approach promotes loose coupling, improves maintainability, and enhances code reusability in large-scale applications.

What are the different access specifiers present in Java? Can you explain their significance?

The following are the different access specifiers in Java:

- **Private**: When we declare any member as private, it is said to be the highest secure member. Such a member is accessible within the class in which it is declared. Even if you import a class, such data members are not accessible. Only inner classes can access the private data members of the outer class in which they are declared.
- **Default**: As the name indicates, it is a default access specifier. There is no specific way to declare it, but if you do not mention any specifier, the member is said to have default access. The members with this specifier are accessible within the same package.
- **Protected**: When we declare a member as protected, the member is accessible within the package. It is also available outside the package as well, but only to the subclasses of that class.
- **Public**: When we want to declare any member that is exposed to the entire world, we can declare that member with a public access specifier. Of course, even though we use a public access specifier, it is compulsory that we import that class if we are using the member outside the package.

Can we apply a private modifier to a class?

This is a tricky question. If you state that you can apply a private modifier to a class, the answer is generally incorrect. Top-level classes in Java cannot have the private access specifier. However, from a different perspective, you can apply the `private` keyword to a class if it is an inner class.

A **`private`** inner class is accessible only within the enclosing outer class and is completely hidden from the outside world. This technique is often used to achieve stronger encapsulation and to restrict class usage to a specific detail within a class.

How to achieve abstraction in Java?

There are different ways to achieve the abstraction in Java listed as follows:

- By using abstract class
- By using interfaces

Note: **Abstract classes and interfaces are discussed in the later sections of this chapter.**

Encapsulation

The famous poet *Fernando Pessoa* once said:

If after I die, people want to write my biography, there is nothing simpler. They only need two dates: the date of my birth and the date of my death. Between one and another, every day is mine.

Everyone enjoys privacy in the real-world. The same is the case with objects. After all, they represent the real-world. Objects are recommended to be designed in a way that hides the way they are built and the way they process the data to achieve something through encapsulation.

What is encapsulation, and how to achieve that?

Every object consists of data members and member functions. The value of data members denotes the state of an object, and the member functions define the behavior of an object. Behavior is normally controlled by the value of data members. Therefore, if we want an object to behave as designed by the creator, then the data members should not be exposed directly to the end users. This hiding of internal structure or data members from the external world is termed encapsulation.

We can achieve encapsulation by declaring the data members as private and member functions as public. In this way, the users of the system will be able to access only the member functions and not the data members.

Can you explain why we should follow encapsulation, with a real-time example?

Consider the class **Rectangle**, in the code as follows:

```
public class Rectangle {
  int width,height;
  double area;
  public Rectangle(int width) {
   height=width*2;
  }
  public double calculateArea() {
   area=width*height;
   return area;
  }
}
```

Here, we are expecting that the user will initialize the width of the rectangle, while the height is calculated internally based on the logic implemented by the developer:

```
public class RectangleApp {
  public static void main(String[] args) {
   Rectangle rectangle=new Rectangle(10);
   System.out.println(rectangle.calculateArea());
  }
}
```

The preceding code initialized the width to **10**, and internally, the height is calculated as twice the width, resulting in the value **20**. However, the major drawback with this approach is that, as encapsulation is not properly enforced, the object of the rectangle can initialize the data member height directly as:

```
Rectangle rectangle=new Rectangle(10);
rectangle.height=200;
```

We do not want this manual modification for the height data member from outside the class. To enforce this restriction, we need to declare the width and height as private data members so that they are not accessed outside the class directly as:

```
public class Rectangle {
 private int width,height;
 //implementation code
}
```

By declaring the data members as private, direct access to width and height from outside the class is restricted. Controlled access can then be provided through public getter and setter methods, ensuring proper validation and maintaining data integrity.

To achieve complete encapsulation, can we declare the class itself with a private access specifier?

One may find the luxury to declare the entire class as private to achieve the encapsulation automatically. However, it is not permitted. The reason is quite obvious. If you declare a class with a private access specifier, then it is not accessible to the outside world, not even to JVM. Due to this, JVM will not be able to load and execute the main method, which is the starting point of the execution.

Inheritance

Java provides many concepts as part of its inheritance mechanism. In fact, most of the interviewers will invest at least 60% of their interview duration on the concept inheritance. You must be well prepared about the topic of inheritance if you want to be successful in your Java interview. The next few pages are dedicated to inheritance-related questions.

What is association in Java?

When we develop an application, we deal with many objects. These objects can interact with each other. In other words, the objects can utilize the services that are defined by other objects. Such a relationship between the objects is called an **association**.

What is composition in Java?

Designing a class is always a creative job. You define properties and behavior that control the overall working of an object. Some of the properties of an object itself can contain some behavior. Let us take an example where a `Car` contains an `Engine`. The `Engine` is one of the properties of a `Car`, but the `Engine` itself can have its own attributes and behavior. Therefore, we can define `Engine` as a separate class with its own properties and behavior, which can be declared as a property of the `Car`. This concept is termed as *composition* or *has-a-kind* relation.

The following code snippet demonstrates how the composition can be implemented:

```
public class Car {
 String color;
 Engine engine;//composition
 public void drive() {

 }
 public void start() {

 }
}

public class Engine {
 //data member
 //member functions
}
```

In the code snippet, we have designed a **Car** object, which contains the **Engine** object, which is a classic example of containment.

What is the difference between composition and aggregation?

Both of these are types of association in Java. Both these concepts use the other object as a part of it. However, there is a key difference between the two. In composition, if we destroy the main object, the object that is associated with it also gets destroyed or becomes meaningless. In the case of aggregation, even if we delete the main object, the other object still continues to exist in the system.

Can you give one example of composition and aggregation?

One of the simple examples of composition is about a **Car** and an **Engine**. A **Car** is composed of an **Engine**. However, if we destroy the **Car**, the **Engine** on its own cannot perform. On the other hand, if we take an example of a **School** and **Students**, where the **School** will have students associated with it. In this case, even if we destroy the **School** object, students can still exist and perform their role in the system.

What is the difference between is-a-kind relation and has-a-kind relationship in Java?

Java supports two types of inheritance approaches: *is-a-kind* and *has-a-kind* relationship. The *is-a-kind* relationship demonstrates a classical approach of inheritance where you create a new type that behaves similarly to the existing type. In this approach, you create a new object that essentially inherits all the properties and behavior of an already existing object, which is termed its super class. The newly created object is termed a subclass. For example, a **`Car`** is of type **`Vehicle`**. Here, **`Vehicle`** defines the common attributes for different types of vehicles. A **`Car`** is a subclass that can be designed as *is-a* type of **`Car`**. This achieves reusability of the code, which is defined in **`Vehicle`**. Therefore, you do not have to redefine the common properties or methods that are already defined in the **`Vehicle`**.

On the other hand, *has-a-kind* represents composition. In this approach, one object has a reference to another object as part of its attribute. Here, the newly created object does not inherit the properties and behavior of an existing object. However, it can use its services by reference that is declared within it. For example, a **`Car`** has a **`Steering Wheel`**, or a **`Car`** has an **`Engine`** inside it.

How does constructor chaining work in inheritance in Java?

Java facilitates constructor chaining in the inheritance approach. As we are aware, if we create and object of any class, its constructor gets invoked. However, if such a class is a subclass of another class, then it invokes the superclass constructor via the **`super()`** keyword, through its own constructor. When you are invoking **`super()`**, you have to ensure that it is the first line of your constructor of the child class; otherwise, the compiler complains.

In some cases, it is observed that if you do not write the super keyword, the compiler does not complain. In other cases, the compiler complains. Why is there a different behavior of the super keyword?

Fundamentally, **`super()`** is added implicitly in every constructor. This ensures that the default constructor of the superclass is invoked implicitly. So, even if you do not add the **`super()`** keyword, the compiler does not complain. However, if you have a parameterized constructor in the superclass, then even though the **`super()`** is added implicitly, it refers to the default constructor of the superclass, which is not available, and the compiler complains. In such cases, the developer has to explicitly write the **`super(arg1,arg2...)`** in the constructor to invoke the parameterized constructor of the superclass explicitly.

What is the concept of flexible constructor bodies? (Java25)

The flexible constructor bodies feature was finalized in Java25 under the **Java Enhancement Proposal 513**. In this feature, a developer can add the code prior to the **`super()`** or **`this()`** keyword in the constructor of the class. In the earlier version, the mandate was **`super()`** or **`this()`** must be the first line in the constructor. This facilitates the validation of the data before passing it to the super class constructor via the **`super()`** method or passing the validated data to another constructor of the same object using the **`this()`** keyword.

How do you explain the term coupling?

Software development is a complex scenario. As we are moving more toward advanced features of programming, it is getting more and more complex. **Software** is essentially a collection of different components communicating with each other to achieve a desired outcome. This communication often requires the relationship to be established between different components of a system with each other. This relationship or connection is termed as **coupling** in the OOP language.

What do you mean by loose coupling?

Often, when we create software, the components are dependent on each other, which is coupling. **Loose coupling** is the type of coupling in which, if one component is modified, the other component of the system does not get impacted. In a nutshell, the components are independent of each other, though there is some relationship between them.

What do you mean by tight coupling?

If two components in a system are dependent on each other in such a way that changes made in one component impact the other component, then such coupling is termed **tight coupling**. In this case, if we change one component, the other component is also forced to be changed.

How do you achieve tight coupling, and can you explain with a real-time example?

Tight coupling is a scenario in which a component is dependent on another component. If we change one component, the other component is required to be changed.

To explain this concept, consider two objects **A** and **B**, where object **A** is using the services of object **B** using the concept of composition, as shown in the code:

```
1. class A {
2.     B b;
3.     public A() {
4.         b = new B();
5.     }
6.     public void display() {
7.         System.out.println("In A");
8.         b.display();
9.     }
10. }
11.
12. class B {
13.     public B(){}
14.     public void display() {
15.         System.out.println(„In B“);
16.     }
17. }
```

As mentioned, **A** is utilizing the services of **B**, which is tightly coupled with it. If you look at the **display()** method in class **A**, it is internally invoking **display()** of **B**. Therefore, any change in the implementation of the **display()** method of **B** will produce a different output for **A**. Moreover, the code will completely fail if we rename the **display()** method from class **B**, as the method is invoked from class **A**.

What if, instead of using the services of class **B**, class **A** now wants to use the services of class **C**? Then, we need to modify *line number* 2 of the preceding code as:

```
2.    C c;
```

This will obviously require recompilation of class **B**. This scenario explains tight coupling in a real sense.

Could you explain loose coupling in Java with a real-time example?

Flexibility is the main reason why loose coupling is introduced in OOP. When you design a component in such a way that you can plug in and plug out the components within another component, you are essentially talking about loose coupling.

Consider the following code snippet:

```
interface Print {
  public void display();
}

class A {
  Print s;
  public A(Print s) {
    this.s = s;
  }
  public void display() {
    System.out.println("In A");
    s.display();
  }
}

class B implements Print {
  public B() {
  }
  public void display() {
    System.out.println(„In B");
  }
}

class C implements Print {
  public C() {
  }
  public void display() {
    System.out.println("In C");
  }
}
```

In the preceding code, we have introduced the interface **Print**. The **Print** interface is implemented by classes **B** and **C**. And, if you observe class **A**, instead of referring to **B** or **C**, which will create the glue code, it refers to the type of **Print**, which could be either **B** or **C** dynamically. This is a classic example of loose coupling. Thus, at runtime, we can decide which object **A** can refer to, as shown in the following code:

```
public class LooseCouplingDemo {
 public static void main(String args[]) {
  Print b = new B();
  Print c = new C();

  A a = new A(b);
  a.display();

  A a1 = new A(c);
  a1.display();
 }
}
```

In this snippet, we have referred to the object of the subclass with the superclass, which demonstrates the loose coupling.

Can you explain when to use is-a-kind and has-a-kind relationships in Java?

Whenever you want to create a new entity that behaves like an existing entity, you can create an *is-a-kind* relationship. This is termed **inheritance**. On the other hand, when one object requires the services of another object within our object, then we need to create a *has-a-kind* relationship. This is termed **containment** in Java.

What is an abstract class?

An **abstract class** is said to be an incomplete class. This class declares a skeleton and not a stub. This means that the class declares methods but does not define their bodies. The class declares the incomplete methods by declaring them as abstract. Such abstract methods need to be overridden by the subclass that extends the abstract class.

What is a final class, and why does one need to declare it?

A class, when declared as **`final`**, cannot be extended. When you want to make sure that your services cannot be modified by a subclass, you can declare the class as final. By declaring a class as **`final`**, all the methods implicitly become final. If you wish, you can apply the final keyword to selective methods.

This approach is commonly used to enforce immutability, maintain consistent behavior, and enhance security by preventing unintended method overriding.

What is a final method?

When a method is declared with the `final` keyword, we are restricting overriding. That means the method is not permitted to override. A subclass cannot override such a method.

Declaring a method `final` is useful when you want to preserve critical business logic, ensure consistent functionality, or prevent accidental modification of the existing methods.

Can the abstract class contain constructors?

Yes. An abstract class can have a constructor as part of its definition. This constructor is used to initialize common state and resources required by all subclasses.

Although an abstract class cannot be instantiated directly, its constructor is always executed when a concrete subclass object is created.

Why do abstract classes provide constructors even though they are not instantiated?

An abstract class does not represent only a skeleton. Sometimes, it may have concrete methods with some business logic. In order to execute the business logic of that method, the abstract class may require the local variables or even the data members. So, to have some default value for the data member, the abstract class gives you constructors where you or JVM can initialize the data members.

What are concrete and abstract methods?

Normally, when we define a class, we write the methods that describe the behavior of an object. These methods have a body associated with them within the boundaries of curly braces. Such methods are termed *concrete methods*.

In some cases, instead of a class defining the behavior, it delegates the implementation to its subclasses. In such cases, the methods are declared, but the body is not defined. Such methods are termed *abstract methods*, which are terminated by a semicolon (;) instead of curly braces.

Even if the method is declared with empty curly braces, the method is still treated as a concrete method and not an abstract method.

Can we declare all the methods of an abstract class as concrete method?

Yes. We can have a class where all of its methods are concrete and still declare such a class as an abstract class. However, as we know, we cannot instantiate an abstract class. Due to this, if you want to use the services provided by this class, you need to subclass this class and then instantiate it.

Can we declare an abstract class as final?

The objective of declaring any class as an abstract class is to subclass it. We always extend the abstract class and instantiate the subclass. A subclass also overrides the abstract methods that are declared by the abstract class. The **final** keyword makes the class ineligible for the subclass; one cannot extend the class if the class is declared as final. Due to this, the declared abstract class as final is not permitted.

Can we have abstract methods as private?

When we declare any method as private, we are taking away visibility from it. The method is not visible to the outside world. Abstract methods need to be overridden by the subclass, for which they must be visible to the subclass. As private methods are not visible outside the class where they are declared, you cannot override them. Therefore, it is not permitted to declare abstract methods as private.

Can we declare abstract methods as static?

The **static** keyword is associated with a class and not with an object. On the other hand, the concept of overriding establishes relations between the objects where you can override the methods of a superclass. Due to this, anything that is not part of an object cannot be overridden, so the **static** keyword is not used while declaring an abstract method.

Who takes the responsibility to invoke the constructor of an abstract class, if the abstract class cannot be instantiated?

An abstract class is extended by the subclass. Every subclass, while getting instantiated, invokes its own constructor implicitly. Furthermore, the constructor provides the **super** keyword, which calls the constructor of the superclass. The following code demonstrates the implicit invocation of the constructor of the **abstract** class by the subclass:

```
public abstract class A{
  int x;
  public abstract void method1();
}

public class B extends A{
  public void method1(){
    //body of method 1
  }
}
```

The preceding snippet is equivalent to:

```
public abstract class A{
   int x;
   public A(){
      //initialization of data members
   }
   public abstract void method1();
}

public class B extends A{
   public B(){
      super(); // calls the default constructor of super class i.e. abstract class A
   }
   public void method1(){
      //body of method 1
   }
}
```

The code snippet shows how the subclass's constructor implicitly invokes the constructor of the superclass, though the superclass is abstract.

Can interfaces have a constructor? How is it different from abstract classes?

Unlike abstract classes, an interface cannot have a constructor. As an interface does not have data members, there is no need for a constructor for it. One major difference between an abstract class and an interface is that an interface contains only abstract methods, whereas an abstract class can contain a combination of concrete and abstract classes.

What is the need for interfaces?

Java does not support multiple inheritance. Due to this, you cannot utilize the services declared or defined from multiple resources. Interfaces are a solution to this problem. You can extend a single class and multiple interfaces for your classes. Interfaces are a real-time implementation of complete abstraction where you declare the methods, and implementation is left to the subclass. Interfaces also play a major role in implementing loose coupling.

What is a polymorphic reference?

A polymorphic reference is used to control the behavior of a subclass dynamically. When the subclass object is referred to by the superclass reference, such a reference is termed a *polymorphic reference*. Any instance that takes part in *is-a kind* of relationship can take part in a polymorphic reference. Therefore, any object can be referred to by its immediate super class, indirect super class, interface it is implementing, or even the cosmic super class object.

What is the significance of a polymorphic reference, and how would you achieve the same?

When we use an object reference to invoke a method, JVM searches for that method in the object to which we are referring, and it executes that method. In case the method is not present in the subclass, then the method of the superclass gets executed if it is present in the superclass. Therefore, prima facie, a subclass is flexible enough to write and execute a method that is not present in the super class. A subclass is a supreme boss, traditionally, unless someone controls it.

Consider the following code snippet, where **Dog** is a subclass of **Animal**:

```
public class Dog extends Animal{
 public void talk() {
  System.out.println("Dog is barking");
 }
}
```

`Dog` extends **`Animal`**, and it can override the methods from the **`Animal`** class. So, the reference to **`Dog`** when invokes method **`talk()`**, will invoke the implementation from **`Dog`**, and when the method **`breath()`** is invoked, then the method from the **`Animal`** class is invoked, as the method is not present in the **`Dog`** class. Let us consider the implementation of **`Dog`** as follows:

```
public class Dog extends Animal{
 public void talk() {
  System.out.println("Dog is barking");
 }
 public void read() {
  System.out.println("Dog is reading Economic Times");
 }
}
```

Here, you can see the intelligent **`Dog`** can even read the *Economic Times*. You may like that, but economists might hate that. Furthermore, the most interestingly, as the subclass is being independent, nobody can object to this.

Let us now change the reference of **Dog**, which is shown as follows:

```
1. Animal d=new Dog();
2. d.read()
```

The preceding code fails as the object of **Dog** is referred to by **Animal**, and it is trying to invoke the method that is not known to **Animal**. This way, we can control the behavior of the subclass using the polymorphic reference.

If Object is a cosmic super class, what is wrong with referring to every object by it?

Technically, there is nothing wrong in referring every object by the **Object** superclass. However, this will create a very weird situation dynamically. Imagine the following statements:

```
1. Object one=new Employee();
2. Object two=new Car();
3. Object three=new Student();
```

Here, all three objects are referred by the **Object** super class, which is perfectly fine for a compiler. However, when you try to invoke the methods of **Employee**, **Car**, or **Student** using the respective references, it will fail. The reason is quite obvious. Since all the objects are polymorphically referred to **Object**, only those methods can be invoked that are known to the **Object** class.

Can we extend more than one class?

No, in Java, multiple inheritance is not supported. Though you can create hierarchical inheritance, you cannot create multiple inheritance.

This restriction avoids ambiguity and complexity, such as the *diamond problem*, where a class may inherit conflicting implementations from multiple parent classes.

However, Java allows multiple inheritance through **interfaces**, since interfaces do not carry state and resolve method conflicts explicitly.

How do you achieve multiple inheritance in Java?

The only way by which you can achieve multiple inheritance in Java is by using the concept of interfaces. You can create an interface and implement it in the class where you would like to have multiple inheritance. Your class can extend one class, and it can implement any number of interfaces.

Can you implement more than one interface?

Yes, we can. One of the important reasons for using an interface is to achieve cohesion effectively. You can implement more than one interface, even if all the interfaces are not related to each other.

Additionally, interfaces can extend other interfaces, enabling the creation of a hierarchical inheritance structure. This allows common behavior contracts to be defined at higher levels and reused across more specific interfaces.

Observe the following code snippets for interfaces **First** and **Second**:

- **First.java**:

```
public interface First {
  public void methodFirst();
}
```

- **Second.java**:

```
public interface Second extends First{
  public void methodSecond();
}
```

In the preceding snippet, interface **Second** is extended from **First**. You can extend one interface from another, as discussed earlier:

InterfaceDemo.java:

```
public class InterfaceDemo implements Second{
  //implementation of methods from interface First,Second
}
```

In the preceding snippet, the class **InterfaceDemo** implements the interface **Second**. However, as the **Second** interface extends **First**, the implementation class **InterfaceDemo** must implement the methods from interfaces **First** and **Second**.

If your class implements two interfaces and both the interfaces declare similar methods, which method will be invoked? Is it permitted?

Nothing wrong with this. You can have two interfaces with similar abstract methods, which can be implemented by any class. Once the class implements both interfaces, it must override the method from both interfaces. Therefore, ideally, when a class implements or overrides such a method, the method becomes the behavior of the class and not of the interface. When you create an object of such a class and invoke the method, it becomes irrelevant to the invoker about the interface in which the method is declared. Even if you refer to the object by any of the interfaces, it does not make any difference for execution.

Consider the following code snippet:

```
interface First {
 public void method1();
}
interface Second{
 public void method1();
}

class DemoInterface implements First,Second{
 @Override
 public void method1() {
  // TODO Auto-generated method stub
 }
}.
```

In the preceding snippet, there are two interfaces, **`First`** and **`Second`**. Both these interfaces declare the same method as **`method1()`**. When **`DemoInterface`** implements the **`First`** and **`Second`** interfaces, it must override methods from both interfaces. However, as both interfaces contain the same method, the class can have a single method that suffices the method declared in both the interfaces, so the program compiles fine.

Note: **If the question is framed differently, like, can you have different interfaces with the same method signature implemented by a single class? The answer to this is still yes. However, if you come across a scenario like this, then there is something wrong with the design of your application. Make sure that you talk about this in front of the interviewer.**

What is the use of the final keyword?

In Java, there is no **`const`** keyword, which is present in earlier programming languages like C and C++. The keyword **`final`** is used to mark something that cannot be modified. You can declare variables as **`final`**, which makes them constants. You can also declare classes as **`final`**, which makes them ineligible for extension. You can even declare a method as **`final`**. If you declare a method as **`final`**, the subclass is not permitted to override it.

Can we make the reference as final? What does it mean?

We can make the reference **`final`**. Making the reference final does not mean that you are making the object that it refers to **`final`**. When you declare any reference as **`final`**, you cannot reassign the object to the same reference.

Consider the code snippet as follows:

```
1. final String x="abc";
2. x="xyz"; //compilation error
3. x.concat("xyz");
```

In the snippet, **String x** is declared as **final**. This means we cannot reassign any object to the same. Due to this, *Line* 2 will fail at compilation. However, as you can see, you can make the changes in the actual object by invoking the **concat()** method on the object to which it is referring.

What is the use of a static variable?

Static keywords are used to declare class variables. Normally, when we declare any data member, it is instantiated independently for different objects. It has different copies of variables allocated to different objects. Therefore, if one object makes any changes in that variable, the other object does not have any relation with that. The other object will have its own copy of that variable on which it can process.

On the other hand, if we declare a variable as static, the copy of such a variable is shared across all the objects of the same type. So, if one object makes a modification in such variables, the other object will get the updated copy of that variable.

What is the use of a static method?

As we are aware, we can declare the static variables in a class. Static variables are class variables that have only one copy of the variable shared across all the objects. When we want to process static variables, it is recommended to use the static method. So, essentially, static methods are used to process or return the static variables.

Can we use a non-static method to process static variables?

Yes. We can use a non-static method to process static variables. Though this might create confusion in a developer's mind, technically, it is permitted. This is because static variables belong to the class and are accessible from both static and non-static contexts.

However, using instance methods to modify static data should be done cautiously, as it may lead to poor design and unexpected behavior in multi-object scenarios.

Can we use a static method to process instance variables?

No. Whenever we declare static methods, the keyword this is never used within them. The instance variables are always prefixed with **this** keyword by the compiler. However, static methods are not dedicated to any specific objects; they are termed as class methods, and they cannot process any business logic that is dedicated to a specific object. So, we cannot use non-static members within the static method.

Can we declare static and instance variables with the same name?

No, you cannot have the same name for a static and an instance variable, as it will create confusion for the compiler. Java does not allow this because both variables would belong to the same namespace within the class, making references ambiguous.

This restriction ensures code clarity and prevents accidental access to the wrong variable, thereby improving maintainability and readability.

In what scenario can you use a static variable?

There are numerous scenarios in which you can use a static variable. Let us assume that you have an **Employee** class. If you are interested in counting how many **Employee** objects are created, you would require a counter variable that can be increased by one every time the object is created. However, if we declare a counter variable as an instance variable, then if one object increases the value of the counter variable, the other object will still get the original value of the counter. In such a case, you can declare the counter as static so that all the updates on the counter variable will be shared across all the objects of **Employee** as follows:

```
public class Employee {
 int empId;
 String empName;
 static int counter;
 public Employee(int empId,String empName) {
  this.empId=empId;
  this.empName=empName;
  counter++;
 }
 public static int getCounter() {
  return counter;
 }
```

```
public static void main(String[] args) {
 Employee e1=new Employee(101,"John");
 Employee e2=new Employee(102,"Smith");
 Employee e3=new Employee(103,"Derek");
 System.out.println("Total Employees :"+Employee.getCounter());
}
}
```

If we execute this code, we will get the count for total employees as 3. This clearly indicates the role of the **static** keyword in the program.

Can the static keyword be applied anywhere apart from variables?

Certainly, apart from the variables, you can apply the **static** keyword at numerous locations. You can make any method static. You can declare the **static** block, which executes before the **main()** method. Apart from this, there is a concept called a static instantiation block, which is executed just before the creation of an object. You can also use the static keyword with a class that is termed a static class. However, you cannot make any class static unless it is nested in some other class. Such a class is called a static nested inner class.

What is the use of this keyword?

The keyword **this** refers to the current object. Fundamentally, it is used to call another constructor of the same object. This is the only way to call the constructor of the same object. You can call a parameterized constructor from a default or from a default to a parameterized constructor using the keyword **this**.

Moreover, if there is any ambiguity with the local variables and instance variables, you can use **this** keyword to denote the instance variables differently from the local variables.

Explain the significance of the super keyword

The **super** keyword refers to the super class. If you want to invoke the members of the super class explicitly from a subclass, you can use this keyword. You can invoke data members or member functions of a super class using the **super** keyword. Not only that, but you can also invoke the constructor of the super class explicitly from a subclass constructor.

Another use of the **super** keyword is done by JVM when it calls the default constructor of super class implicitly from the constructor of the subclass.

The **super** keyword must be the first line of the constructor.

Why must the super keyword be the first line of the constructor?

When we say that we are in a subclass, it obviously contains some data members. Many times, the data members of the subclass are dependent on the data members of the super class. So, unless the data members of super classes are initialized, the subclass data members cannot be initialized. So, to ensure that the super class data members are initialized prior to any member of the subclass, the **super** keyword is placed as the first line of the constructor.

In what sequence will the constructors be invoked if we create an object of a subclass?

When we create an object of any class, implicitly, the constructor of the same object gets invoked, but internally, that constructor invokes the constructor of the super class by using the **super** keyword. So, practically, though we can observe that the constructor of the super class is invoked first, theoretically, it is not like that. It is *not everything as it seems*. Always, the constructor of the subclass executes first, which internally invokes the super class constructor.

Do we have destructors in Java?

Unlike traditional programming languages like C++, we do not have a destructor in Java that matches the class name. However, the method **finalize()** is termed a destructor in Java. This method is invoked implicitly by JVM when the object memory gets deleted from the virtual memory. We can override this method to write the customized code to free up the resources connected with the current object.

Which methods are present in the Object class that can be overridden?

The following methods are part of the **Object** class that can be overridden by a subclass protected object **clone()**:

- **public boolean equals(Object o)**
- **protected void finalize()**
- **public int hashCode()**
- **public String toString()**

Once you list out different methods from the **Object** class, next, you can expect a series of questions based on these methods.

What is the use of the toString() method?

As the name indicates, the **`toString()`** method represents the object in the String format. It returns a string that consists of information about an object, which is easy to read for the user. If it is not overridden, it returns the hexadecimal representation of the hash code of the object. We can override this method so as to return the string that we want to represent as object information, as per the business need.

What is the use of equals() method, and how is it used?

This method is used to check the equality of an object. Developers can override this method to implement the business logic to check the equality of the object. In this method, a developer can check member-wise equality and return true or false depending on the result. If this method is not overridden, then the **`Object`** super class considers every object as unequal and returns **`false`** to the invoker.

Can we declare an interface with the abstract keyword?

We can declare an interface with the **`abstract`** keyword, but it is not required. Interfaces are internally, by default, abstract classes, so we can declare an interface as an abstract interface.

If an interface is internally a class, does it extend the cosmic super class by default?

There is no cosmic super class available for interfaces. As there is no scope for any business logic because of its abstraction approach, there is no need for the **`Object`** super class.

What is the default method in an interface?

The default method concept is introduced in JDK1.8. Fundamentally, interfaces provide full abstraction, but default methods in an interface are implemented methods in an interface. It is as good as creating an abstract class with a combination of concrete as well as abstract methods. We can have more than one default method in any interface.

Why is a default method required in an interface?

Sometimes, we have an interface implemented by some classes. Let us assume that now the interface wants to declare one more method because of some business need. However, the moment we add some additional method in an interface, the class that is connected with that interface will fail, as it is not aware of the new method that is introduced in that interface.

In such cases, the newly created method or methods can be created as the default implemented method. By doing so, the existing class, which is dependent on the interface, does not need to modify itself as the method in the interface has a body associated with it. The new class where your interface is going to be implemented can override the method if required.

What is a static method in an interface, and what is its significance?

Static methods in an interface are similar to default methods, which means that they have a body associated with them. However, the difference between the two is that, as the method is static, the subclass that implements that interface does not have permission to override it; on the other hand, the default method can be overridden.

What is the significance of private methods defined in interface? (Java 9)

As we know, we can use the default methods in the interface. These default methods obviously possess some business logic, and an interface can have multiple default methods. Private methods can be utilized to provide common internal functionalities to such default methods. As the method is private, it cannot be used outside of the interface, nor is it visible to the implementor class. Such methods are only available internally in the interface, so they can serve the default method and ensure code duplication.

What is a functional interface?

Function interfaces are interfaces with a sole purpose. This means that the functional interface declares only one method as part of its content. Any class that implements this interface will need to override this method so as to make sure that it provides the meaning to the service that is declared by the functional interface.

Which is a cosmic super class in Java?

The emperor **`Object`** class is termed as a cosmic super class of every object in Java. Even if you do not explicitly mention any class extending **`Object`**, by default, JVM makes **`Object`** as a super class for each and every class.

As a result, all Java classes inherit common methods such as **`toString()`**, **`equals()`**, **`hashCode()`**, **`wait()`**, **`notify()`**, and **`getClass()`**.

This design ensures uniform behavior across all objects and enables polymorphism at the root level of the class hierarchy.

What is the difference between the equal operator = = and the equals() method?

The equality operator `==` is normally used with primitives to check the equality of the variables. On the other hand, the **`equals()`** method checks the equality of object comparing the data members. To check if the two objects are equal, we need to override the **`equals()`** method from the **`Object`** super class. We can also use the `==` operator with object references, but instead of checking the object, it will check the equality of references.

The `==` operator will return **`true`** only if both the references are pointing towards the same object.

What is a var argument? Where can it be used?

When we overload a method, we modify the arguments of the method. Either we change the type of argument or the number of arguments. If we want to overload a method that takes a different number of parameters of the same data type, instead of declaring different methods with different numbers of arguments, we can use **`var`** arguments, shown as follows:

```
public class Calculator {
 public void add(int a,int b) {
  //body of method
 }
 public void add(int a,int b, int c) {
  //body of method
 }
 public void add(int a,int b, int c, int d) {
  //body of method
 }
}
```

In the preceding code snippet, we have overloaded three different methods taking different numbers of integer arguments. This code snippet can be replaced with the **`var`** argument as follows:

```
public class CalculatorWithVarArg {
 public void add(int... values) {
  //body of method
 }
}
```

In this code, as we have replaced the arguments with the **`var`** arguments, we can pass any number of integers as arguments while invoking the method.

What do you mean by method overloading?

Method overloading is also termed compile-time polymorphism, where the method signatures are identified at compile time. Method overloading is essentially the same method name with different arguments. The arguments may differ in terms of the number of arguments or the type of arguments. The return type of the method, or the access specifier of the method, does not have any impact on the concept of method overloading.

What are the different rules for declaring the var argument method?

The following rules must be followed while using the **var** argument:

- There must be one and only one **var** argument in the given method.
- If you are using the **var** argument along with other primitive arguments, the **var** argument must be declared as the last argument of the method.

What is the difference between using the var argument and array as a method argument?

Technically, there is no difference. The **var** argument internally arrays in Java. The only difference is the way the method is invoked. If you have a method with a **var** argument, you can invoke the method by passing the comma-separated values. However, if you have a method with array as an argument, then the invoker must first create an array and pass that array as an argument while invoking that method.

What is method overriding?

Method overriding is termed as dynamic polymorphism in Java. In this concept, the method declared or defined in the super class is redefined in the subclass. We need to make sure that the method signature must remain same, which includes the arguments and return type. Method overriding is observed only in the case of inheritance.

What are the rules of method overriding in Java?

The following are the rules for method overriding:

- The overridden method must have the same name and the same argument list.
- The overridden method must have the same return type or the covariant return type (covariant return type is a subtype of the original method's return type).
- The overridden method must not have a more restrictive access specifier.

- The final method cannot be overridden.
- Private methods cannot be overridden as they are not visible outside the class where they are declared or defined.
- The overridden method must not throw new or broader checked exceptions.
- The **synchronized** modifier has no impact on the overriding process.
- The **strictfp** modifier has no impact on the overriding process.
- Static methods cannot be overridden.

Can we overload or override a static method?

A **static** method can be overloaded, as the overloading concept is limited only to the types or number of arguments. The other keywords applied to the method do not make any sense when you overload the method. On the other hand, if you have a **static** method in the parent class, the subclass can have the same method signature, but technically, it is not termed as overriding.

What is a co-variant return type?

When we override the method in a subclass, we must keep the return type of the method the same or a subtype of the original **return** type. This subtype of return type is termed a *co-variant* **return** type.

The following code snippet shows how we can use the co-variant **return** type effectively:

```
public class A {
 public Number returnSomething() {
  return 10;
 }
}
public class B extends A {
 public Integer returnSomething() { // overridden method with covariant return type
  return 10;
 }
}
```

In the preceding snippet, class **B** is a subclass of **A**, and it overrides the **returnSomething()** method, which is defined in its super class **A**. If you observe the **return** type of the method in the super class, it returns **Number**. However, in the subclass, the method is returning **Integer**, which is a subtype of **Number**. Such a **return** type is termed a co-variant return type.

Can we change the return type of the overridden method?

By the rule, the `return` type of the overridden method must be the same. However, there is one alternative available to you. Instead of having the `return` type exactly the same, you can keep the method `return` type as a subtype of the method that is defined in the super class.

Do we have any restrictions on the access modifier when we implement method overloading?

Precisely, the concept of method overloading is only connected with the method signature. In method overloading, we need to strictly maintain the same method name with a different argument list. Method overloading has nothing to do with an access modifier, so there is no restriction on whether you need to keep the access modifier the same or different while overloading.

Note: **Sometimes, the interviewer might share some code with you on a white paper where method overloading is implemented with different access modifiers, so make sure that you know what has to be observed while reading the overloaded method.**

What is the difference between an abstract class and an interface?

The following are the differences between an abstract class and an interface:

- An `abstract` class can contain abstract as well as concrete methods; an interface can contain only abstract methods.
- An `abstract` class may contain a constructor, but an interface cannot contain a constructor.
- An `abstract` class may contain data members, but an interface can declare and initialize only constants.
- An `abstract` class does not support multiple inheritance, but an interface can extend multiple interfaces.
- An `abstract` class can have members that may be private, protected, or even public. Interfaces, on the other hand, have everything public by default.

What is a marker interface?

A marker interface is a special type of interface that does not have any methods declared within it. It does not even have the field associated with it. This interface is also termed a *tagging interface*.

What is the use of a marker interface?

Marker interfaces are used to instruct the compiler about the special behavior that can be applied to a class at runtime. You do not have to override any method to implement an interface; it is just some extra information provided to the compiler. Of course, there are certain other ways than a marker interface to provide extra information to the compiler, like declaring some flag inside the class. However, if we use a marker interface, it adds more readability to the class.

Can you name some commonly used marker interfaces in Java and explain their purpose? There are several marker interfaces commonly used in Java, such as **`Serializable`**, **`Cloneable`**, **`RandomAccess`**, and **`EventListener`**. These interfaces do not define any methods but are used to indicate specific behaviors to the JVM or the compiler.

Can you create your own marker interface? How to declare it?

There is no special magic in creating a marker interface. We can just create an interface without any methods, which will be treated as a marker interface. Then, you can implement this interface on some class so as to denote that the class is of the type of a marker interface you have denoted. Furthermore, in your business logic, you can check if the class is of the type declared by you and then permit the object to do some processing.

What is typecasting in Java, and what are the different types of typecasting available in Java?

Converting one data type to another is termed typecasting. There are two types of typecasting available in Java:

- Down-casting
- Up-casting

Down-casting is changing the type from the current data type into the lower data type. This has to be done explicitly by a developer, as converting the data type to a lower data type might generate data loss or precision.

On the other hand, **up-casting** is converting the current data type into a higher data type. This can happen implicitly, as there is no precision loss in this process.

Can you elaborate on any situation where you can apply up-casting to objects or references?

One of such scenarios, in which we can use up-casting, is implementing the **equals()**method from the **Object** super class. The **equals()** method from the **Object** super class declares the argument of type **Object** as its signature, which is shown as follows:

```
public boolean equals(Object obj)
```

That means, any object can be referred to by the **Object** reference, as **Object** is the cosmic super class for all the objects.

Consider the **Employee** class, which is shown as follows:

```
package casting;
public class Employee {
 int empId;
 String empName;
 public Employee(int empId,String empName) {
  this.empId=empId;
  this.empName=empName;
 }
}
```

If we want to check the equality of the **Employee** object, we need to override the **equals()** method:

```
1. public boolean equals(Object o) {
2.    if(this.empId==o.empId)//error
3.     return true;
4.    else
5.     return false;
6.  }
```

If you observe, *Line* 2 uses the reference of the **Object** class to access the data member of **Employee**, which is not possible because of the polymorphic reference. So, to achieve this, you need to down-cast the reference of the **Object** class to **Employee**, which is shown as follows:

```
public boolean equals(Object o) {
   Employee e=(Employee)o;//Downcasting
   if(this.empId==e.empId)
    return true;
   else
    return false;
 }
```

Line 3 of this code shows the way to down-cast the `Object` reference to `Employee` reference.

What are the types of variables in Java? Could you also explain their scope?

Java provides the following types of variables:

- **Instance variables**: An instance variable is a variable that is declared within a class and not in any method. When we create an instance of that class, a copy of such a variable is created for each instance. Modifications done by one instance do not impact the value of the same instance variable in another object. One of the most important features that an instance variable provides is that it is accessible within all the member functions of the class. The instance variables always have a default value.
- **Local variables**: When the variables are declared within a method or block, they are termed local variables. The main property of local variables is that they are visible only within the block or method where they are declared. You can declare a local variable in a method, loop, or even if condition. Unlike instance variables, local variables do not have a default value.
- **Static variables**: Static variables look almost similar to instance variables, but with one difference; they need to be declared with the `static` keyword. The static variables are also called class variables, as they do not have a separate copy for each object. A single copy of the variable is shared across all the objects of the same class. Modification made by one object will be reflected in other objects of the same class. Similar to the instance variable, all the static variables have a default value.
- **Reference variables**: Reference variables are the variables that point to an object. We can declare these variables locally in a method, or we can use them as instance variables in the concept of composition. If they are used as instance variables, they are accessible to all the methods of that class. However, if declared within any method, they are accessible only within that method.

What is an instance initializer block in Java?

An **instance initializer** block is a block that gets executed before the creation of an object. The moment JVM identifies a new keyword while execution, it immediately jumps to the static initializer block and executes it.

What is the difference between a static initializer block and an instance initializer block in Java?

A **static initializer** block is used to initialize the static members, and an instance initializer block is used initialize the instance variables. The major difference between the two is that a static initializer block is called only during the life cycle, while an **instance initializer** block is called each time the object of that class is created.

Can you explain the concept of wrapper classes in Java?

Wrappers, as the name implies, wrap the data. They wrap data and convert it to an object. So, essentially, a wrapper class is an object form of the primitives. For instance, for an int primitive, there is an **Integer** wrapper. Similarly, we have **Byte**, **Short**, **Long**, **Double**, **Float**, **Character**, **Boolean**.

What is the significance of wrapper classes?

Wrappers provide two important facilities:

- There are some concepts in Java, like collections, where you can use objects and not the primitives. In such a location, if we want to make use of primitives, we can use the wrapper form of the same.
- Wrappers provide methods for parsing the data types from one type to another.

What is auto-boxing and auto-unboxing? In which scenarios are they observed?

Auto-boxing is the process of converting the primitive into a wrapper automatically, and auto-unboxing is the process of converting the wrapper into primitive.

If you push primitive to collection, then primitives are automatically converted into wrappers and then they are added to collections, as collections only permit an object to be part of them.

Auto un-boxing happens when you try to access or modify or process the wrappers. For example, consider two Integer wrappers and you want to add them, which is shown as follows:

```
Integer i1=new Integer(10);
Integer i2=new Integer(20)
int add=i1+i2;
```

In this case, you cannot add **i1** and **i2** directly as they are objects. However, at runtime, JVM unboxes the wrappers and pulls the value out of it, and then, it does the process of addition.

What is the use of an immutable object?

Immutable objects are created when you want to ensure that object do not get modified after its creation. Typically, in a multi-threaded application, sometimes an object created by one thread can be modified by other thread because of which the system might perform in an unexpected way. So, to make sure that your object is not modifiable by other thread, you can create an immutable object. Since their state cannot be changed once created, they can be safely shared across multiple threads without requiring additional synchronization.

Can you create your own immutable object and how to to create it?

We can create an immutable object. To create an immutable object, we need to follow the following norms while designing a class:

- All the data members of the class should be private. If they are not private, they might get modified outside the class.
- You must have a parameterized constructor for your class so as to initiate the data members.
- Convert your class to final so that no one will be able to subclass it and try to modify the data members. (Though this is not assumed to be very strict norm, it is better to have it.)
- The class must not have the setter methods. It may contain the getter methods.
- If the class contains other object reference, then the getter method should not return direct reference of an existing object; instead, the cloned copy of that reference should be returned.

What is an enum to you?

An **`enum`** in Java is a special class that contains a group of named constants. This **`enum`** class is a subclass of a predefined **`Enum`** class. In Java, **`enum`** can also contain variables, methods, and constructors.

Enums are commonly used when a fixed set of values is required, such as day of week, directions, or status code. They improve code readability, provide type safety, and help prevent invalid values from being assigned.

Can enum extend any other class?

No, **`enum`** cannot extend another class as it is already extending the **`Enum`** class. This is against the policy of Java, which says *multiple inheritance is not supported in Java.*

Can we write an enum that implements an interface?

Yes, **`enum`** can implement any other interface like a class, as it is internally a class. The only thing that you need to remember is that you must override the methods that are declared in that interface.

What is the connection of the toString() method with enum?

When you try to access the constants that are present in `enum`, Java provides you the `toString()` method internally, which returns you the string representation of those constants or objects. You can even override the `toString()` method and return the customized string to represent the object.

Can we declare constructors within enum?

We can declare constructors in `enum`. However, the constructor must be private. For each constant, this constructor is executed while the `Enum` class is loaded.

Why is the constructor of enum kept private?

An `enum` is kept private so that the values or constants that are present within it should not be modified outside `enum`. As `enum` does not have a public constructor, it cannot be instantiated using the `new` keyword.

Could you explain some important methods of enum in Java?

There are three important methods in `enum` of Java:

- **values():** This method returns all the values that are present in `enum`.
- **ordinal():** This method returns the index numbers of all the constants that are present in `enum`.
- **valueOf():** This method returns the constants in `enum`, which are specified as an argument.

Packages

Packages are used in Java to group related classes together. The services that are written inside classes can be utilized by importing the packages into other classes. We will discuss a few interview questions based on packages.

Which package is available as a default package for every Java class?

Whenever we create any class in Java, the `java.lang` package is available by default for that class. So, all the interfaces, classes, and their methods are implicitly available to all the classes that we declare.

If you import the parent package, does the compiler automatically import sub-packages as well?

No. If you want to use the class from the sub-packages, you have to explicitly import them. Importing a parent package does not automatically import its sub-packages. Each package in Java is treated as an independent namespace, so classes from the sub-packages must be imported separately.

What is the use of static import?

When we define a class, we use static members inside it. To import such static members, we can use static import statement. When you use static import, you do not need to write the complete class name while using that member inside the class where you have imported it. Here, instead of importing the entire class, we import only the members that we want to use in our class.

Record classes (Java 16 update)

Record class concept was introduced in Java14 as a preview feature and was standardized in Java16 version. **Record** class is a model for an immutable data carrier. The main feature of **Record** is that it generates **constructor**, **getter**, **equals()**, and **toString()** implementations automatically. The following code snippet shows the standard declaration of the **Record** class **Employee**:

```
public record Employee(int id, String name, double salary) {
}
```

Can we override the equals() and toString() methods in Record?

Records are implicitly final. It has internal implementation of **equals()** and **toString()** methods. While you can implement your own **equals()** and **toString()**, it is not recommended. Doing so breaks the fundamental purpose of the Records.

If you declare the Record, what details are implemented implicitly by the compiler?

For any Record, the compiler generates:

- Private final fields
- Canonial constructor

- Public accessor methods
- `equals()`, `hashCode()` and `toString()` methods

Note: Records do not generate the setter methods, and the members are final or immutable by nature.

What is the difference between Canonical constructor and Compact constructor in Records?

Canonical constructor explicitly declares all the record components as parameters. These parameters must follow the same order as they appear in the **Record** header. In the **Canonical** constructor developers get full control over initialization of the data members, and developers can perform validations on the data if required.

On the other hand, the **Compact** constructors are really compact in nature. It omits the parameter list. Here, developers do not have any control over the data member initialization. The compiler automatically assigns the parameters to fields.

Can we add any instance or static method in the Record?

Records can have any additional instance or static method. The only rule that you have to follow is not to add any instance variable in the class body. It is not absolutely permitted in **Record** class.

Record looks similar to the Lombok framework that we are using traditionally. What is the difference between them?

Lombok is a third-party library, while the **Record** is a language-level feature which does not require any dependency to be included in your classpath. Lombok allows both mutable and immutable classes, where **Records** are implicitly immutable. Lombok generates both getters and setters, while **Record** generates only the accessor method.

Sealed classes

Sealed classes were introduced in Java15 as a preview feature, and finalized and released as a full feature in Java17. As the name suggests, these classes are designed in order to control the inheritance behavior of classes.

By using sealed classes, a developer can explicitly specify which classes are permitted to extend or implement a given class or interface. This leads to more predictable and maintainable code, improves type safety, and works especially well with modern Java features such as records and pattern matching.

The sample code shows a simple sealed class **Shape**, which can be extended by **Circle**, **Rectangle**, and **Triangle**:

```
public sealed class Shape
        permits Circle, Rectangle, Triangle {
}
```

Why is there a need for sealed class, although we have final keyword and access modifiers?

The **final** keyword completely blocks the inheritance, and the access specifiers control the visibility. On the other hand, the sealed classes ensure that only specific classes can extend the given class. This permits the developer to write a controlled class hierarchy in the given software design.

Is there any rule about the way we declared the permitted subclass of a sealed class?

The permitted subclass of the sealed class must explicitly declare using the keyword sealed, non-sealed, or final. Otherwise, the compiler complains.

This explicit declaration makes the inheritance behavior clear and intentional. It ensures that the class hierarchy remains well-defined and prevents accidental or uncontrolled extension of sealed types.

Apart from controlling the inheritance does sealed classes provide any other services?

Sealed classes also improve the pattern matching in the switch expression. As the compiler already knows about which classes are permitted, there is no need for the default case for pattern matching in a switch expression. This ensures the compile-time type safety, as we already know all the allowed or known subtypes.

Why do we need to declare the non-sealed classes in the hierarchy of sealed class?

Declaring the sub-type of sealed class as non-sealed creates channel for future extensibility. It ideally removes the overall control on the inheritance hierarchy created by the sealed class. You can use the non-sealed when a sub-type can work as extension point for further inheritance.

Can you explain the pattern matching in instanceof operator? (Java 17)

Pattern matching in the **instanceof** operator was introduced in Java16 and it was launched a full feature in Java17. This feature combines the type checking and the casting of the data type into single step making the whole process simpler and more readable. The following code shows how to use the pattern matching in **instanceof** operator:

```
if (obj instanceof String s) {
    System.out.println(s.length());
}
```

Here, the compiler checks if the object is of type **String**. If it is of type **String**, it automatically casts it to **String** and binds it to the variable.

Conclusion

In this chapter, we explored different concepts of object orientation that can be implemented in Java. We started the journey from very basic building blocks like class and object and then discussed every detail about their structure, purpose and relevance. Then we dived in different concepts like abstraction, inheritance, and polymorphism and the different questions that can be asked on these concepts. We also discussed a few concepts that are important, like enum, wrapper classes, which will give an added advantage at the time of actual interview. In addition, we extended our discussion to include the modern Java features introduced in the recent versions such as record classes, sealed classes and pattern matching with the instanceof operator, highlighting how Java continues to evolve while strengthening the object-oriented design. By mastering these concepts, you not only gain a solid foundation for writing clean and maintainable Java code but also develop confidence to explain design decisions effectively during interviews and real-world discussions. In the next chapter, we will focus on exception handling in Java. We will discuss how to face the different interview questions on exceptions handling in Java.

Chapter 4
Handling Exceptions

Introduction

To err is human, and everyone accepts this fact. We as humans are generous enough to forgive the errors made by others. Most of us live in a culture of *forgive and forget,* which is the key to a happy and longer life. Unfortunately, things are different when we talk about software systems. Clients always prefer to have reliable, robust software for their business. Error-prone software may cost the client millions in their business. It is a developer's prime responsibility to develop software that will not fail or generate unwanted results for which they are paid. One must question why developers would intentionally produce faulty software. In reality, developers always make their best efforts to create flawless software. Despite this, there might be some cases in which the software might fail. Software is created by human beings, installed on machines, and used by human beings. Owing to this, there might be something wrong with the hardware or some error on the part of the user of the system, which will cause the system to fail. Such situations are termed exceptions. As developers, we need to ensure that we control such abnormal situations. Even if it occurs, we need to make sure that the application should not be abruptly terminated. This process of controlling the abrupt termination of applications is termed *exception handling.*

Structure

We will be covering interview questions based on the following topics in this chapter:

- Types of exceptions
- Handling an exception
- User-defined exceptions
- Updates in exception handling

Objectives

Exception handling is one of the most important topics in a Java interview process. The candidate must understand the need for exception handling and the way to implement it. In this chapter, you will learn the fundamentals of exception handling. You will also explore the recent updates in exception handling. Additionally, you will know how to answer real-time interview questions, which could be asked during interviews.

Types of exceptions

Exceptions in Java can be broadly classified into different types based on how they occur and how they are handled by the program. The main types include **checked exceptions**, **unchecked exceptions**, and **errors**. Understanding these categories helps developers identify different kinds of runtime problems and handle them appropriately to make programs more robust and reliable.

Explain the hierarchy of an exception

The top-most class in the hierarchy of exceptions is `Throwable`. The `Throwable` class is further extended by two different classes, `Error` and `Exception`. Both `Error` and `Exception` classes further have their subclasses.

The following figure shows the hierarchy of exceptions in Java:

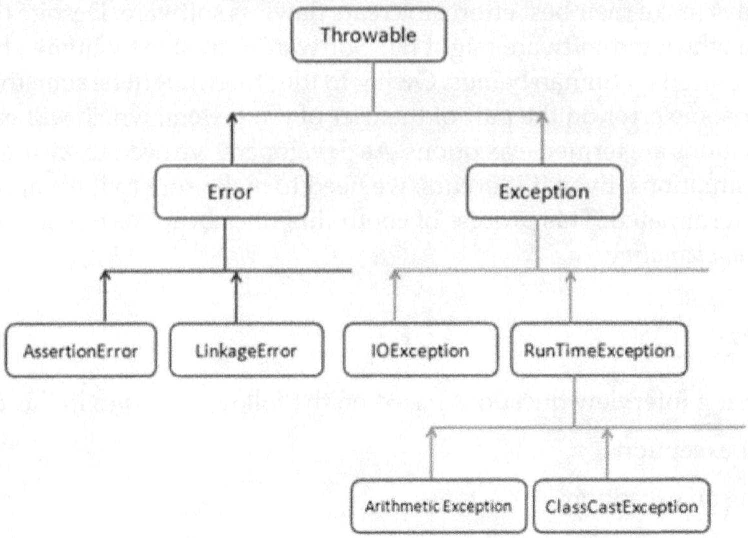

Figure 4.1: Hierarchy of exceptions

Note: **This figure is not complete, as it is not possible to show all the classes at a single glance. However, if you are able to explain even these classes, this would be enough for the interviewer.**

What is the difference between an error and an exception in Java?

`Error` and **`Exception`** are subtypes of the **`Throwable`** class. Thus, both may cause the program to terminate abruptly if not handled. However, a point to remember is that errors are not recoverable. That means there is no practical way to handle the errors if they occur at runtime, and the program usually terminates abruptly. However, whenever you feel that the exception might cause the abrupt termination of your application, you can control the abrupt termination by providing the exception handling code.

Could you tell me something about the Throwable class?

Throwable is the super class for all the exception classes in Java. Only the objects of this class or subclass can be thrown and handled by Java. The **`Throwable`** class or its subclass provides two commonly used constructors: a default constructor and a parameterized constructor with a String argument. This String argument is used to store the complete information about the exception. If we wish to get the exception message, we can use the **`getMessage()`** method of this class.

How do you classify exceptions?

Exceptions are classified into two different types:

- **Checked exception**: These types of exceptions are checked by the compiler at the time of compilation. The compiler verifies whether the exception is properly handled. If it is not handled, then a compilation error is generated. Typically, such types of exceptions are generated when Java programs communicate with resources from a Java program. Such exceptions need to be handled either by using the **`try-catch`** block or by using the throws keyword at the method declaration. **`IOException`**, **`SQLException`** are types of such exceptions.

- **Unchecked exception**: These types of exceptions are checked at runtime. If the exceptions are not handled, the compiler does not complain. However, the program may end abruptly if an exception occurs. Whether to handle such an exception or not is entirely dependent on the programmer. Some of the examples of such exceptions are **`ArithmeticException`**, **`ArrayIndexOutOfBoundsException`**, **`NullPointerException`**, **`NumberFormatException`**, etc.

Can you list out different exceptions that you know and the scenarios when they are thrown?

The following table highlights some common exceptions and the situations in which they arise:

Exception	Description
`ArithmeticException`	This is RunTimeException and occurs when exceptional arithmetic operations are performed, which are not permitted.
`ArrayIndexOutOfBoundsException`	This exception occurs when an array element is accessed with an invalid index number.
`NullPointerException`	This exception occurs when the reference tries to invoke the methods or members of an object, though it is not referring to any object.
`NumberFormatException`	This exception occurs when a String is converted into a number, but it is not convertible to a number.
`ClassCastException`	This exception occurs when we try to convert one type to another when it is not convertible.
`CloneNotSupported`	This exception occurs when we try to clone the object, but it does not implement the Cloneable interface.
`InterruptedException`	This exception is thrown when the Thread is in the waiting or sleeping mode.

***Table 4.1**: Types of exceptions*

Handling an exception

Handling an exception is not rectifying an exception. By handling, we mean providing sufficient information to the client about the type of and reason for an exception. Moreover, it avoids the abrupt termination of a program. Exception handling allows the program to manage unexpected situations in a controlled manner. It also helps maintain the normal flow of the application by executing alternative code when an error occurs.

What is the need for exception handling?

When the exception is raised, the program is terminated abruptly. Along with this, it also generates a technical message about the exception, which is difficult for the user of the system to understand. Moreover, because of this abrupt termination, the code segments after the exception, which are not dependent on the exception, also get terminated.

We must take care of the following:

- A clear and meaningful message should be displayed to the end user.
- Code that follows the exception (if it is not related to the code that generates the exception) should execute smoothly.

To achieve this, we can perform exception handling.

How to handle an exception?

To handle an exception, you must first identify the block that may generate an exception. Once you know which block generates an exception, you need to put that code in the **`try`** block. The **`try`** block is followed by the **`catch`** block, where we handle the exception. The **`catch`** block in its argument takes the reference of the exception object, which may be thrown by the **`try`** block. If the **`Exception`** object, which is thrown by the **`try`** block, matches the **`catch`** argument, then the **`catch`** block executes.

The following syntax shows how to use the **`try-catch`** block:

```
try{
//code block
}
catch(Exception e){
//exception handling block
}
```

In this structure, the **`try`** block contains the code that may generate an exception during execution. If an exception occurs, it is caught by the **`catch`** block, where appropriate handling logic can be written. This mechanism prevents the program from terminating abruptly and allows the developer to handle errors in a controlled manner.

Can you use the try block without the catch block?

Though it is not recommended, you can use the **`try`** block without **`catch`**. In that case, you need to compulsorily use the **`finally`** block as an alternative to the **`catch`** block. The **`finally`** block always executes, irrespective of whether the exception occurs or not. However, in the absence of **`catch`**, if the exception occurs, the program will be terminated abruptly. This is a very uncommon practice that overrides the whole reason for the exception handling concept.

Can we use a single try block to handle multiple types of exceptions?

We can have a single **try** block, which may raise multiple types of exceptions. This **try** block may be followed by a single **catch** block that handles all the exceptions generically, or multiple **catch** blocks matching the types of exception, which are generated within the **try** block.

Can a single catch block handle multiple types of exceptions?

Yes, we can use a single **catch** block to handle multiple exceptions. To achieve this, the **catch** block must be generic. This means that instead of handling a specific exception, it uses the **Exception** object as an argument, which accepts all the types of exceptions that are thrown from the **try** block. However, to handle the specific exception types, you need to check the type of exception, as shown in the following code snippet of the **catch** block:

```
catch(Exception e){
if(e instanceof ArithmeticException){
//handle the exception of type ArithmeticException
}
if(e instanceof NullPointerException){
//handle the exception of type NullPointerException
}
}
```

In this example, a generic **Exception** object is caught in the **catch** block. The **instanceof** operator is then used to determine the specific type of exception that has occurred. Based on the type of the exception, the program executes the appropriate handling logic for **ArithmeticException** or **NullPointerException**.

What is the cascading of an exception?

Cascading of an exception is the propagation of an exception. When the exception is raised, it needs to be handled in the same method block. However, sometimes, if we do not handle that exception, the exception is carried forward to the other method from which the original method is called. Such an approach of forwarding the exceptions to the next method is termed cascading exceptions or propagation of exceptions.

What is a chained exception?

Chained exceptions were introduced in JDK 1.4. Chained exceptions allow you to re-throw a new exception when an exception occurs. While doing so, you can still maintain the cause of the earlier exception, which can be chained to the next exception. To achieve this, the **Throwable** class is modified with two additional methods and constructors listed as follows:

- **New methods**:

  Throwable getCause()

  Throwable initCause(Throwable t)

- **New constructors**:

  Throwable(String s, Throwable t)

  Throwable(Throwable t)

The following code snippet illustrates how we can use the chained exception:

```
try {
//some code
} catch (IOException e) {
throw new MyException("IOExceptionoccurred", e);
}
```

In the preceding example, the **catch** block handles the **IOException**, but instead of completing the handling, it re-throws another exception **MyException**.

How do you handle the exception in a generic way?

Normally, to handle an exception, we use the **catch** block. In the **catch** block, we use the specific type of **Exception** object as an argument. Once the exception object is thrown, it will be caught by the corresponding **catch** block. However, instead of handling the specific exception object, we can use the super class **Exception** as an argument. This is considered to be a polymorphic reference in which the super class reference can refer to its subtype. Since all the exception types are subtypes of the **Exception** super class, the **Exception** super class can refer to all types of exceptions.

The following **catch** block illustrates the use of a generic way of handling an exception:

```
catch(Exception e){
//catch block to handle exception
}
```

This **catch** block handles any exception that may occur within the corresponding **try** block. Since **Exception** is the superclass of most exception classes in Java, it can **catch** different types of exceptions. This approach provides a generic way of handling errors when specific exception types are not handled separately.

When do you recommend handling the exception in a generic way? What is the complexity of using this approach?

Typically, when we are not aware of what kind of exception might be generated, we can use the generic approach to handle an exception. One of the complexities of using this approach is that the **catch** block becomes generic, so we need to take extra measures to display the exception message according to the type of exception. We have already discussed how to achieve this in earlier questions.

Can we use a generic approach of exception handlers along with other exception handlers?

Yes, we can definitely do so. However, you need to follow the important rule, where you combine both the generic and specific **catch** blocks. According to standards, the generic **catch** block must be placed at the end of all the specific **catch** blocks.

The following code snippet gives a compilation error as the generic exception handler is written at the beginning:

```
catch(Exception e){
//catch block to handle exception
}
catch(ArithmeticException ae){
//catch block to ArithmeticException
}
catch(NullPointerException ne){
//catch block to handle NullPointerException
}
```

This happens because if we place the generic exception handler at the beginning, then all exception objects thrown by the **try** block are caught by this **catch** block. This makes the other **catch** blocks unreachable because the generic **catch** block will handle all exceptions thrown by the **try** block before the specific **catch** blocks get a chance to execute.

The following code snippet shows the actual way to combine the generic and specific exception handlers:

```
catch(ArithmeticException ae){
//catch block to ArithmeticException
}
catch(NullPointerException ne){
//catch block to handle NullPointerException
```

```
}
catch(Exception e){
//catch block to handle exception
}
```

This code demonstrates the correct ordering of multiple **catch** blocks. Specific exceptions, such as **ArithmeticException** and **NullPointerException**, are handled first, followed by the generic **Exception** handler. This ensures that each specific exception is processed by its corresponding **catch** block, while the final **catch** block handles any other exceptions that are not explicitly covered.

What is the use of the finally block?

The **finally** block is used to write the code that we wish to execute, irrespective of whether an exception occurs or not. The **finally** block is normally used to close the resources that are opened during the **try-catch** block. Of course, we can close the resource within the **try-catch** block as well, but that is not recommended, as we cannot guarantee the complete execution of either the **try** or **catch** block. If the exception occurs, then the **try** block is terminated, and JVM executes the **catch** block. However, if no exception occurs, then JVM never goes to the **catch** block. Owing to this, we need one block of code that is always confirmed to get executed, irrespective of the exception status. The **finally** block serves this purpose.

Can you use the finally block without using the catch block?

Yes, we can use the **finally** block after the **try** block even without a **catch** block. As we know, the **finally** block is always executed; it does not matter whether the **catch** block exists.

This approach is commonly used when we want to ensure that certain cleanup code, such as closing the resources, releasing the locks, or freeing the memory, is executed under all circumstances. However, in such cases, any exception thrown from the **try** block will propagate to the invoking method after the **finally** block is executed.

If we use the finally block without the catch block, what happens if the exception is thrown by the try block?

In such a case, the **try** block throws an exception, and a generic message will be generated. The actual exception is handled within the **finally** block, even if the **finally** block does not have any facility to catch the exception as part of the argument:

Observe the following code snippet:

```
public class Exception1 {
public static void main(String[] args) {
    int a, b, sum, div, mul;
    a=10;
    b=0;
    try {
        sum = a + b;
        System.out.println(sum);
        div = a / b;
        System.out.println(div);
        mul = a * b;
        System.out.println(mul);
    } finally {
        System.out.println("Finally called !!");
    }
  }
}
```

In the preceding code, the try block will generate **ArithmeticException**. However, we do not have the **catch** block to handle this exception. So, the **try** block will be terminated. However, while doing so, it will print that the exception is generated. JVM then executes the **finally** block, and the detailed exception trace will be returned as shown:

```
10
Exception in thread "main" Finally called !!
java.lang.ArithmeticException: / by zero
	at Exception1.main(Exception1.java:11)
```

What is the difference between ClassNotFoundException and NoClassDefFoundError?

Both of these exceptions are related to locating a class at runtime. If we are loading a class by using **Class.forName()** and the specific class is not found in the classpath, then **ClassNotFoundException** is generated. On the other hand, **NoClassDefFoundError** occurs if the class was present at compile time, and is not available at runtime.

In simple terms, **ClassNotFoundException** is a *checked exception* that usually occurs due to an incorrect class name or missing dependency at runtime, whereas **NoClassDefFoundError** is an *error* that typically occurs due to classpath issues, version mismatches, or missing libraries during application execution.

What is the use of the throws keyword?

In some situations, we come across a situation in which a method may contain code that may generate an exception. Normally, we need to handle such an exception by using the **`try-catch`** block within that method. However, if we do not want to handle that exception ourselves, we may use the throws keyword in the declaration of the method. This denotes that the method contains some code, which may generate the exception. However, the method had not handled it internally, and it is the caller's responsibility to handle the exception.

The following code snippet shows how to use the **`throws`** keyword:

```
public static void displayContent(File f) throws IOException {
  FileInputStream fis;
  fis = new FileInputStream(f);
  while (fis.read() != -1) {
    // business logic to read the file
  }
}
  public static void main(String[] args) {
    // TODO Auto-generated method stub
    File f = new File("d:\\sample.txt");
    try {
      displayContent(f);
    } catch (IOException io) {
      System.out.println("IO Exception occurred!!");
    }
  }
```

The preceding code snippet declares a method **`displayContent(File f)`**, which reads the content of the file. Reading a file may generate **`IOException`**, which is a checked exception. However, the method does not put the code of the file reading in try-catch; instead, the method declares itself as it throws **`IOException`**. This forces the invoker of the method to handle the exception. If you observe the invocation of **`displayContent()`** in the **`main()`** method, it is wrapped within the **`try-catch`**. This **`try-catch`** handles the **`IOException`**, that is thrown by the actual method.

Could you give a scenario where the throws keyword can be used?

When the code snippet within a method generates any exception, we must handle that exception in some way. If we handle the exception in the method itself, it will be a concrete way of dealing with the exception for all the other users who are invoking that method. However, if the method does not handle that exception and it is delegated to the invoker, then the invoker gets more flexibility to handle the exception in its own way.

This approach promotes better separation of concerns and makes the method more reusable and adaptable across different use cases.

What is a multi-catch block statement?

This is another important update in JDK1.7. Often, in an application, we come across a situation in which a single **try** block can generate more than one exception. To handle such multiple exceptions, earlier, we used to write multiple **catch** blocks one after another, forming a ladder of **catch** blocks. This approach is replaced in JDK1.7 by implementing a **multi-catch** block statement. In this case, we can club all the exception types in a single **catch** block separated by a pipe (|). This works in a similar manner to the logical OR (||) condition used in the **if** statements.

The following code snippet shows how to use a multi-catch block to handle **ArithmeticException**, **ArrayIndexOutOfBoundsException**, and **NullPointerException** in a concise and readable way:

```
catch(ArithmeticException | ArrayIndexOutOfBoundsException |
   NullPointerException e){
   //exception handler code
}
```

You can also use the generic exception object inside this **catch** block, but you should use it at the end.

In some cases, we observed that the main() method throws an exception. What do you mean by that?

When you have a code that may throw any exception, you need to handle it. There are a couple of approaches to do that. Either you wrap the code in a **try-catch** block inside a method or declare the method with the throws clause. If you declare a method with the throws clause, the invoker must handle it. However, at times, even the invoker may not handle the exception. In such a case, your code may get terminated abruptly if an exception arises. To avoid this, you can declare the **main()** method to throw that exception. It means that the exception is not handled within main, but it is propagated to the invoker of the **main()** method. In other words, the exception is propagated to JVM, and it will handle that exception.

What is the use of the printStackTrace() method?

Fundamentally, when we handle an exception in the **try** block, we often display the information about that exception to the user. One of the ways to do that is to print the **Exception** reference directly. However, a limitation of this approach is that while the user can see the reason for the exception, they do not get the exact line of the code that caused the exception.

The **printStackTrace()** method overcomes this limitation. It prints the complete stack trace of the exception, including the **Exception** type, error message, method call sequence, class names, and the exact line numbers where the exception occurred. This makes debugging easier and helps developers quickly identify the root cause of the problem.

Consider the following code snippet:

```
class ExceptionDemo {
    public static void divideNumber() {
      try {
        int ans = 5/0;
      }
      catch (Exception e) {
        System.out.println(e);
      }
    }

    public static void main( String args[] ) {
      divideNumber();
    }
}
```

Here, we know that the program is going to fail because of the invalid arithmetic operations it is trying to perform. When we execute the program, it gives the following information about the exception:

```
java.lang.ArithmeticException: / by zero
```

Therefore, instead of using the printing of the **Exception** reference, we can invoke the **printStackTrace()** method of the **Exception** reference in **catch**, as shown:

```
catch (Exception e) {
e.printStackTrace();
      }
```

This will return us the output as:

```
java.lang.ArithmeticException: / by zero
     at ExcecptionDemo.divideNumber(ExceptionDemo.java:4)
     at ExcecptionDemo.main(ExcecptionDemo.java:12)
```

Can we use the throw keyword for both the checked and unchecked exceptions?

The `throw` keyword is used to throw an exception explicitly. The `throw` keyword is used to manually create and throw the exception object at runtime. Although it is commonly used for custom (user-defined) exceptions, we can use this with a pre-defined exception as well. We can throw both the checked and unchecked exceptions provided by Java.

When a checked exception is thrown using the throw keyword, the method must either handle it using a `try-catch` block or declare it using the throws keyword. In contrast, when an unchecked exception is thrown, there is no such compile-time requirement to handle or declare it.

This flexibility makes the `throw` keyword useful for enforcing business rules, validating input, and signaling exceptional conditions explicitly in application logic.

Can we use the throws keyword for both the checked and unchecked exceptions?

Yes, we can use the `throws` keyword for both the checked and unchecked exceptions. It is used in the method declaration to indicate that the method may pass an exception to its caller instead of handling it internally.

For **checked exceptions**, using the `throws` keyword is often mandatory if the exception is not handled within the method. The `calling` method must then either handle the exception using a `try-catch` block or further declare it using `throws`.

For **unchecked exceptions**, using the `throws` keyword is optional and not enforced by the compiler. However, declaring unchecked exceptions can improve code readability and serve as documentation to inform callers about possible runtime issues.

Overall, the `throws` keyword helps in clearly defining a method's exception handling contract and promotes better separation of concerns.

What happens to the finally block if the try block returns a value to the invoker? Does it still execute?

The `finally` block works as a guarantor in exception handling. No matter what happens in the `try` block, the `finally` block always executes. Therefore, even if the `try` block returns some value successfully to its invoker, `finally` still executes. In this case, `finally` will be executed first, and then the value will be returned to the invoker function. This ensures that critical operations, such as closing resources, releasing locks, or performing cleanup activities, are always performed.

The **finally** block is commonly used for resource management and cleanup logic because of this guaranteed execution, making applications more robust and reliable.

What happens if the try and finally blocks execute different boolean values?

If you have a method that returns boolean, then your **try** block must return a Boolean value. However, it is not compulsory that the **try** and **finally** blocks should return the same Boolean value. That means your **try** block can return true, while the **finally** block can return false. In such a case, as **finally** executes even before the **return** statement is generated by the **try** block, the method returns from finally itself and returns false to the invoker.

Note: **This is a tricky question. Normally, when we implement the finally block, we write the resource closing code into it. So, the interviewer is expecting a common-sense approach in your answer.**

Is there any way by which you can avoid the execution of the finally block?

As we know, the **finally** block is always executed irrespective of the status of the **try** block. The only way to avoid the execution of the **finally** block is to use **System.exit(0)** in the **try** block, as shown in the following code:

```
public class RejectFinally {
  public static void main(String[] args) {
    try {
       System.out.println("Hello world");
       System.exit(0);
     } finally {
       System.out.println("Goodbye world");
  }
 }
}
```

The preceding code exits from the **try** block because of **System.exit(0)**, which in fact exits the entire application. The code generates **Hello World** output as the **finally** block is not executed.

What is the reason for OutOfMemory error? Do you have any ways to solve it?

This error occurs whenever JVM goes out of the heap memory. In other words, when JVM is unable to allocate heap memory for a newly created object, then this error is generated.

This situation may arise due to several reasons, such as creating too many objects, holding object references for a long time (memory leaks), inefficient data structures, or insufficient heap size configuration.

`OutOfMemoryError` is a subclass of `Error` and is generally **not meant to be handled at runtime** using `try-catch`, because recovery from it is difficult and unreliable. Instead, corrective actions are usually taken at the JVM or application design level.

Some common ways to address this issue include increasing the JVM heap size using options like `-Xms` and `-Xmx`, optimizing code to release unused object references, fixing memory leaks, and using memory profiling tools to analyze heap usage.

If a method does not throw any checked exception, can we invoke such a method in the try-catch block where the catch block handles the checked exception?

No, we cannot invoke any method in the `try-catch` block using the checked exception if the method does not throw that type of exception. This is because Java performs compile-time checking for checked exceptions, and the compiler will report an error if a checked exception is caught but is never thrown by the code inside the try block.

However, this restriction does *not* apply to unchecked exceptions. A `try-catch` block can catch unchecked exceptions even if the invoked method does not explicitly throw them, because unchecked exceptions are not verified by the compiler at compile time.

User-defined exception

A **user-defined exception** is a custom exception created by the programmer to represent specific error conditions in an application. It is created by defining a new class that extends the `Exception` or `RuntimeException` class. User-defined exceptions help make the program more meaningful by allowing developers to handle application-specific problems in a clear and organized way.

How to create a user-defined exception?

To create a user-defined or custom exception, we need to create a class that extends **Exception**. As **Exception** is a superclass for this class, the object of this class can be thrown and catch, similar to other built-in exception types.

This class may also contain a constructor to initialize a **String** member, which will contain the information about the exception. Along with this, it should also implement the **toString()** method to return meaningful information to the exception handler.

The following code snippet shows how to create a user-defined or custom exception:

```
public class MyException extends Exception{
   String str;
   public MyException(String str) {
      this.str=str;
   }
   public String toString() {
      return "MyException occurred";
   }
}
```

This code defines a user-defined exception named **MyException** by extending the **Exception** class. The constructor accepts a message and stores it in the **str** variable, allowing additional information about the exception to be passed when it is created. The **toString()** method is overridden to return a custom message when the exception object is printed.

How to use a user-defined exception?

User-defined exceptions are not known to JVM, so they are not automatically thrown by it. It is the responsibility of the developer to throw the object of such an exception based on the specific scenario for which such exceptions are created. We need to make use of the **throw** keyword to throw the object of a user-defined exception explicitly.

Typically, user-defined exceptions are used to represent business logic violations or application-specific error conditions. Once thrown, these exceptions can be handled using standard **try-catch** blocks or propagated to the calling method using the **throws** keyword.

The code snippet shows how we can throw and handle the exception of type **MyException,** which we have created earlier:

```
public void doSomething() {
   int x=10;
   if(x<10)
   try {
    throw new MyException("Number not matching");
```

```
    } catch (MyException e) {
    // TODO Auto-generated catch block
      System.out.println(e);
    }
}
```

This method checks the value of `x` and throws a user-defined exception if the condition `x < 10` is satisfied. The **`throw`** statement creates an object of **`MyException`** and transfers control to the corresponding **`catch`** block. The **`catch`** block then handles the exception by printing the message returned by the **`toString()`** method of the **`MyException`** class.

Can a subclass method throw a broader checked exception than its superclass method? Why or why not?

No, a subclass method cannot throw a broader checked **exception** than the one declared in its superclass method. This restriction exists to preserve polymorphism and maintain compile-time safety.

If a subclass were allowed to throw a broader checked exception, code written to the superclass type could unexpectedly encounter exceptions it is not prepared to handle, breaking the contract established by the superclass.

For example, if the superclass method declares **`throws IOException`**, and the subclass method declares throws **`Exception`**, any code calling the method via a superclass reference would be forced to handle all possible exceptions, violating the principle of substitutability.

Therefore, the compiler enforces this rule to ensure that any subclass method remains compatible with the exception handling expectations of the superclass, preventing runtime surprises.

Updates in exception handling

Exception handling in Java has improved gradually since Java 7 to make programs more robust and easier to maintain. Java 7 introduced important features such as try-with-resources for automatic resource management and multi-catch to handle multiple exceptions in a single **`catch`** block.

Java 9 enhanced try-with-resources by allowing effectively final variables declared outside the **`try`** block to be used as resources. Later versions of Java also improved exception messages and diagnostics, such as better **`NullPointerException`** messages, helping developers identify errors more easily. Up to Java 25, the core exception handling mechanism remains stable, with improvements mainly focused on better readability, debugging, and developer productivity.

What are the updates in exception handling provided by JDK 7?

JDK1.7 introduced 2 features in the exception handling mechanism:

- Automatic resource management
- Multi-catch block statement

What is automatic resource management?

Automatic resource management, or **try-with-resources**, is a new mechanism introduced in JDK1.7, to implement a more robust and reliable way to handle exceptions that deal with resources.

Normally, when we deal with resources in exception handling, we need to close the resources. To do this, we implement the **finally** block and close the resource inside that block. However, the problem is that as the resources are within the **try** block to close it outside the **try** block, the developer needs to take extra efforts that might make the code bulkier. Instead, JDK1.7 provides a way to open the resources in the arguments of the **try** itself, which can be closed automatically by JVM when we are done with the **try** block.

The following code block shows the **BufferedReader**, which is opened as a resource as an argument in the **try**, which will be closed automatically by JVM:

```
try (BufferedReader reader = new BufferedReader(
                                new InputStreamReader(System.in)))
```

By this approach, we do not need to use the **finally** block to close the **BufferedReader**. **BufferedReader** is opened within the **try** argument, as a resource that will be closed automatically by JVM after completion of the **try** block.

How are the resources closed automatically in the automatic resource management concept in Java?

From JDK 1.7 onward, the **AutoCloseable** interface was introduced. This class is implemented by different classes that can be used as resources. Classes related to I/O, networking, and **Remote Method Invocation** (RMI) implement this interface. The interface exposes the **close()** method for all implementer classes. When such resources are used within the **try** block as resources, the **close** method is implicitly invoked by JVM. We do not need to close such resources explicitly in **finally**.

How do enhanced NPE messages affect debugging and exception stack trace interpretation? (Java 14)

Starting from **Java 14**, **NullPointerException** (NPE) messages were introduced to provide more precise information about the null value that caused the exception. Traditionally, an NPE only indicated the line number where the null reference was accessed, but it did not specify which variable was null, making debugging a little difficult for the developer. This complexity was increased if you had multiple method calls or a chained reference.

With enhanced NPE messages, the JVM now pinpoints exactly. For example, consider the code as:

```
String cityName = person.getAddress().getCity(); //Line No. 14
```

In this code, if **getAddress()** returns null, prior to Java14, the **NullPointerException** was thrown and displayed for *line number 14*. With NPE now, the JVM will throw a clear exception message like:

```
java.lang.NullPointerException: Cannot invoke "Address.getCity()" because "person.getAddress()" is null
```

How does try-with-resources work with effectively final variables declared outside the try block? (Java9)

Starting from Java 9, the **try-with-resources** statement was enhanced to allow effectively final variables, that is, variables whose values are assigned once and never changed, to be used directly as resources inside the **try** block.

This means that resources can be declared outside the **try** statement and still be managed automatically, without needing to redeclare them inside the **try** parentheses. The only requirement is that such variables must not be reassigned after initialization.

The following code uses the object of **BufferedReader**, which can be termed as effectively final, as the file path it is referring to will not change during the business logic in the **try** block:

```
BufferedReader br =
                new BufferedReader(new FileReader("data.txt"));
try (br) {
    System.out.println(br.readLine());
}
```

In this example, the **`BufferedReader`** object **`br`** is declared before the **`try`** block and then used inside the **`try-with-resources`** statement. Since **`BufferedReader`** implements the **`AutoCloseable`** interface, it is automatically closed when the **`try`** block finishes execution. This eliminates the need to explicitly close the resource and helps prevent resource leaks.

How do recent JVM optimizations improve exception handling performance in resource-heavy applications? (Java25)

Recent JVM improvements make exception handling faster in applications that use many resources by avoiding unnecessary work upfront. Earlier, the JVM would immediately collect detailed error information (the full stack trace) even if that information was never used. Now, it waits and collects those details only when they are actually needed, such as when the error is printed or logged.

The system spends less time and CPU effort handling errors because of this, especially in situations where exceptions are frequent but not always examined in detail. This results in smoother performance and better efficiency in large, resource-intensive applications.

How does structured concurrency influence exception propagation across tasks? (Java 21)

Structured concurrency makes exception handling easier to understand by ensuring that errors in one task are automatically shared with the group of tasks it belongs to. Instead of exceptions being lost or handled in unexpected places, they are reported in a clear and predictable way within a defined task scope.

In simple terms, if one background task fails, the system knows exactly where that failure belongs, can stop related tasks if needed, and reports the error at a single, well-defined point. This makes debugging simpler and prevents hidden failures in concurrent programs.

How do records impact exception handling in immutable data carriers? (Java16)

Records in Java 16 encourage immutability, meaning that once a record object is created, its data cannot be changed. In simple terms, this removes the risk of accidentally modifying an object into an invalid or inconsistent state, one of the common causes of runtime exceptions.

Since record fields are final and set only at construction time, developers are forced to validate data upfront, which helps catch problems early rather than failing later with unexpected exceptions. This significantly reduces exception-prone state changes during program execution.

How does pattern matching for instanceof simplify exception handling logic? (Java17)

Pattern matching for **instanceof**, introduced in Java 17, simplifies exception handling logic by combining type checking and casting into a single step. This eliminates the need for explicit casting after a type check, reducing boilerplate code and the risk of `ClassCastException`.

With this feature, once an object matches a particular type, it is automatically cast and safely available within the same scope. This leads to cleaner, more readable, and less error-prone code, especially when handling different exception types or response objects.

Conclusion

In this chapter, we discussed what an exception is and how to handle it. We also talked about the different types of exceptions and the situations that are responsible for such exceptions. We studied different keywords like try, catch, finally, throws, and throw that take an active part in different mechanisms of exception handling. During this chapter, we discussed different interview questions that you may face about exception handling. You must now be in a better position now to answer many such interview questions. Additionally, we also explored how the new features introduced in different versions help to improve the way we can write efficient exception handling code. In the next chapter, we will discuss how to work with file handling and I/O in Java.

Join our Discord space

Join our Discord workspace for latest updates, offers, tech happenings around the world, new releases, and sessions with the authors:

https://discord.bpbonline.com

Chapter 5
I/O and File Handling

Introduction

Accepting the data from the user and processing it is a fundamental requirement of any application. It is hard to find an application that does not work with either taking input from the user or writing data to some destination. After all, applications are meant for that; they are meant to produce results based on some inputs. For all traditional programming languages like C, taking the input and formatting the output is the simplest task to do. However, Java developers are often heard complaining about the complex **input/output** (**I/O**) API for working with input/output, but often, what is heard may not be true. I/O API in Java is rich in size, and it is specific to a specific need. It provides many classes to perform basic operations, and also decorators on top of it that provide additional functionality. Just as cooking becomes difficult without knowing the ingredients, working with Java I/O feels complex, if one is unfamiliar with its building blocks.

Therefore, as developers, it is essential to understand this rich I/O ecosystem and how different classes work together to handle various I/O scenarios effectively. It is not enough to know how to read input from the console; it is equally important to understand how to store and retrieve data from flat files and other output destinations.

Structure

We will be covering interview questions based on the following topics in this chapter:

- Classification of I/O hierarchies
- File I/O operations
- Serialization and de-serialization
- Java NIO

Objectives

This chapter covers the rich set of Java I/O API in detail. During this entire chapter, we will study different classes that take an active part in reading/writing data, which is one of the most important requirements of any application. Additionally, you will also learn different input and output operations that you perform. At the end of this chapter, you will be able to work with different I/O statements and perform read/write operations on a file.

Classification of I/O hierarchies

In the Java I/O API, input and output operations are organized into a well-structured hierarchy to handle different types of data and use cases efficiently. This classification is primarily based on the nature of data being processed and the abstraction level provided by the streams. At the top level, Java divides I/O into **byte streams** and **character streams**, catering to binary data and text data, respectively.

Further, the I/O hierarchy is categorized into **low-level (node) streams** that directly interact with data sources such as files and **high-level (filter) streams** that provide additional functionality like buffering, data conversion, and object serialization. Classes such as `InputStream`, `OutputStream`, `Reader`, and `Writer` form the foundation of this hierarchy, enabling flexibility and extensibility in handling I/O operations.

This structured classification not only simplifies the development of robust I/O applications but also allows developers to chain multiple streams together, achieving enhanced performance and functionality while maintaining clean and maintainable code.

What are the different types of I/O streams?

There are two types of I/O streams:

- Byte-based I/O streams
- Character-based I/O streams

Could you explain the hierarchy of byte-based classes?

These classes directly work with streams. The two main classes of this API are `InputStream` and `OutputStream`. Both of these are abstract classes that provide different implementations, such as `BufferedInputStream`, `BufferedOutputStream`, `FileInputStream`, `FileOutputStream`, `DataInputStream`, `DataOutputStream`, `PipedInputStream`, and `PipedOutputStream`.

Could you explain System.in, System.out, and System.err?

A system normally represents a console to JVM, on which the program is executing. Through this console, the JVM facilitates standard input, output, and error handling mechanisms, which are exposed via the following streams:

- **System.in**: This is a static field of the predefined **`java.lang.System`** class and instance of **`InputStream`**. This is a standard instance that is used to take input from the user. This provides the **`read()`** method to accept the data from the user.
- **System.out**: This is a static field of the predefined Java class **`java.lang.System`**. As a hierarchy, a **`System`** is an instance of the **`PrintStream`** class, and **`PrintStream`** is a subclass of **`OutputStream`**. This is used to print the output to the console.
- **System.err**: This is almost similar to **`System.out`**; **`System.err`** is a static field of **`java.lang.System`**. This is also an instance of **`PrintStream`**, which is a subclass of the **`OutputStream`** class. Normally, this statement is used to print the error message on the console. Mostly, you would see this statement in a **`catch`** block of exception handlers.

Could you explain the hierarchy of character-based classes?

The reader and writer hierarchy is used to input/output the data in the character format. Though internally they are processed as bytes, they are exposed to a developer as character handlers. **`Reader`** and **`Writer`** are the top-most abstract super classes in this hierarchy. **`BufferedReader`**, **`BufferedWriter`**, **`FileReader`**, **`FileWriter`**, **`StringReader`**, and **`StringWriter`** are some of the implementation classes of these super classes.

What is the necessity of two types of streams? Why do we need byte streams and character streams?

Byte streams help in operating on the files containing ASCII characters. Sometimes, files also contain Unicode characters. To read such resources, Java introduced **character-based streams**. ASCII is a subset of Unicode. Therefore, to read the files with the English characters, we can use either byte streams or character streams.

In your opinion, which is better to use, byte streams or character streams?

It is often better to work with character streams. Character-based streams have more features than byte-based streams, such as using **`BufferedReader`**. We can use **`BufferedReader`** instead of **BufferedInputStream** or **DataInputStream**. The **BufferedReader** has a **newLine()** method to go to the next line. This is something that byte-based streams like **BufferedInputStream** or **DataInputStream** cannot provide directly and would require additional coding to implement.

Using character streams also simplifies encoding handling, as they are designed to work with Unicode characters, whereas byte streams require manual conversion between bytes and characters. Overall, character streams reduce boilerplate code, improve readability, and make working with text data much more intuitive and efficient.

What are filter streams, and which are those?

Filter streams add an extra functionality to the existing streams, such as giving line numbers to the destination, data formatting, or buffering, even though they do not exist in the source. The filter streams also help in increasing performance, particularly in copying operations, by reducing the number of I/O interactions with the underlying source or destinations.

Some commonly used filter stream classes are as follows:

- **LineNumberInputStream**: This class enables adding line numbers to the destination file.
- **DataInputStream**: The class offers methods such as **readInt()**, **readDouble()**, and **readLine()**, using which we can read an **int**, a **double**, and a **String** at a time.
- **BufferedInputStream**: The class offers a buffering effect, which increases performance to the peak.
- **PushbackInputStream**: The class enables pushing the required character back to the system.

What are PrintStream and PrintWriter? Are they the same? What is the difference between them?

Both these classes offer the functionality of displaying data using the **println()** method. However, both these classes belong to two different categories, byte streams and character streams.

In what scenarios is the Scanner class used?

The **Scanner** class was introduced in Java 1.5. It is used for reading a data stream from the input. Before **Scanner** to read the input, developers were using **DataInputStream**; then, after reading the stream, developers converted it into the respective data type, such as String, integer, or double, and so on. However, the **Scanner** class is a more flexible class that provides direct methods to scan different data types like **nextFloat()**, **nextDouble()**, **nextInteger()**, and so on.

What is the use of Buffered streams?

Buffered streams are used to store a larger amount of data in a buffer. To input the data, we can use `BufferedInputStream`, and to generate the output, we can use `BufferedOutputStream`. When the `read()` method is invoked on `BufferedInputStream`, the data is not removed from the stream, but it is removed from the buffer. Similarly, if we use `BufferedOutputStream`, the data is stored in the internal byte array, and instead of writing the data byte-by-byte, the entire array is pushed as an output. This approach is considered to be more efficient than the traditional I/O approach.

What is the BufferedWriter class in Java. Could you describe the purpose of the flush() and close() methods?

The buffer is a temporary storage area where data is stored. The `BufferedWriter` class is an output stream class that creates a Buffered character-output stream:

- The `flush()` method is used for clearing all the data characters stored in the buffer and making it empty.
- The `close()` method is used to close the opened character output stream.

How and when is the buffer cleared while using the BufferedWriter class?

Buffer is cleared in the following situations:

- Naturally, when the buffer is filled completely
- Explicitly, when the `flush()`method is invoked

We need to invoke the `flush()` method at the end of the file writing operation, so that all the residual content will be dumped to the file.

Could you explain the hierarchy of data streams?

These are the classes that are specialized to read different primitives like integers, floats, or even strings. The two important implementing classes are `DataInputStream` and `DataOutputStream`, which are subclasses of `FilterInputStream` and `FilterOutputStream`, respectively. Additionally, these also implement an interface. `DataInput` is implemented by `DataInputStream`, and `DataOutput` is implemented by `DataOutputStream`. These interfaces provide different methods like `readBoolean()`, `readInt()`, `readLine()`, `write()`, `writeInt()`, `writeDouble()`, and so on, which are implemented by these classes accordingly.

Can we read the data from multiple sources at the same time?

Yes, it is possible to read the data from multiple sources at the same time through the Java I/O API. Java provides **SequenceInputStream**, which can chain multiple input streams together to read the data from different sources. This is also a subclass of **InputStream**. The **SequenceInputStream** reads all the bytes from the resources in a sequence, and at the end, the stream is closed.

The following are the two constructors of this class:

- **public SequenceInputStream(Enumeration en)**
- **public SequenceInputStream(InputStream ins1, InputStream ins2)**

Here, in the second constructor, the **InputStreams**, **ins1** and **ins2**, can be of type **SequenceInputStream**.

The following code snippets show you how you can open different streams to read the data from the home pages of websites **http://www.rediff.com** and **http://www.bpbonline.com**:

```
try {
    URL u1 = new URL("http://www.rediff.com/");
    URL u2 = new URL("http://www.bpbonline.com");
    SequenceInputStream sin = new SequenceInputStream(u1.openStream(),
                                                      u2.openStream());
    }
    catch (IOException e) {
      //exception handler block
}
```

The code demonstrates how to combine input streams from multiple web sources into a single continuous stream using the **SequenceInputStream** class in Java. It opens streams from two URLs and reads their data sequentially, meaning the data from the first website is read completely before continuing with the second. This approach is useful when you want to process multiple input sources as a single stream without manually handling each one separately.

File I/O operations

File I/O operations in Java provide a mechanism to read data from and write data to files stored on the system. These operations are an essential part of application development, enabling programs to persist data, process large datasets, and interact with external resources such as text files, binary files, and configuration files.

Java offers a comprehensive set of classes under the java.io and **java.nio.file** packages to perform file handling efficiently. Developers can use byte streams (**FileInputStream**, **FileOutputStream**) for handling binary data and character streams (**FileReader**, **FileWriter**) for text-based data. Additionally, higher-level classes like **BufferedReader** and **BufferedWriter** improve performance by reducing the number of I/O operations.

With the introduction of the Java **New Input/Output (NIO) operations** API, file handling in Java has become more powerful and flexible, offering features such as non-blocking I/O, file manipulation using **Path** and **Files**, and better exception handling. Overall, Java's File I/O capabilities provide a robust and scalable way to manage data storage and retrieval in modern applications.

What is the purpose of the File class?

The **File** class is a non-stream class. The class is used to find the properties of a file, such as file creation and modification time, read/write permissions of the file, the size of the file, and so on. This normally points to a file location, which can be used further to open the file in read or write mode. The **File** object does not ensure that the file is present or not; when we use this reference with **FileWriter** or **FileOutputStream**, then only JVM checks the existence of the file.

What is the use of FileInputStream class?

The **FileInputStream** class is used to read the content of a file. It is a concrete implementation of **InputStream**. Thus, this provides the implementation for methods like **read()**, **available()**, **close()**, and so on. This class provides the following constructors to open the file in read mode:

- **public FileInputStream(String fileName) throws FileNotFoundException**
- **public FileInputStream(File file) throws FileNotFoundException**
- **public FileInputStream(FileDescriptor fd)**

What is the use of FileOutputStream class?

The **FileOutputStream** class is used to write to a file. It is a concrete implementation of **OutputStream**. So, this provides implementation for methods like **write()**, **flush()**, and **close()**. The **write()** method can take the **int** or **byte[]** array, which can be passed to a file. This class provides the following constructors:

- **public FileOutputStream(String filename) throws FileNotFoundException**
- **public FileOutputStream(File file) throws FileNotFoundException**
- **public FileOutputStream(FileDescriptor fd)**
- **public FileOutputStream(String name, boolean append) throws FileNotFoundException**

Can we read the data from a webpage?

Java provides the **java.net** package, which consists of different classes to communicate with the network. To communicate with the web page, we can make use of the URL class, which takes a URL in the format of String as an argument to which we can connect. Once we get connected with the specified URL, we can use the **openStream()** method of **InputStream**, which downloads the data from the server, and then, using the **read()** method, we can read the data.

Have you dealt with random access files?

The **RandomAccessFile** class is designed to work with files, offering random access to the contents of the file. Working with the **RandomAccessFile** class offers the functionality of **DataInputStream** and **DataOutputStream** combined in one class. In addition to the functionalities offered by them, the class offers another method, **seek()**. This method enables us to move to the specific position in the file and then change the value stored there.

We need to keep in mind the file structure while using the **RandomAccessFile** class. The **RandomAccessFile** class has methods for reading and writing primitives and UTF-8 strings.

Which class should be used to create a directory?

We have the **File** class to create the files, but there is no **Directory** class. The **File** class itself is used to create files as well as directories.

We can create a directory named **mydir** using the following code:

```
File dir = new File("/path/mydir");
if (!dir.exists()){
      dir.mkdirs();
}
```

This code first checks whether the directory already exists to avoid unnecessary creation. The **mkdirs()** method ensures that all required parent directories are also created if they do not already exist, making it suitable for creating nested directory structures.

What is the use of the mismatch() method introduced in Java12?

Java12, introduced a new feature in the file API to check the equality of the files. The **mismatch()** is a static method of the **Files** class, which checks if the files are equal or not. This reduces the burden on the developer to check the contents of the file character by character. This method takes two file paths (Path references) as an argument and returns:

- First mismatch position between the files
- -1L, if no mismatch found

How to create and delete the temporary files?

We can create the temporary files using the **createTempFile()** method of the **File** class. When an application terminates, the created file can be deleted using the **deleteOnExit()** method. This file deletion will be attempted only if the virtual machine is terminated normally. In case of the abnormal termination of the application, the file may not be deleted. Also, once deletion is requested, it is not possible to cancel that request.

We can use the following code to create and, after use, delete the temporary file:

```
File tem = File.createTempFile("myfile", ".txt");
tem.deleteOnExit(); //This will delete when JVM exits
```

This approach is useful when you need a temporary file for intermediate processing without worrying about manual cleanup. The **deleteOnExit()** method ensures that the file is automatically removed when the JVM terminates, helping prevent unnecessary file accumulation on the system.

What is the use of the property file, and how to create property files dynamically in Java?

The property file is used to store the configuration-related data of the application. An application can pull this data at runtime.

The file can be dynamically created as follows:

```
Properties props = new Properties();
//Populating the properties file
props.put("driver_class_name", "com.mysql.cj.jdbc.Driver");
props.put("username", "root");
props.put("password", "mypass");
FileOutputStream os= new
            FileOutputStream("D:\\mydir\\myfile.properties");
//Storing the properties in the file
props.store(os, "This is a sample properties file");
```

This code creates a **Properties** object and populates it with key-value pairs representing configuration data such as database driver, username, and password. It then writes these properties to a **.properties** file using a **FileOutputStream**, making the configuration available for the application to read at runtime.

Serialization and de-serialization

Serialization is the process of maintaining the state of an object in the form of a sequence of bytes for a longer duration. **Deserialization** is the opposite of serialization. It restores an object from these bytes. The **`java.io`** package offers an API for the serialization and deserialization process. To serialize any object, the class representing that object must implement the **`Serializable`** interface.

Which methods are declared within the Serializable interface?

`Serializable` is a marker interface that does not have any methods declared within it. This only makes the object of that class eligible for the process of serialization.

Can you explain the process of serialization and deserialization?

We can serialize and deserialize the object as follows:

1. Let us consider that we have Person as the POJO class.
2. We can serialize the object as follows:

    ```
    FileOutputStream fos= new FileOutputStream("persons.txt");
    ObjectOutputStream oos = new ObjectOutputStream(fos);
    // Method for serialization of object
    oos.writeObject(person);
    oos.close();
    fos.close();
    ```

    This code creates a **`FileOutputStream`** and wraps it with an **`ObjectOutputStream`** to enable object serialization. It then writes the person object to the file **`persons.txt`**, converting it into a byte stream, and finally closes the streams to release resources.

3. Deserialization can be achieved as follows:

    ```
    FileInputStream fis= new FileInputStream("persons.txt");
    ObjectInputStream oin = new ObjectInputStream(fis);
    // Method for deserialization of object
    Person person = (Person)oin.readObject();
    oin.close();
    fis.close();
    System.out.println("name = " + person.getName());
    System.out.println("age = " + person.getAge());
    ```

This code uses a **FileInputStream** and **ObjectInputStream** to read a serialized object from the file **persons.txt**. It deserializes the object back into a **Person** instance, and then prints its name and age after closing the streams.

What is SerialVersionUID?

A version number that is associated with each serializable class is termed as a **SerialVersionUID**. This number is used during the process of deserialization. The number is used to verify whether a serialized object has been loaded for the classes that are compatible with respect to serialization. **InvalidClassException** will be thrown in case the receiver loads a class of the object that has a different UID than that of the corresponding sender's class during deserialization.

Why is it that sometimes, even if you implement Serializable for a class, you cannot serialize an object?

Yes, sometimes you may encounter **NotSerializableException**, even if the class implements the **Serializable** interface. This happens because of the following reasons:

- If you are using containment within that object, and the contained object is not serializable.
- If the superclass of the class does not implement the **Serializable** interface, and it does not even have a default constructor.
- If someone is deliberately throwing **NotSerializableException**, just to ensure that the object should not be serialized.

How to customize the process of serialization?

To customize the process of serialization, instead of implementing the **Serializable** interface, we need to implement the **Externalizable** interface. Unlike the **Serializable** interface, this interface is not a marker interface; it declares the methods **readExternal()** and **writeExternal()**, which must be overridden. In this way, instead of JVM taking the entire responsibility of the serialization process, developers can write their custom logic to serialize an object.

How to protect the data from being serialized?

If you need any data member to get protected from the process of serialization, you can declare that data member with the **transient** keyword. Members declared with the **transient** keyword are not serialized even if the object is serialized.

What is the deserialization filter process? (Java17)

The process of deserialization is quite risky as it can deserialize the object from any untrusted resources. We must ensure that such deserialized objects are safe. This can be achieved by filtering the deserialization process.

The deserialization filtering allows the developer to whitelist or blacklist the classes based on the application's needs. This promotes tight security and avoids the entry of vulnerable objects in applications generated from the deserialization process.

Can you explain how deserialization filtering works? (Java17)

Java17 uses the **ObjectInputFilter** interface to filter the objects in the process of serialization. The **ObjectInputFilter** provides the following status values, which can be used to control and enforce deserialization filtering rules during the deserialization process:

- **ALLOWED**: This indicates that the class or object being deserialized is allowed.
- **REJECTED**: This indicates that the class or object being deserialized is not permitted.
- **UNDECIDED**: This indicates that there is no decision yet about the filtering. The decision is pushed to the next filter condition or business logic scenario.

Can you explain the difference between the InputStream and OutputStream classes?

InputStream is used to read data from a source such as a file, a socket, or the standard input. On the other hand, **OutputStream** is used to write data to destinations such as a file, a socket, or standard output.

Can you explain the difference between the BufferedReader and FileReader classes?

FileReader is specifically used to read the data from the specified file if it exists. However, **BufferedReader** acts as a decorator. **BufferedReader** offers buffering for faster I/O.

The **FileReader** class offers a **read()** method to read the data from the file. We can use it to read data from the **myfile.txt** file as:

```
FileReader fr=new FileReader("C:\\myfile.txt");
```

BufferedReader acts as a decorator, which offers the **readLine()** method to read the data as follows:

```
FileReader fr=new FileReader("C:\\myfile.txt");
BufferedReader br=new BufferedReader(fr);
```

As **BufferedReader** is a decorator, it can also be used to read data from the standard input. We can use the following code to read the standard input:

```
InputStreamReader isr=new InputStreamReader(System.in);
BufferedReader br=new BufferedReader(isr);
```

This setup allows efficient reading of character input from the console by buffering the input stream. Methods like **readLine()** can then be used to read user input line by line, making it convenient for handling text-based input.

What is the use of the PrintStream class?

The **PrintStream** class is used to write data to the standard output. We all very frequently use **System.out.println()** to display something on the console. In this, out is an object of the **PrintStream** class on which we are invoking the **println()** method.

Can we close the stream in a try block? Why should we close the streams in a finally block? What change happened in JDK 7 to close the stream?

We should close the stream in a **finally** block because the **finally** block is always executed irrespective of whether the exception occurred or not in the **try** block.

If we close the stream in the **try** block, it can be closed only if the code gets executed without an exception.

From JDK 7 onward, we do not need to explicitly close the stream if we open it within try-with-resources. This is possible because it now implements the **Autoclosable** interface:

```
try (BufferedReader br = new BufferedReader(
                new FileReader("C:\\myfile.txt"))) {
//code here
 } catch (IOException e) {
            e.printStackTrace();
}
```

In this approach, the JVM automatically closes the resource once the **try** block is executed, even if an exception occurs. This improves code readability and helps prevent resource leaks by ensuring proper cleanup of streams.

Can we convert a file into a string? Can you explain how?

The following code snippet shows how we can convert a file into a string:

```
FileInputStream fi = new FileInputStream(name_of_file);
byte[] buffer = new byte[10];
StringBuilder sb = new StringBuilder();
while (fi.read(buffer) != -1) {
  sb.append(new String(buffer));
  buffer = new byte[10];
}
String file_to_string = sb.toString();
```

This code reads the file in small chunks of bytes using a buffer and appends each chunk to a `StringBuilder`. After the loop completes, the accumulated content is converted into a single `String`, representing the entire file content.

Can we set permissions on a file? Which permissions can be set on a file? How to set permissions on a file?

The file permissions are required to be changed whenever the user wants to restrict the operations on a file. There are a number of methods that offer checking and setting the permissions of a file. For example, a read-only file can be set to permit the permissions of writing data to it.

We can check the permission with methods such as:

- **canExecute()**: The function checks whether the application is allowed to execute the file. It will return true if the path name exists, and the application is allowed to execute the specified file.
- **canRead()**: The function checks whether the application is allowed to read the file or not. The method returns true if it can be read by the application.

The following methods are used to modify or set the permissions on a file:

- **setExecutable()**: The method allows setting the owner's execute permission for the path name.
- **setReadable()**: The method is used to set the owner's read permission.
- **setWritable()**: The method is used to set the owner's write permission.

Have you ever encountered java.io.FileNotFoundException for Access is denied? Do you know how to fix that?

Normally, this exception occurs while creating a file on the C drive where the OS is installed.

To fix this, we can change its permission as follows:

1. Go to `C:\Program Files\`.
2. Right-click **Java** on the folder and click on **Properties**.
3. Now select the **Security** tab.
4. Click on the **Edit** button.
5. A pop-up **PERMISSIONS FOR JAVA** window will open.
6. Click on **Add**.
7. One more pop-up will open. Here, in the **Enter object name** box, enter your user account name, and after that, click **OK**.
8. In the **PERMISSIONS OF JAVA** window, you will find several clickable options such as **CREATOR, OWNER, SYSTEM,** and so on. One of them is your username. Select it, and check the **FULL CONTROL** option in **Permissions for** the sub-window.
9. Hit **Apply** and **OK**.

This will grant the required permissions to your user account, allowing file creation and modification in the specified directory. However, it is generally recommended to avoid writing files in system-protected locations like `C:\Program Files` and instead use user-specific directories (such as documents or application-specific folders) to prevent permission-related issues.

What is a memory-mapped file? Could you explain the advantages and disadvantages of a memory-mapped file?

Memory-mapped files are the files in Java that allow an application to access contents directly from memory. This is achieved by mapping the whole file, or some part of the file, into memory. The operating system will take care of loading the page requested and then writing that into the file while the application deals with the memory. This allows very fast I/O operations. The memory used to load the memory-mapped file is from outside of the Java heap space. The `java.nio` package offers memory-mapped file operations. `MappedByteBuffer` can be used to read and write from the memory.

The advantages are as follows:

- The performance is important to build a high-frequency electronic trading system. The memory-mapped file is a faster way than using a standard file access using normal I/O operations.
- The memory-mapped file allows the developers to load a potentially larger file, which is not accessible otherwise.
- Most of operating system supports memory-mapped I/O operations. Furthermore, with the 64-bit architecture, it is possible to map almost any file into memory and also access it directly using the Java application.
- The file can be shared; it gives the developers shared memory between processes, and this can be more than 10x lower latency using a socket over loopback.

The disadvantage is that as the operating system only loads a portion of the file into the memory, when the requested page is not present in the memory, then it will result in a page fault.

What is the output for a given code? Will the physical file will be available at the location after the execution of the code?

Consider:

```
File f = new File("myfile.txt");
```

The code will only be executed without an exception, but no physical file will be created. In case if the file needs to be created, we need to execute the code as follows:

```
f.createNewFile();
```

This method explicitly creates a new empty file on the file system if it does not already exist. It returns a boolean value indicating whether the file was successfully created, helping in validating the operation.

How can you pull specific types of files for processing?

Java provides the **FilenameFilter** interface, which lets you to provide the information about which kind of files can be accepted. This interface, which is present in the **java.io** package, declares the **accept()** method as follows:

```
public abstract boolean accept(File directory, String name);
```

This method takes two arguments; the **`File`** object, which points to the directory, and file name. This method returns true if the file that you have declared has passed through this filter and matches the condition, else returns false.

Java NIO

Java NIO is an advanced I/O API introduced in JDK 1.4 to provide faster and more efficient data processing compared to traditional I/O. It is designed to handle large volumes of data using buffers, channels, and selectors. Unlike the conventional stream-based approach, NIO supports non-blocking I/O operations, allowing a single thread to manage multiple tasks. This makes it highly suitable for scalable and high-performance applications such as servers and real-time systems.

What is the difference between I/O and NIO?

NIO is an advanced I/O API in Java designed to provide faster and more flexible data processing compared to traditional I/O. The key differences between traditional I/O and NIO can be understood as follows:

- Java new input-output is known as NIO, which was introduced with JDK 1.4. The NIO offers high-speed, block-oriented I/O to the library.
- I/O is blocking I/O; however, NIO is non-blocking I/O. It means the thread will be blocked until it completes the I/O operations. However, the thread can perform some other operation if the data is not available and does not block the process.
- The traditional I/O is stream based; however, the NIO is buffer-oriented. It means the NIO first reads the data in a buffer and then makes it available for asynchronous processing. Moreover, it is possible to move back and forth in the buffer, but in older stream-based operations, it was not possible.

What are the fundamental components of NIO?

The following are the fundamental components of NIO:

- **Channel buffers**: In standard IO, operations are either character or stream-based, but NIO uses channels and buffers. It means the data is always written from a buffer to the channel and then read from the channel into the buffer.
- **Selectors**: The selector is an object that is used to monitor multiple channels for events such as connection opened, data arrived, etc. It makes it possible for a single thread to monitor multiple channels for the data.
- **Non-blocking I/O**: The application must have a mechanism to find when the data is ready so that the operation will not be blocking to wait till the data is arrived.

What are selectors?

Selectors are introduced in NIO, which enables a single thread to monitor multiple channels of the input. We can register multiple channels with the selector. After that, we can use a single thread to select the channels that have input available for processing. Furthermore, we can select the channels that are ready for writing. The mechanism of a selector makes it very easy for a single thread to manage multiple channels.

What are channels?

Channels are used to perform NIO operations. They act as a tube through which the data will be transported between the buffer and the entity. The data is read from the entity via channels and placed in the buffer to consume. The best part of channels is that they can be used for both read and write operations. It means the channels read the data from the entity in the buffer and then write the data from the buffer to the destination asynchronously as well.

Could you explain the NIO channel classes?

The following are the types of channel classes:

- **FileChannel**: This is a file-based channel used for reading as well as writing operations that cannot be placed in non-blocking mode. We can get the instance of `FileChannel` by invoking the `getChannel()` method on the instance of the file.
- **SocketChannel**: These are the channels that can be used to operate in the non-blocking mode. `SocketChannel` is mainly divided into the following three types of channels:
  - **DatagramChannel**: This class can be used to perform read and write operations over the network using UDP.
  - **SocketChannel**: The `SocketChannel` class can be used to read and write data over the TCP network.
  - **ServerSocketChannel**: This class is used to perform I/O operations over TCP connections.

When would you prefer I/O over NIO and vice versa?

If your I/O operations are pretty simple and predictable, you should always prefer the Java I/O API. It is like reading a book line by line. This approach suits best if you wish to write code to read a configuration file, write a log file, or process a CSV file.

On the other hand, if your requirement is to handle many I/O operations at the same time, then you should always prefer the Java NIO API. For example, if you are dealing with chat applications of your program that handle many connections at the same time, then NIO is the best choice for you.

How does Java NIO support event-driven programming?

Earlier, when developers were utilizing the traditional I/O operations, the program was of a blocking nature. In other words, the program waits for the operation to complete. In NIO, developers can utilize concepts like channel and selector. The channels are registered with a selector, and the program waits for the event to occur. Once the event occurs, it is notified to the program via a selector. This way, NIO supports the classical event-driven programming.

What is the use of CompletionHandler in Java NIO?

As the name implies, `CompletionHandler` is a handler that handles the completion of an asynchronous task in a program. It is invoked automatically when the task is completed associated with it.

`CompletionHandler` consists of the following methods:

- **completed**: Invoked when the operation is completed successfully.
- **failed**: Invoked when the operation fails or abruptly terminates because of some error.

Conclusion

In this chapter, we discussed the different classes and interfaces that are used in an I/O operation. Java IO API is vast in number, but we have tried to cover many classes and interfaces that play a vital role in the interview questions, which is the prime goal of this book. Additionally, we also discussed the NIO API in Java, which was introduced to work with non-blocking I/O operations. In this chapter, we have discussed many such questions that can be asked in a Java interview. In the next chapter, we will discuss how you can create multi-threaded applications and interview questions related to the same.

Join our Discord space

Join our Discord workspace for latest updates, offers, tech happenings around the world, new releases, and sessions with the authors:

https://discord.bpbonline.com

CHAPTER 6
Concurrency

Introduction

Right from the early days of programming, developers have been writing sequential programs to develop an application. Often, such programs were executed on a system that had to perform a single task throughout its life. Though initially it was not a big concern, in the later stages of hardware development, when hardware and operating systems evolved to their next stages, such programming was considered to be inefficient as well as expensive. Sequential programs do not utilize the power of the operating system and hardware to their full extent. This gave rise to the concept of multithread or concurrent programming, where different programs can run simultaneously on the operating system. To understand the concept of a multithreaded program, you can take real-time examples from your day-to-day life. While boiling water for tea, you can fetch a newspaper that is on your doormat, or while having a cup of tea, you can even read the newspaper; these tasks are typically asynchronous in nature. Similarly, there are many tasks in applications that do not depend on each other. Such tasks can be executed simultaneously by using the concepts of threads.

Structure

We will be covering interview questions based on the following topics in this chapter:

- Concept of multithreading
- Inter-thread communication
- Thread lifecycle
- Concurrency API
- Recent updates in concurrency

Objectives

In this chapter, you will learn what a thread is and how to create it. We will also discuss how different threads can communicate with each other to create an efficient application. In the later stages, we will discuss the concurrency API of Java, which makes the multithreaded programming way simpler than the traditional programming approach.

Concept of multithreading

Multithreading is a programming technique in which multiple threads are executed concurrently within a single process. Multithreading consumes less memory and system resources compared to creating multiple processes, as they share the same address space. As threads are lightweight, they enhance the performance of an application.

What is a thread?

A **thread** is a lightweight sub-process and represents the smallest unit of execution within the program. It provides a separate path of execution because each thread runs in a different stack frame. A process may contain multiple threads. Threads share the process resources, but still, they execute independently and can perform different tasks simultaneously. This enables efficient multitasking, improved application performance, and better utilization of CPU resources, especially in multi-core environments.

What are the advantages of multithreading?

The advantages are as follows:

- The thread is lightweight, so it enhances the application performance.
- Multithreading reduces the number of servers, as one server can execute multiple threads at a time.
- Even though some background tasks are running, multithreading allows an application to always be reactive to accept input.
- As multithreading includes the execution of multiple threads independently, it allows the faster execution of tasks.
- The threads share the common memory resources, so multithreading provides better utilization of cache memory.

What is a process? Can you differentiate between a process and a thread?

A program in execution is termed as a **process**, and a **thread** is a subset of the process.

The differences between them are as follows:

- Processes are independent, but the threads are a subset of a process.
- The processes have different address spaces in the memory. However, the threads contain a shared address space of the process.
- The inter-thread communication is faster and easier than the inter-process communication.
- The context switching is faster between the threads as compared to the processes.

What is the difference between synchronous and asynchronous programming in multithreading?

The following are the differences between synchronous and asynchronous programming:

- **Synchronous programming**: It is a blocking programming model. In synchronous programming, a thread is assigned to complete a task. Once the thread starts working on the task, it is only available for other tasks after the completion of the assigned task. The tasks are executed in a predictable and sequential manner, making the program easier to understand and debug. This model is more suitable in scenarios where execution order is critical.
- **Asynchronous programming**: This follows a non-blocking execution model. In the asynchronous programming model, one job can be handled by more than one thread in the background. While one task is waiting, the thread can execute the other tasks, which enhances the application's performance and hence provides maximum usability.

Is it possible to predict the thread behavior?

No one can predict the thread behavior with certainty. It is said so because it is the thread scheduler that does the execution of threads. The developer has no direct control over choosing which thread to execute at any given moment. The thread scheduler may have a different implementation on different platforms. This depends on several factors like CPU availability, system load, thread priorities, etc. Thus, it may happen that the same threading program may produce different outputs in subsequent executions on the same platform as well. Owing to this inherent non-deterministic behavior of the threads, we need to ensure that we implement proper thread synchronization and thread-safe programming practices in multi-threaded applications.

What is context switching?

Whenever we work with multiple threads, the CPU switches from one thread to another. This switching is so rapid that it creates the illusion of parallel execution. In **context switching**, the states of the executing threads, such as the program counter, register values, and the stack information, are saved. This stored state is restored, and the thread is resumed from that point onward when the thread gets a chance to execute again.

Could you differentiate between the Thread class and the Runnable interface for creating a thread?

A thread can be created in two ways:

- By defining a class that extends the **Thread** class
- By defining a class that implements the **Runnable** interface

The differences between these two ways are as follows:

- When we use an extension of the **Thread** class, the class cannot extend another class, as Java does not support multiple inheritance. However, when we use the implementation of the **Runnable** interface, the class can still extend another class to utilize its services.
- Once we write a class extended from the **Thread** class, each thread creates a unique object and is associated with it. However, if we use the implementation of the Runnable interface, multiple threads share the same object.
- The **Thread** class has inbuilt methods such as **getPriority()**, **isAlive()**. However, the **Runnable** interface has a single method, **run()**.

What is the relationship between Thread and Runnable?

The **Thread** class implements the **Runnable** interface, which establishes a close relationship between the two. The **Runnable** interface declares the single abstract method **run()**, which represents the task to be executed by a thread.

The **Thread** class implements an empty implementation of the **run()** method. If a **Thread** object is created by passing a **Runnable** instance to its constructor, the **run()** method internally delegates the execution to the **Runnable** object's **run()** method. If no **Runnable** is provided, the default implementation of **run()** in the **Thread** class performs no operation.

This design promotes the separation of concerns, where the task logic is defined in the **Runnable** implementation, while the thread management is handled by the **Thread** class.

What are the different overloaded constructors that Thread provides?

The **Thread** class provides the following types of constructors:

Constructor	Description
`Thread()`	Creates a new **Thread** object
`Thread(Runnable r)`	Creates a new **Thread** object for **Runnable** target object
`Thread(String s)`	Creates a new thread with a title
`Thread(Runnable r,String s)`	Creates a new thread for **Runnable** target object and also adds a title to it
`Thread(ThreadGroup t, Runnable r)`	Creates a new thread for **Runnable** target object, which belongs to a particular thread group
`Thread(ThreadGroup t, Runnable r,String s)`	Creates a new thread for **Runnable** target object, which belongs to a particular thread group and with a title for the thread

Table 6.1: Constructors of a thread

What is thread starvation?

Thread starvation is a condition in which a thread does not have enough CPU time for its execution. It may be caused by several different reasons, such as:

- Low-priority threads get less CPU time for execution compared to high-priority threads. As a result, the lower-priority thread may starve away waiting to get enough CPU to perform the task.
- In the deadlock situation, two or more threads wait for each other to release the lock. Since none of the threads can proceed, they efficiently starve and are unable to obtain CPU time.
- The thread might be waiting for a long time for the lock on an object's monitor, as no other thread is calling the `notify()` or `notifyAll()` methods. This results in indefinite waiting and eventual starvation.

What are daemon threads?

Daemon threads are low-priority threads. The daemon threads provide the background support and services to the user threads. These threads perform auxiliary tasks that help the application run smoothly but are not essential to the core execution of the program. The JVM terminates the daemon thread automatically if the program remains with the daemon thread only. The common examples of daemon threads are the garbage collector, memory management threads, and other background maintenance tasks managed by JVM.

The **Thread** class provides the following methods to work with the daemon threads:

- **setDaemon(boolean status)**: The method is used to mark the thread as a daemon thread or a user thread. This method must be invoked before starting up the thread; otherwise, it results in **IllegalThreadStateException**.
- **isDaemon()**: The method does a check for the thread whether it is a daemon or not.

How to create a daemon thread? Can we make the user thread a daemon thread if the thread is started?

If a thread is already started, and after that we try to make that a daemon, it will throw **IllegalThreadStateException**. We can only create a daemon thread before starting that thread.

The following code snippet demonstrates how to create the daemon thread:

```
public class DaemonThread extends Thread {
   public DaemonThread(String name) {
      super(name);
   }
   public void run() {
      // Checking the thread is Daemon or not
      if (Thread.currentThread().isDaemon()) {
      System.out.println("The " + getName() + " is Daemon thread");
   } else {
      System.out.println("The" + getName() + " is User thread");
    }
 }
public static void main(String[] args) {
   DaemonThread thread1 = new DaemonThread("thread1");
   // Set user thread to Daemon
   thread1.setDaemon(true);
   thread1.start();
 }
}
```

What is a shutdown hook?

The **shutdown hook** is a thread that is invoked implicitly before JVM shuts down. We can use it to perform cleaning up of the resource to save the state when JVM shuts down either normally or abruptly. The shutdown hooks can only be started when JVM shuts down. Shutdown hooks are registered using the **addShutdownHook** (thread hook) method of the **Runtime** class. Once registered, they are executed concurrently, and the JVM does not guarantee the order in which multiple shutdown hooks will run. The shutdown hooks are more reliable than the **finalize()** method, as there is very little chance that shutdown hooks will not run. The **halt(int status)** method of the **Runtime** class can be invoked to stop the shutdown hook.

Inter-thread communication

Multithreaded applications essentially consist of different threads performing the assigned task to achieve the business need. While achieving this, multiple threads can communicate with each other. They may have data or method invocation, which is shared across them. This is normally required to make sure that the CPU always remains utilized, reducing its idle time. Such communication between threads generates the information exchange between them. This information exchange is sometimes complex, as the information might get exchanged even before the business logic is completed. To control this confusion, inter-thread communication is controlled by different methods like **wait()**, **notify()**, and **notifyAll()**.

What is the purpose of the wait() method in a thread?

The object class has the **wait()** method, which is primarily used for inter-thread communication in Java. The method allows for pausing the current thread temporarily, and it waits until a specific condition is met.

When a thread invokes a **wait()** method on an object, it releases the monitor lock of that object and enters the waiting state. The thread remains in this state until another thread invokes the **notify()** or **notifyAll()** method on the same object.

Are you aware of the synchronized block? Why is the wait() method invoked from the synchronized block?

Yes, the synchronized block is a fundamental construct in Java to control access to shared resources in a multithreaded environment. It ensures that only one thread at a time can execute a critical section of the code by acquiring the monitor lock associated with a specific object. The **wait()** method comes into play to perform inter-thread communication. If we do not use the synchronized block while invoking the **wait()** method, the JVM throws the **java.lang.IllegalMonitorStateException** exception. Additionally, when a thread calls **wait()**, it releases the monitor lock and enters the waiting state, allowing other threads to acquire the lock and invoke **notify()** or **notifyAll()** to resume execution. This coordination mechanism ensures safe and predictable communication between threads.

How would you maintain the sequence of execution of a thread in Java? If you have multiple threads, how would you control the flow so that a particular thread executes first and others execute later?

This can be achieved by invoking the `join()` method on a particular thread. Suppose you have three threads: `thread1`, `thread2`, and `thread3`, and you want `thread1` to complete its task first, then you can invoke `join()` on `thread1`. Remember that you must have invoked the `start()` method on `thread1` before invoking the `join()` method. Once the `join()` method is invoked, the invoking thread enters a waiting state until `thread1` completes its execution. After `thread1` finishes, the remaining threads are allowed to execute in the desired order.

What does the join() method do?

The `join()` method causes the currently running thread to pause its execution until the thread it joins completes its task.

The `join()` method comes with three overloaded versions as follows:

- **join()**: This method will put the current running thread on wait until the thread on which the method is invoked is dead. In case the thread is interrupted, then it will throw `InterruptedException`.
- **join(long milliseconds)**: This method works similarly to the `join()` method, but it waits for the specified time, as denoted in arguments.
- **join(long milliseconds, int nanoseconds)**: In this overloading method, along with the milliseconds, nanoseconds are also added to denote the waiting period for join.

Could you explain the difference between the wait() and sleep() methods? What is the difference between the wait() and sleep() methods?

The `wait()` and `sleep()` methods are both used to pause the execution of a thread, but they differ significantly in purpose, behavior, and usage. One of the most important differences is the class hierarchy of these methods. The `wait()`method is defined in the `Object` class, and the `sleep()`method is defined in the `Thread` class. This reflects their intended use: `wait()` is meant for inter-thread communication, while `sleep()` is used to pause a thread for a fixed duration. Another difference is in terms of lock handling. The `wait()` method releases the lock acquired by a thread; however, the `sleep()` method does not release the lock and simply pauses the execution of the thread for the specified time.

Additionally, the **wait()** method must be invoked within a synchronized block or method. On the other hand, the **sleep()** method does not require any synchronization and can be invoked anywhere in the code.

How do threads communicate with each other? Which methods can the developer use to achieve inter-thread communication?

More than one thread can communicate with each other with the help of the **wait()**, **notify()**, and **notifyAll()** methods provided by the **Object** class. The **wait()** method can be used to wait for the result from another thread. The **notify()** and **notifyAll()** methods are used to send the notifications to the threads that are in the wait state. The **notify()** method is used to wake up a single waiting thread, while the **notifyAll()** method wakes up all threads that are waiting on the same object's monitor. Once notified, the awakened threads compete to re-acquire the monitor lock before resuming the execution.

Why are wait(), notify(), and notifyAll() in the Object class and not in the Thread class?

In Java, synchronization and inter-thread communication are fundamentally object-centric and not thread-centric.

Every object in Java has a monitor associated with it, and multiple threads can access one object. Only one thread can hold the object's monitor at any given time. The **wait()**, **notify()**, and **notifyAll()** methods being supplied by the **Object** class allow all the threads created on the same object to communicate with each other easily.

If the **Thread** class provides the **wait()**, **notify()**, and **notifyAll()** methods, then the thread communication will be problematic. The synchronization is performed on the shared object and not on the threads. If each thread has its own monitor, then there will not be a reliable way of achieving synchronization, which will lead to inconsistency in the state of the object. This design aligns with Java's core concurrency model, where objects act as a medium of coordination and communication between threads.

Thread lifecycle

A thread lifecycle in Java represents the various states a thread goes through during its execution. A thread is not always running; instead, it transitions through different stages from creation to termination.

In Java, a thread typically passes through states such as New, Runnable, Running, Blocked/ Waiting, and Terminated. These states help manage thread execution, synchronization, and resource utilization effectively.

Understanding the thread lifecycle is essential in concurrent programming, as it enables developers to control thread behavior, avoid issues like deadlocks, and build efficient multi-threaded applications.

What are the states in the lifecycle of a thread?

Each thread goes through the following states during its lifetime:

- **New thread**: In this state, a new instance of the `Thread` class is created. However, the thread is not alive.
- **Runnable thread**: The thread becomes runnable once a `start()` method is invoked on the thread. It makes the thread ready to run. The thread is not in the running state as it is not yet selected by the thread scheduler.
- **Running thread**: When the thread scheduler selects the thread from the thread pool, its `run()` method is invoked. This method execution denotes that the thread is running.
- **Thread is waiting or blocked**: In this state, the thread is alive but is not running or it might be waiting for an other thread to finish.
- **Thread is dead or terminated**: This state is achieved when the execution of the `run()` method is complete. The thread is said to be dead or terminated after this.

Can we start a thread twice? What happens if the start() method is invoked twice on a thread?

No, it is not possible to restart the thread multiple times. Once a thread is started, it is executed by the thread scheduler, and it completes the `run()` method. After this, it enters the dead state. If we still try to start a thread, it will give a `java.lang.IllegalThreadStateException`, which is a type of `RuntimeException`.

As a thread follows a well-defined lifecycle, to execute the same task again, a new Thread instance must be created. This ensures the proper thread lifecycle management and predictable execution behavior.

Is it possible to invoke the run() method instead of start() directly?

The `run()` method is a valid public method. So technically, it is possible to invoke the `run()` method directly. However, we need to understand the difference between invoking `start()` and `run()`. When we invoke the `run()` method directly, it does not work as a thread. It will be considered as a normal object invoking the `run()` method. A new stack will not be created because of this. In contrast, when we invoke the `start()` method, it internally invokes the `run()` method. This creates a new stack for the thread.

Is it compulsory to override the run() method? What will happen if we do not override the run method?

The **Thread** class is a concrete class, so when we extend a class from **Thread**, there is no compulsion to override the **run()** method. As we are not overriding the method, no application-specific code is available to the newly created thread to execute, and therefore, no application-specific logic will run when the thread is started.

However, if we are writing a class that implements the **Runnable** interface, then we do not have a choice, and we must override the **run()** method of the **Runnable** interface. Without this implementation, the class will fail to compile.

Can we override the start() method? What will happen if we override it?

The **Thread** class has the **start()** method, which is not final. Thus, it is legal to override this method. However, this is strongly discouraged because when we invoke the in-built **start()** method on the thread, it internally invokes the **run()** method, where our application-specific code has been written for the newly created thread. If we override the **start()** method, then the **run()** method will not be invoked internally. Hence, we need to explicitly invoke the **run()** method, which will be treated as a normal method invocation. Otherwise, the **run()** method will never be invoked.

Why are the suspend() and resume() methods deprecated?

The **suspend()** method is deadlock-prone. When the target thread holds the lock on an object, and it is in a suspended state, no other thread can lock that object until the target thread is resumed. The new thread tries to acquire the lock on an object or monitor that is already owned by another thread, and if that thread is suspended, then we must invoke the **resume()** on that thread; this will result in a deadlock condition. Such a deadlock is also termed as a **frozen process**. The **suspend()** method puts the thread from the running state to the waiting state. Now, the thread can go from the wait state to the runnable state only when the deprecated **resume()** method is invoked on the thread. The **resume()** method is used only with the **suspend()** method, and that is the reason it is also deprecated.

Why is the destroy() method deprecated?

The **destroy()** method is also deadlock-prone. When the target thread holds a lock on an object that is destroyed, no thread can lock this object. It is very similar to the deadlock formed when the **suspend()** and **resume()** methods are used improperly. Once the deadlock is formed, one must call the **`destroy()`** method. When the destroy method is invoked on Threads, it will throw a runtime exception, and the **`destroy()`** method puts the thread from running to the dead state.

When should we interrupt a thread?

A thread is said to be blocked or paused once a **`wait()`** or **`sleep()`** method is invoked on it. In such a situation, one can interrupt a thread to break the sleep or wait state of that thread by calling the **`interrupt()`** method.

The **`interrupt()`** method is used to signal the thread that it should stop the task it is performing and handle the interruption. Such an interruption throws **`InterruptedException`**, which needs to be handled.

In a nutshell, we interrupt the thread in scenarios such as:

- Graceful shutdown of long-running or background threads
- Canceling the tasks that are taking much time to complete
- Responding to timeouts for the registered event

What is synchronization? How to achieve synchronization?

Sometimes, the application has some shared resources that are required to be accessed by multiple threads. **Synchronization** is the capability of controlling the access of multiple threads to shared resources. Synchronization is used to prevent thread interference and data inconsistency, which may lead to incorrect results. To avoid such a scenario, synchronization can be used. In synchronization, only one thread is allowed to execute a critical section of the code at a given time.

Synchronization can be achieved by using:

- Synchronized method
- Synchronized block
- Static synchronized method

Can you give any real-time example of synchronization in an application?

One common example could be reading and writing a file concurrently. Imagine a scenario in which one user is trying to read from the file and another user is trying to update the file. So, if the file is accessed by both users simultaneously, then the end result would be very complicated and weird. In such cases, you can control the entry of the second user to update the file while the first user is still reading the file using the concept of synchronization.

What is the purpose of the synchronized block?

Synchronization allows a single thread to execute the code written in the function to avoid the side effects. However, sometimes, only a couple of lines of code may cause the side-effect and not the entire function. This means it is unnecessary to make the entire function synchronized. The synchronized block can be used under such conditions to lock a specific object in a critical section of code that operates on a shared resource. Only one thread at a time can perform operations on a particular resource used inside the synchronized block, and all other threads that attempt to enter the synchronized block are blocked until the lock is released.

Can we declare a constructor as synchronized?

No, we cannot declare the constructor as synchronized. A constructor is used for creating an instance of an object. It means that when the constructor is invoked, the process of object creation is ongoing. So, until an object is created, it does not need any synchronization. If we try to declare the constructor as synchronized. It will result in a compilation error.

Important point to note is that a constructor cannot be synchronized; however, it is possible to write a synchronized block inside the constructor.

Can you explain an intrinsic lock?

When synchronization is built around an entity, it is termed the **intrinsic lock** or **monitor lock**. The intrinsic locks play a vital role in enforcing exclusive access to an object's state as well as establishing the relationships that are essential for visibility. A **lock** is associated with every object. When a thread needs exclusive and consistent access to an object's state before accessing it, the object should acquire its intrinsic lock.

Note that after the completion of the task, the lock should be released. The thread owns the intrinsic lock only between the time it has acquired the lock and released the lock. Once a thread owns an intrinsic lock, no other thread can acquire the same lock. It means the other thread will be blocked when it attempts to acquire the lock. Once the thread releases an intrinsic lock, another thread can acquire it.

What is reentrant synchronization?

When a thread has a lock, another thread cannot acquire a lock. However, a thread can acquire a lock that it already owns. **Reentrant synchronization** is a situation in which a thread is allowed to acquire the same lock more than once. Reentrant synchronization describes a situation in which the synchronized code, directly or indirectly, invokes a method that also contains synchronized code, and more importantly, both sets of code use the same lock. In case no reentrant synchronization is used, then the synchronized code takes many additional precautions to avoid thread blocking.

What is a deadlock?

In multithreaded applications, it is quite normal to have inter-thread communication. **Deadlock** is a situation in which one or more threads are waiting for a resource and the resource is currently held by some other thread, which is also in the waiting state. That means none of the threads are executing or getting a chance to execute. Thus, all the threads are universally in the waiting state. Deadlock is a very complicated situation, and while writing a multithreaded application, it is essential to carefully manage lock acquisition, maintain consistent locking order, and apply best practices such as lock timeouts or avoiding unnecessary nested locks to prevent deadlock situations.

How to detect a deadlock condition? How can it be avoided?

We can detect a deadlock condition by running the code on the command prompt and collecting the thread dump. This can be done by executing the application from the command prompt and capturing the thread dump using tools such as **jstack** or by sending a thread dump signal to the JVM. In case any deadlock is present in the code, then a message will appear on the command prompt indicating the threads involved and the locks they are waiting for.

There are certain ways to avoid the deadlock condition, such as:

- **Avoid the use of the nested lock**: The nested lock is one of the common reasons for coming across a deadlock. The deadlock occurs when we provide the locks to various threads. So, make sure one gives only one lock to only one thread at any particular time.
- **Avoid the use of unnecessary locks**: If not required, one must avoid locks.
- **Using thread join**: The thread join enables waiting for a thread until another thread finishes its execution. The proper use of the `join()` method can help in avoiding a deadlock.

What happens when the object that has the lock calls the sleep() or wait() method?

When the `sleep()` method is invoked, the thread does not leave the object locked, though it goes from the running state to the waiting state. Now, the thread waits for the specified sleep time to be complete, and once it is completed, the thread continues in the runnable state.

When the **`wait()`** method is invoked, then the thread leaves the object's lock, and it goes from the running state to the waiting state. Now, the current thread waits for other threads on the same object to invoke either the **`notify()`** or **`notifyAll()`** method. When either of the **`notify()`** or **`notifyAll()`** method is invoked, the current thread leaves the waiting state and goes to the runnable state. Once a thread is in runnable state, it re-acquires the object's lock.

Could you explain the thread scheduler?

A developer creates the threads. Then, they are under the supervision of a **thread scheduler**. The thread scheduler, which is a part of JVM, schedules the threads and decides which thread to execute at any given point in time. The thread scheduler uses preemptive scheduling and time slicing as two mechanisms to perform this scheduling of the threads. The thread scheduler decides which thread to choose depending on the priority of a thread. The scheduler is also responsible for determining the waiting time of the thread.

Thread selection is influenced by the **priority assigned to each thread**, although thread priority serves as a scheduling hint rather than a strict guarantee. The exact scheduling behavior is platform-dependent and may vary across different operating systems and JVM implementations. Additionally, the thread scheduler manages thread state transitions, such as moving threads between runnable, waiting, blocked, and terminated states, thereby ensuring efficient and controlled execution of concurrent tasks.

What are preemptive, non-preemptive scheduling and time slicing? What are the advantages of preemptive and non-preemptive scheduling?

The following are the different algorithms used for thread scheduling:

- **Preemptive scheduling**: Preemptive scheduling is a scheduling method in which the tasks are mostly assigned with their priorities. Under certain scenarios, it is important to run a task with a higher priority before any other lower-priority task. Sometimes, the thread with lower-priority task is running; however, we still want the higher-priority task to be executed. In preemptive scheduling, the tasks that have the highest priority task execute until they enter the waiting state or dead state, or any other higher-priority task comes into existence.

  Advantages of preemptive scheduling:

  - The preemptive scheduling method is a more robust approach, as no single process cannot monopolize the CPU.
  - The choice of running task reconsidered after it is interrupted.
  - Every event causes the interruption of running tasks.

- In this method, the operating system makes sure that the CPU usage is the same by all running processes.
- The preemptive scheduling is beneficial when we use it for the multi-programming environment.

- **Non-preemptive scheduling**: In the non-preemptive scheduling method, the CPU has been allocated to a specific process. The process that keeps the CPU busy will release the CPU either by switching context or terminating. It does not need any specialized hardware, so this type of scheduling is used for various hardware platforms. The non-preemptive scheduling occurs after the process voluntarily enters the wait state or terminates.

  Advantages of non-preemptive scheduling:

  - The scheduling offers low scheduling overhead.
  - It is conceptually a very simple method.
  - It tends to offer high throughput.
  - It needs less computational resources for scheduling.

- **Time slicing**: In time slicing, a particular task executes for a predefined slice of time, and after that, it re-enters the thread pool of ready tasks. The thread scheduler then determines which task should execute next depending on the priority or some other factors.

What is thread priority?

Thread priority is an integer number associated with the thread from 1 to 10. This number provides the scheduling hint to the thread scheduler that denotes the relative importance of the thread compared to other threads. The number 1 denotes the minimum priority, and 10 denotes the maximum priority. The Thread class also provides predefined constants of static int type for setting thread priority. The thread having `MAX_PRIORITY` is likely to get more CPU as compared to the low-priority threads, which are denoted by `MIN_PRIORITY`. The `setPriority(int priority)` method is used for changing the priority of the thread, and the method returns the priority that the thread has.

What is a race condition?

Under multithreaded scenarios, more than one thread might access or modify the same resource simultaneously. The **race condition** is actually a problem that occurs when various threads that are executing simultaneously are trying to access a shared resource at the same time without proper synchronization.

What is the volatile keyword in Java?

The **`volatile`** keyword is used to achieve thread safety in multithreaded programming. The change in one volatile variable is visible to all other threads immediately. However, volatile does not provide mutual exclusion and does not guarantee atomicity. Therefore, it is suitable only for variables that are accessed independently, such as flags, status indicators, or configuration values.

What is ThreadLocal?

When an application uses multithreading or concurrency code, it comes with the cost of synchronization or locking. However, it all comes with a great effect on the scalability of the application. When multiple threads share an object, synchronization is a way to achieve thread safety. **ThreadLocal** is another way to achieve thread safety. It does not require synchronization; instead, it eliminates resource sharing by providing an independent copy of an object to each thread. An object is no longer shared, so there is no requirement for synchronization. Automatically, it improves the scalability and performance of the application.

What is a thread pool?

A **thread pool** is a group of pre-created worker threads that are waiting for a task to be allocated. This reduces the overhead associated with frequent thread creation and destruction. The threads in the thread pool are supervised by the scheduler, which pulls one thread from the pool and assigns a task to it. Once the assigned task to the thread is complete, the thread returns to the thread pool. The size of a thread pool determines how many tasks can execute concurrently and is typically configured based on system resources, workload characteristics, and performance requirements.

What is atomic action in concurrency in Java?

Atomic action is an operation that can be performed in a single unit of a task without any interference from any other operation. The atomic methods are available in the **`java.util.concurrent`** package. It is not possible to stop the atomic action while it is in progress. It will stop only after the completion of the task. All the read and write operations for the primitive variable are atomic operations, except for long and double. All the read and write operations for the volatile variable are atomic operations.

Concurrency API

The concurrency API in Java, introduced in Java 5 under the **`java.util.concurrent`** package, provides a powerful and flexible framework for handling multithreaded programming. It offers high-level constructs such as thread pools, executors, concurrent collections, and synchronization utilities like semaphores and latches. These abstractions simplify thread management and improve performance compared to traditional thread handling. The API helps in writing scalable and efficient concurrent applications by reducing complexity and minimizing common threading issues. It also provides better control over task execution and resource utilization.

What is a lock interface in the concurrency API in Java?

The **`java.util.concurrent.locks.Lock`** interface is part of the Java concurrency API and provides a more flexible and powerful synchronization mechanism as compared to the traditional synchronized block or method.

There are a few differences between the lock and synchronized block that are discussed as follows:

- `The` **`Lock`** interface provides the guarantee of a sequence in which the waiting thread will be given access, whereas the synchronized block does not guarantee it.

- `The` **`Lock`** interface provides the option of a timeout if the lock is not granted access, whereas the synchronized block does not provide that.

The methods of the **`Lock`** interface, that is, **`Lock()`** and **`Unlock()`**, can be invoked in different methods, whereas a single synchronized block must be fully contained in a single method.

Could you list out the main components of a concurrency API?

The concurrency API is available in the **`java.util.concurrent`** package. Some of the key components of Java concurrency API include:

- **`Executor`** and **`ExcecutorService`**
- **`FarkJoinPool`**
- **`ScheduledExecutorService`**
- **`Future`**
- **`TimeUnit(enum)`**
- Synchronization utilities such as **`CountDownLatch`**, **`CyclicBarrier`** and **`SemaphoreThreadFactory`**
- Concurrent Collections such as **`BlockingQueue`** and **`DelayQueue`**
- Lock Framework
- Phaser

These components collectively provide fine-grained control over concurrency, improve resource utilization, and help build robust, maintainable multithreaded systems.

What is the Executor interface in the Java concurrency API?

The **`Executor`** interface is provided by the package **`java.util.concurrent`**, which can be used to execute a new task with the help of the **`execute()`** method. The **`execute()`** method accepts a task and handles its execution using a thread or pool of threads. This is an automotive way to achieve multithreading without the developer taking extra efforts to create and manage threads.

Could you explain the ExecutorService interface from the Java concurrency API?

`ExecutorService` interface is the sub-interface of the **`Executor`** interface in **`java.util.concurrent`** package, and it adds comprehensive features to manage the lifecycle. In addition to executing Runnable tasks, **`ExecutorService`** supports the submission of Callable tasks that can return results and throw checked exceptions. It provides methods to gracefully shut down or forcefully terminate the executor, enabling better control over application resource management. Furthermore, it allows developers to track task completion, retrieve results using Future, and coordinate the execution of multiple asynchronous tasks efficiently.

What is the difference between the ScheduledExecutorService and ExecutorService interface?

The **`java.util.concurrent`** package includes both **`ExecutorService`** and **`ScheduledExecutorService`** interfaces. **`ExecutorService`** enables asynchronous execution of the task in the background. It allows the developers to submit **`Runnable`** and **`Callable`** tasks for immediate execution and obtain the result through Future. The **`ScheduledExecutorService`** interface has some additional methods than its parent **`ExecutorService`**. The methods enable the execution of the **`Runnable`** and **`Callable`** tasks with some delay or repeatedly after a fixed time period. This makes it ideal for use cases such as periodic monitoring, scheduled maintenance jobs, and time-based background processing.

What is the difference between Callable, Runnable, and Future interface?

Both the **Callable** and **Runnable** interfaces are used by the classes that are interested in the execution of multiple threads, with the following differences:

- The **Callable** interface can be used only after Java 5, whereas the **Runnable** interface can be used from the very first version of Java. So, **Callable** is the improved version of **Runnable**.
- The **Callable** interface can return a result, but the **Runnable** interface cannot return any result.
- The **Callable** interface can throw a checked exception, but the **Runnable** interface cannot.

On the other hand, the **Future** interface is used to provide the result of a concurrent process, and it is returned by the **Callable** interface. The interface has the following methods for implementation:

- **cancel(boolean status)**: This method is used to cancel the execution of the assigned task.
- **get()**: The method waits for the time till the execution is completed, and after that, the result is retrieved.
- **isCancelled()**: The method returns a Boolean value. The method returns **true** when the task was canceled before its completion.
- **isDone()**: The method also returns a Boolean value. The method returns **true** if the job is completed successfully; otherwise, it returns **false**.

What is the difference between traditional multithreading and parallel programming?

Multithreading was designed to work with a single CPU and also to utilize the idle time of the CPU. Unfortunately, even though the system has multiple cores, multithreading does not inherently guarantee effective utilization of all available cores unless explicitly designed and managed for parallel execution. The Fork-Join framework uses parallel programming, and it decomposes a large task into smaller independent subtasks, executes them concurrently on different cores, and effectively utilizes multiple processors available in a computer, which enhances the application performance.

What is the Fork-Join framework in Java?

The **Fork-Join framework** is introduced in JDK 7 under the **`java.util.concurrent`** package. The fork and join framework is used to achieve parallel programming. The framework uses the **`divide-and-conquer`** strategy to divide a big task into smaller, manageable tasks.

What is a divide-and-conquer algorithm in the Fork-Join framework?

One big task is divided into smaller tasks in such a way that each subtask is small enough to be solved independently. The divide-and-conquer strategy recursively divides a task into smaller subtasks until the subtask is not small enough to be solved independently.

State the Fork-Join pool features. Why is it necessary to explicitly shut down the Fork-Join pool?

The **Fork-Join pool** is a special thread pool that is designed to work with the *Fork-Join* task splitting. The Fork-Join pool uses the work-stealing approach to manage the threads. A queue of tasks is maintained for each thread in the *Fork-Join* pool. When the queue of one thread is empty, it takes tasks from another thread, which improves the application performance. One needs to shut down the pool explicitly because the pool uses a low-priority daemon, which runs intermittently in the background and dies after all other user threads die. One can use the **`shutdown()`** method for shutting down a pool, if required. Also, one can set the level of parallelism; however, setting the level does not guarantee that that many tasks will be managed simultaneously. Thus, it is possible to execute more tasks than the level of parallelism of the *Fork-Join* pool.

Can you explain the real-world application of the Fork-Join framework?

Let us assume we have an array of 100,000 or more elements. Calculating the sum of all the elements sequentially can be time-consuming and inefficient. To improve performance, *the Fork-Join* framework can be used for this computation in parallel. The framework uses the *divide-and-conquer* strategy for parallel programming. The strategy recursively divides an array into smaller sub-arrays until the sub-array becomes small enough to be processed by a single thread. Once the partial results are computed, they are combined to produce the final result. In case one of the threads is taking more time or is busy, the pool uses the work-stealing approach for managing threads. In this approach f a worker thread completes its assigned tasks early or becomes idle, it can *steal* pending tasks from other busy threads. This dynamic load balancing ensures optimal utilization of available CPU cores and significantly enhances overall performance.

What are the Executors in the Executor framework?

Executors are a part of the concurrency API. Executors act as a factory that provides the static factory methods to return instances of `ExecutorService`, `ScheduledExecutorService`, and `ThreadFactory`.

Executors have the following methods:

- **newFixedThreadPool()**: The method returns the `ExecutorService` that maintains a pool of fixed number of worker threads. The number of threads is specified as a parameter during creation. When tasks are submitted for execution, they are assigned to available threads in the pool. When concurrently submitted tasks are more than the maintained pool size, then the rest of the tasks wait in the queue. The method returns `ExecutorService`.
- **newScheduledThreadPool()**: The method is also used to create a fixed-size pool with an extra facility to schedule the thread, which can run after a specific pre-defined delay. The method is useful to schedule the task. The method creates and returns `ScheduledExecutorService`.
- **newCachedThreadPool()**: It creates a pool without any fixed number of threads. The threads are created at runtime. When there is no task to execute, the thread will be alive for 60 seconds, and eventually, it will die. The method is best to create a thread pool with short-lived threads. The method creates and returns `ExecutorService`.

Could you explain the working of FutureTask in Java?

The `FutureTask` class is a concrete implementation of the `Future` interface provided in `java.util.concurrent` package. The result generated from this can only be obtained if the execution of the task is completed. In case the computation is not yet completed, then the `get()` method will be blocked. However, if the execution is completed, then it cannot be restarted or even canceled. However, the result can be retrieved multiple times using the `get()` method without re-executing the task.

What is the difference between shutdownNow() and shutdown() in the Executor framework of Java?

Both the `shutdown()` and `shutdownNow()` belong to the `ExecutorService` interface. The `shutdown()` method enables the stopping of the thread only after completion of the current task and does not accept a new task to execute. The `shutdownNow()` method also tries to stop the running threads. This is a forceful way to halt all the tasks that are running or scheduled to run. It will not execute any task that has been submitted but not yet started. This returns a list of all the tasks that are in the waiting state for execution.

How to terminate a thread in the Executor framework?

`ExecutorService` has a method `awaitTermination(long timeout, TimeUnit unit)`, which takes the time and unit of time as arguments. After the specified time, the thread pool is terminated. If a task needs to be terminated immediately, the same method can be invoked with a timeout value of zero seconds.

What are the different polices in the Executor framework?

In the Java Executor framework, rejection policies define how a `ThreadPoolExecutor` should handle tasks that cannot be accepted for execution. Task rejection typically occurs when the executor's task queue is full, and the maximum pool size has been reached.

These policies are implemented using the `RejectedExecutionHandler` interface and are provided as predefined strategies in the `ThreadPoolExecutor` class.

The following are the different policies of the Executor framework:

- **ThreadPoolExecutor.AbortPolicy**: This policy is a handler for rejected tasks. It handles the tasks that have been rejected. This is a default rejection policy.
- **ThreadPoolExecutor.CallerRunsPolicy**: This policy handles the rejected task, but it runs the rejected task directly.
- **ThreadPoolExecutor.DiscardOldestPolicy**: This policy handles the rejected tasks that are the oldest and unhandled. It discards the tasks that are the oldest. This policy is useful when the recent tasks are more important than the older tasks.
- **ThreadPoolExecutor.DiscardPolicy**: This policy silently discards the rejected task. The policy is only appropriate when task loss is acceptable.

How can one get a value returned from the Callable thread in the Executor framework?

When a `Callable` task is submitted to an `ExecutorService` using the `submit()` method, the executor returns a `Future` object. This `Future` acts as a handle to the pending result of the asynchronous computation.

By invoking the `get()` method on the `Future`, the calling thread can retrieve the result. If the computation has not yet completed, the `get()` method blocks until the task finishes execution and the result becomes available.

The following code depicts the working of the **get()** method to retrieve the result:

```
1. ExecutorServiceservice = Executors.newCachedThreadPool();
2. Future<Integer> future=service.submit(new CallableThread());
3. int val=future.get();
```

The **submit()** method submits a **Callable** task to the executor service and returns a **Future** object representing the pending result. The **get()** method is then used to retrieve the result of the computation. It blocks the current thread until the task completes and the result becomes available.

Which classes in the collection provide concurrency?

The following classes in the collection provide the concurrency mechanism:

- **BlockingQueue**: The package **java.util.concurrent** provides the interface **BlockingQueue**, which is a child of the **Queue** interface. It provides functionalities such as waiting for the queue to become non-empty before retrieving an element, or waiting for the space to become available in the queue before storing another element.
- **ConcurrentMap**: The package **java.util.concurrent** provides the interface as a child of the **Map** interface, which ensures thread safety and atomicity guarantees. The interface supports atomic operations on the underlying map variable. It has the **get()** and **set()** methods that work for reading and writing operations on the volatile variables.
- **ConcurrentNavigableMap**: **ConcurrentNavigableMapinterface** is included in the **java.util.concurrent** package as a child of the **ConcurrentMap** interface. It supports **NavigableMap** operations such as **lowerKey**, **floorKey**, **ceilingKey**, **higherKey**, and so on.

How can you solve the consumer–producer pattern by using BlockingQueue?

The consumer–producer problem can be solved using the **wait()** and **notify()** methods. The consumer–producer pattern can be optimized using the **BlockingQueue** interface. The **BlockingQueue** interface has the **put()** and **take()** methods for solving the consumer–producer pattern. The **put(i)** method is used by the producer to produce in the shared queue, and the **take()** method is used by the consumer to consume from the shared queue.

What care should be taken while writing a thread-safe code? What are the most important points one must keep in mind while writing a multithreaded application?

The thread unsafe code may cause various issues to the application. And, that is the reason utmost care should be taken while writing a thread-safe healthy code and avoid deadlocks. Some of the things that we can follow are as follows:

- Use the immutable **`String`** in place of **`StringBuffer`**, as whenever a change happens in the value of a string, it produces a new String.
- The unsynchronized method with a multithreaded code may lead to race condition. So, try to use the synchronized block or synchronized methods.
- The final variables are considered to be thread-safe as once a value is assigned, it cannot be altered. Wherever possible, try to use final variables.
- The static variables are also not thread-safe. If such static variables are used in the unsynchronized static methods, then multiple threads may enter the method concurrently, which leads to an issue. One must declare the static methods as synchronized.
- When a field is declared as volatile, all threads can see a consistent value for that variable. The volatile variables can be considered as an alternative to synchronized methods. So, whenever possible, use volatile variables.
- Using thread-safe collections, for example, in place of using **`HashMap`**, use **`ConcurrentHashMap`** or **`HashTable`**; instead of using **`ArrayList`**, use **`Vector`**.

What are the different components of the Flow API introduced in Java9?

Flow API introduced in Java9, is a sophisticated approach of publisher-subscriber model. It consists of following interfaces to support this model:

- **Flow.Publisher**: Used to produce the data items for the **`Subscriber`**.
- **Flow.Subscriber**: Used to consume the data item published by **`Publisher`**.
- **Flow.Subscription**: Controls the entire flow of the data.
- **Flow.Processor**: Acts as both **`Publisher`** and **`Subscriber`**.

How does the Subscriber work in Flow API?

`Subscriber` interface in the Flow API facilitates the subscribing to the publisher. This also facilitates the callback mechanism. When one works in this approach, the subscriber can receive the data only when the data is requested by it. Upon request, the data is pushed from the publisher.

The `Subscriber` interface provides the following methods:

- **onSubscribe(Subscription subscription)**: The method is invoked to generate the `Subscription` object for the `Subscriber`.
- **onNext(T item)**: This method is invoked with the next item of `Subscription`. You need to request the item which is pushed by the Publisher, using the `request()` method.
- **onError(Throwable throwable)**: This method is invoked, if any error occurs in `Publisher` or `Subscriber`. If this method is invoked, then entire flow is terminated.
- **onComplete()**: When the entire data is pushed by the `Publisher` and processed by the `Subscriber` without any error, then this method is invoked. This is considered to be the natural termination of Publisher-Subscriber architecture.

How does the Publisher work in Flow API?

This interface is termed as a functional interface, which is used to generate the items. These items can be utilized or subscribed by the `Subscriber`. The items produced by the Publisher are utilized by `Subscriber` by invoking the `onNext()` method.

The following method is provided by this interface:

```
subscribe(Subscriber<? Super T> subscriber)
```

This method adds the `Subscriber` to `Publisher`.

What is CompletabaleFuture?

The `CompletableFuture` introduced in Java8 supports asynchronous programming. As the name implies the instance of `CompletableFuture` represents result of asynchronous business logic or computation that may complete in future which can be utilized in the later stages. This avoids the blocking property of Future which utilized the data using the `get()` method.

The `CompletableFuture` provides the following methods to perform any action:

- **runAsync()**:
  - Executes a task asynchronously
  - Does not return a result
  - Returns `CompletableFuture<Void>`

- **supplyAsync()**:
    - o Executes a task asynchronously
    - o Returns a computed value
    - o Returns `CompletableFuture<T>`

What is the significance of thenAccept(), thenRun() and thenApply() methods of CompletableFuture?

These methods are used to chain the actions after `CompletableFuture` completes the task assigned to it:

- **thenAccept()**:
    - o Accepts the result
    - o Does not return anything
    - o Used when the result needs to be consumed
- **thenRun()**:
    - o Does not accept any input
    - o Does not return any output
    - o Used for final actions after completion
- **thenApply()**:
    - o Accepts the result of the previous stage
    - o Returns a transformed result
    - o Used when the result needs to be processed or transformed.

What is the difference between thenCompose() and thenCombine()?

Many a time, we require to complete the task in different `CompletableFuture` to provide more optimized way to execute the task. In some cases, we might need to combine the results of two `CompletableFuture` or chain one `CompletableFuture` with another. The `thenCompose()` and `thenCombine()` methods are used for the same purpose.

- **thenCompose()**: This method is used with the second async task is dependent on the first. This creates a chaining approach with `CompletableFuture` and facilitates the asynchronous workflows.

- **thenCombine()**: This method is used when to async tasks runs independently and their results are combined. This method is typically very useful in the scenarios of parallel execution of the tasks and aggregation of the results from the independent tasks.

How do you handle the exceptions in CompletableFuture?

`CompletableFuture` provides different approaches to handle the exceptions, such as:

- **Using exceptionally()**: This approach handles the exception and also provides the fallback value when the exception is thrown.
- **Using handle()**: This approach handles the exception as well as the normal values generated from the computation if completed by the `CompletableFuture` without any exception.
- **Using whenComplete()**: This approach handles the exception without changing the result.

Recent updates in concurrency

Recent versions of Java have introduced significant enhancements to the concurrency API, making concurrent programming more powerful, scalable, and developer-friendly. Starting from Java 9, improvements such as the Reactive Streams-based Flow API and enhancements to `CompletableFuture` enabled better asynchronous and event-driven programming. In later versions, the focus shifted toward simplifying concurrency with higher-level abstractions like virtual threads and structured concurrency. These modern features aim to reduce complexity, improve performance, and make concurrent code more readable and maintainable. Overall, the evolution reflects a move from low-level thread management to more declarative and efficient concurrency models.

What improvements were made in CompletableFuture in Java9?

Java 9 enhanced `CompletableFuture` by adding:

- **orTimeout()**: Automatically completes exceptionally after a timeout
- **completeOnTimeout()**: Completes with a default value when a timeout occurs
- **delayedExecutor()**: Allows delayed asynchronous execution

These additions make asynchronous programs more robust, faulttolerant, and predictable.

What are virtual threads introduced in Java19?

Threads in Java were always platform-specific from the introduction of the concept of the thread in Java. In Java 19, virtual threads are introduced, which are lightweight threads managed by the JVM internally instead of the operating system. As a result of this JVM-dependent nature, we can now handle millions of concurrent tasks while using minimal system resources.

Note: **Virtual threads are standardized from Java21 onwards.**

How to work with the virtual thread?

There are different ways to work with virtual threads as follows:

- **Using Thread.startVirtualThread()**: This is the simplest and most direct way to create and start a virtual thread. It allows you to quickly execute a task without explicitly managing thread creation or lifecycle. It is ideal for lightweight, fire-and-forget tasks.
- **Using Thread.ofThread()**: This approach provides more control over thread creation through a builder pattern. You can configure properties such as thread name before starting the virtual thread. It is useful when you need customization along with the benefits of virtual threads.
- **Using ExecutorService**: Virtual threads can also be managed using an `ExecutorService`, typically created with `Executors.newVirtualThreadPerTaskExecutor()`. This method is suitable for handling a large number of concurrent tasks efficiently. It simplifies task submission and lifecycle management while leveraging virtual threads under the hood.

What is structured concurrency?

Structured concurrency was introduced in Java19 as a preview feature, and as of Java24, it is still a preview feature of the Java API. Structured concurrency treats multiple concurrent tasks as a single unit of work.

It ensures that all the tasks:

- Start together
- Finish together
- Fail together

How to use the structured concurrency?

Java provides the `StructuredTaskScope` API to work with the concept of structured concurrency. This provides methods to manage the multiple concurrent tasks and also ensures that all the tasks are completed within the scope where they were started. This also automatically handles the cancellation and failure.

The following are the key methods from this API:

- **fork(Callable<T> task)**: The following is the behavior of this method:
  - Starts a child task in the new virtual thread
  - Registers the tasks with the given scope of `StructuredTaskScope`
- **join()**: This method ensures that the process waits till all the forked subtasks gets completed.
- **throwIfFailed()**: The following is the behavior of this method:
  - Throws an exception if any subtask gets failed
  - The failure is propagated
- **ShutdownOnFailure()**: This method cancels all the other tasks as soon as any of the tasks in the group fails.
- **ShutdownOnSuccess()**: The following is the behavior of this method:
  - returns first successful result
  - cancels the remaining tasks

What is ScopedValue?

ScopedValue concept is launched as a final feature in Java21. Scoped values are mostly used in the Virtual Thread and structured concurrency concepts. ScopedValues are also considered to be replacement for `ThreadLocal`.

Generally speaking, ScopedValue is a container of immutable data which is available to all the methods which are part of the given scope. This value can be also used within the child threads and gets cleared automatically when the scope ends.

In other words, it is contextual data shared across all the child threads within a scope without usage of any method parameters etc.

How to use the ScopedValue?

The following steps are to be followed if we intend to use the ScopedValue:

- **Declaring a ScopedValue**: To declare a ScopedValue, we need to invoke **`newInstance()`** method of **`ScopedValue`**. As it is only declaration, we should not assign a default value for the same. For example:

  ```
  static final ScopedValue<String> USER_ID = ScopedValue.newInstance();
  ```

- **Binding a ScopedValue**: We can bind a value to **`ScopedValue`** by invoking the **`where()`** method, which is then associated with the actual scope where that **`ScopedValue`** can be shared. For example:

  ```
  ScopedValue.where(KEY, value).run(() -> {
      // code executed within scope
      method1();
  });
  ```

- **Accessing a ScopedValue**: Within the scope, we can invoke the **`get()`** method on the **`ScopedValue`** reference to access the value assigned to **`ScopedValue`**. For example:

  ```
  static void method1() {
      System.out.println("Within a method1: " + REQUEST_ID.get());
  }
  ```

Conclusion

In this chapter, we discussed the concurrency mechanism of Java. There are many tasks in an application that can be executed simultaneously, which improves the performance of the application. We studied how to achieve this by using the different implementations of multithreading. However, while running this multithreading application, sometimes, there might be problems with cross-functioning of threads, which creates unwanted or undesirable outputs, as multiple threads are accessing common data. To avoid this, we must know how to implement synchronization, which we studied through different interview questions during this entire chapter. At the end of this chapter, we talked about the update in the concurrency API introduced in Java. Additionally, we discussed relatively new concepts like virtual threads, structured concurrency, and ScopedValue. In the next chapter, we will discuss Java Database Connectivity.

Join our Discord space

Join our Discord workspace for latest updates, offers, tech happenings around the world, new releases, and sessions with the authors:

https://discord.bpbonline.com

Chapter 7
Java Database Connectivity

Introduction

Data has become a fundamental asset in the modern world, with an ever-increasing volume being generated, processed, and analyzed across various domains. This data can be in different formats. Even our brain consists of huge amounts of data. Every day, in and out (even at night), our brain receives a lot of data, and to our surprise, we can recall that data as and when we require it. On similar lines, our application deals with a lot of data. This data could be generated by an application or entered by a user. However, this data is not immortal. The data dies when an application exits. At times, it is still acceptable. Now imagine a scenario where an account holder deposits some amount in their bank account through an application. Obviously, when an application is restarted, the account holder would like to see the reflection of that amount in their bank account, but that cannot happen as data is erased automatically when an application is terminated. That means there must be a way to store this data somewhere permanently, even if the application is terminated. To add to it, the application should be able to pull that data whenever the application restarts. Another example would be the identity proof that the account holder provides at the account's opening. The account holder would expect that once such information is provided to the bank, the bank authorities should never ask for the same identity proof for each transaction. We can store such data in either flat files or a database. We have already discussed how to store the data in a file in *Chapter 5, I/O and File Handling*, but the file lacks storing the data in a structured format, which makes it more difficult to find the data based on some condition. In order to achieve this, Java introduced the **Java Database Connectivity** (**JDBC**) API, which can communicate with the database to store, retrieve, or update the data in a structured format.

Structure

We will be covering interview questions based on the following topics in this chapter:

- Persistency

- Java Database Connectivity API
- Transaction management

Objectives

At the end of this chapter, you will be able to learn different interview questions based on JDBC. Working with JDBC is always complex, as we need to remember many interfaces and their sequence, so as to achieve the desired result. In this chapter, we will start our journey from very basic concepts. We will begin our journey by understanding the concept of persistency, and then we will learn how to achieve the same using the JDBC API. We are not targeting any specific database to explain JDBC, but in a few code snippets, we have used MySQL as the underlying database. You are free to change those database-specific code snippets as per your choice of database. Understanding JDBC is very important to study Hibernate in future topics.

Persistency is one of the most important segments of any application, so an interviewer is always keen to know whether you know the basics of persistency. Let us discuss some of the very basic questions that you might come across in an interview related to JDBC.

Persistency

Persistency refers to the capability of an application to store data for a long duration so that it remains available even after the application terminates or the system is restarted.

In software systems, persistency ensures that data is saved in a stable storage medium such as a database, file system, or external storage, rather than being held only in memory. This allows applications to reliably retrieve, update, and maintain data across multiple executions and user sessions.

What are the ways for persistency?

Java provides various ways to store data:

- The very initial way to store the data is file handling. Java objects can be saved in a file using serialization.
- Java objects can be stored in XML files, and using **Java Architecture for XML Binding (JAXB) APIs**, developers can deal with them within Java applications.
- JDBC API enables persisting data in databases.
- **Object Relational Mapping** (**ORM**) provides a mechanism to perform **Create, Retrieve, Update, and Delete** (**CRUD**) operations with data in the database.

Java Database Connectivity (**JDBC**) is a **Java API for Database Connectivity**. The API developed by Sun Microsystems, now part of Oracle, is used to deal with a database. JDBC API facilitates a mechanism for the connection to the database. It also provides the methods to execute the CRUD operations on the database.

Can you explain the architecture of JDBC?

Figure 7.1 represents the architecture of JDBC:

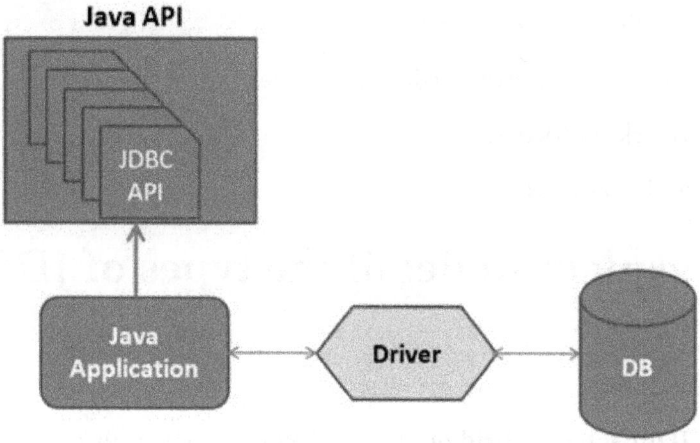

***Figure 7.1**: JDBC architecture*

As you can observe from *Figure 7.1*, the Java application communicates with the JDBC API to establish connectivity with the database. However, the Java application cannot communicate with the database directly. To bridge this gap, a JDBC driver layer is required between the Java application and the database. The JDBC driver acts as an intermediary that translates JDBC API calls into database-specific API calls and converts the database responses back into a format understood by the Java application.

What is a driver in JDBC? Why is it required?

The **JDBC driver** is a component of software that enables a Java application to interact with the underlying database. It provides the concrete implementation of different interfaces defined in JDBC API. Typically, JDBC drivers are distributed as **Java Archive** (**JAR**) files, such as `mongo.jar` or `mysql-connector-XXX.jar`, which must be included in the application's classpath to enable database access.

Why is a JDBC driver required? What is the use of the JDBC driver?

JDBC drivers are client-side adapters that are installed on the client machine. The drivers help to convert JDBC API requests from Java programs to a dv-specific protocol that the database can understand. Similarly, it transfers the response generated from the database vendors into a format that can be processed by the Java application. In this way, the JDBC driver serves as a bridge between the Java application and the database, ensuring seamless and standardized database interaction.

How many types of JDBC drivers are available?

There are four types of JDBC drivers, as listed:

- Type 1 or JDBC-ODBC bridge driver
- Type 2 or native API driver or partial Java driver
- Type 3 or network protocol driver
- Type 4 or pure Java driver

Could you explain in detail the types of JDBC drivers?

The following are the different types of drivers:

- **Type 1 or JDBC-ODBC bridge driver**: **Type 1 driver** uses the Open Database Connectivity driver installed on each client machine to connect to the database. We need to configure **Data Source Name** (**DSN**) on the system to use ODBC. The JDBC-ODBC bridge driver converts the JDBC method calls into the ODBC function calls. The conversion of data takes place from JDBC to ODBC, making it slower. As no extra download or installation is required, it is easy to use. However, we cannot overlook the process of configuring DSN on every system, which makes it tedious to migrate from system to system.
- **Type 2 or native API driver or partial Java driver**: **Type 2 driver** uses the client-side libraries of the database. In the Type 2 driver, the JDBC API calls are converted into native C/C++ API calls, which are unique to the database. Whenever we change the database, we have to change the native API, as it is specific to a database. Its performance is better than the JDBC-ODBC bridge driver. These drivers are provided by the database vendors and must be installed on each client machine.
- **Type 3 or network protocol driver**: **Type 3 driver** is extremely flexible and uses a three-tier approach to access databases. The network protocol driver uses middleware, which converts JDBC calls into the vendor-specific database protocol. The driver is entirely written in Java and does not require any client-side library.

  JDBC clients use standard network sockets to communicate with a middleware application server. Now, the socket information is translated by the middleware application server into the call format required by the **Database Management System** (**DBMS**) and forwarded to the database server. As no code is installed on the client and a single driver can actually provide access to multiple databases, it is very flexible.
- **Type 4 or pure Java driver**: **Type 4**, or **pure Java-based driver**, communicates directly with the database through a socket connection. It directly converts JDBC calls into the

vendor-specific database protocol, hence providing the highest performance driver available for the database. It is entirely written in Java and is usually provided by the vendor. As the driver is database-specific, we need to remember to add a new driver definition every time we change the DB.

Can you explain the procedure to connect to a database? What are the steps to connect to a database?

The following are the steps to connect to a database:

1. Get the connections to the database.
2. Create a statement instance.
3. Perform CRUD operations.
4. Close the opened connection.

Java Database Connectivity API

Java provides the **JDBC API**, using which we can connect to the underlying database. It contains many interfaces, and as a developer, you must be aware of that. You can expect a few questions related to different interfaces, which are discussed in the following section.

If JDBC is an API, who provides the implementation?

The vendors implement the JDBC API and provide it in a JAR file. For example, MySQL provides the **`mysql-connector-**.jar`** file as a driver; we can add this JAR file to communicate with **`MySQL DB`**. The driver JAR contains concrete implementations of the JDBC interfaces, such as **`Driver`**, **`Connection`**, **`Statement`**, and **`ResultSet`**. At runtime, the JDBC **`DriverManager`** (or the Service Provider mechanism in modern JDBC versions) uses these implementations to translate JDBC method calls into database-specific operations.

Can you list different interfaces of JDBC API?

JDBC API provides different interfaces such as **`Connection`**, **`Statement`**, **`PreparedStatement`**, **`CallableStatement`**, **`ResultSet`**, **`ResultSetMetaData`**, and **`DatabaseMetaData`**. Together, these interfaces form the foundation of the JDBC API and allow developers to perform database operations in a database-independent way.

What is the standard process to obtain a database connection?

The standard process of obtaining a database connection in JDBC involves using the **DriverManager** class to establish a connection between the Java application and the database.

Before requesting a connection, the appropriate JDBC driver must be available on the application's classpath. In modern JDBC versions, the driver is automatically loaded using the Service Provider mechanism, so explicit driver registration is usually not required.

A connection can be obtained using the following statement:

```
1. Connection conn = DriverManager.getConnection(URL, USER, PASS);
```

In this statement, URL specifies the database location and JDBC driver details, while **USER** and **PASS** represent the database credentials. If the connection is successful, a **Connection** object is returned, which can then be used to create Statement or **PreparedStatement** objects and perform database operations.

Now, the **Connection** is ready to use. Once the database operations are completed, we can close the connection as follows:

```
1. conn.close();
```

Closing the connection releases database resources and helps prevent memory leaks, ensuring efficient resource management within the application.

What is connection pooling, and why is it important?

Connection pooling is a technique in which a pool of database connections is maintained and managed by a pool manager. A pool manager is ideally a software or a tool that creates readily available connections and provides them as and when requested. Instead of creating a new database connection for every client request, the application provides an existing connection from the pool, uses it, and then returns it to the pool for future reuse.

This significantly improves the application performance, specifically in scenarios where multiple users are requesting database connections.

Can you explain how connection pooling is different from returning the connection instances from methods like getConnection()?

Developers can create the **getConnection()** method and return the **Connection** object from that. Though this may sound like connection pooling, it is way different from the actual connection pooling. The method **getConnection()** creates a new physical connection every time it is invoked. On the other hand, if we use the connection pooling approach, the connection pool providers create a fixed number of database connections at startup and facilitate the users to reuse these objects as and when required. This means that, typically, if you are working on a small demo application or your application has limited users, then the traditional approach of creating a connection is feasible. While working with web applications or microservices, however, we need to use the approach of connection pooling.

How to obtain a generated primary key from a database?

Whenever we insert a record into a table, the application either sends a **primary key** (**PK**) of that row to the database or asks the database to generate the PK for the row, such as an auto-incremented column.

We can retrieve the values of the particular column using the **getGeneratedKeys()** method of **Statement** object as follows:

```
stmt.executeUpdate(INSERT_QUERY,Statement.RETURN_GENERATED_KEYS);
ResultSet rs = stmt.getGeneratedKeys();
```

The **ResultSet** returned by the **getGeneratedKeys()** method contains the generated key values produced by the database for the executed statement. The application can iterate over this **ResultSet** to access the generated PK and use it for further processing, such as maintaining relationships between tables or confirming the successful insertion of the record.

Which interfaces are used to execute queries that perform CRUD operations on a database?

This question can be rephrased as:

What is the difference between Statement, PreparedStatement, and CallableStatement?

To perform CRUD operations on a database, we can use different interfaces provided by JDBC API, such as **Statement**, **PreparedStatement**, or **CallableStatement**, each of which is based on specific application requirements and scenarios:

- **Statement**: **Statement** is a general-purpose method to communicate with a table. It is used to execute the static queries.
- **PreparedStatement**: **PreparedStatement** is a very useful way to execute the same SQL queries again and again with different parameter values at runtime. It is useful to execute dynamic or parameterized queries. **PreparedStatement** is a precompiled SQL query, where the SQL query is parsed and compiled only once by the database, which saves time. Thus, it improves the performance of the application.

- **CallableStatement**: **`CallableStatement`** is used to execute the stored procedures. We can pass three types of parameters to **`CallableStatement`** as follows:
    - **IN parameter**: The **`IN`** parameter is used to pass input values from a Java application to the stored procedure. These values are read-only within the procedure.
    - **OUT parameter**: The **`OUT`** parameter is used to hold the result that is returned from the procedure. The procedure assigns values to these parameters, which can be retrieved after the execution of the procedure.
    - **INOUT parameter**: The **`INOUT`** parameter holds both **`IN`** and **`OUT`** parameters. The Java application provides an initial value, and the stored procedure updates and returns it.

Though we can pass the **`IN`** parameter without any additional settings, the **`OUT`** and **`INOUT`** must be explicitly registered using **`registerOutParameter()`** before executing the **`CallableStatement`**.

How to use CallableStatement? How to invoke a procedure using CallableStatement?

Working with **`CallableStatement`** typically involves the following steps:

1. Creating a **`CallableStatement`** object using **`Connection.prepareCall()`**.
2. Use the **`setter`** methods such as **`setInt()`**, **`setString()`**, etc., to set **`IN`** parameters.
3. Use the **`registerOutParameter()`** method to register the **`OUT`** or **`INOUT`** parameters.
4. Executing **`CallableStatement`** using **`execute()`** or **`executeQuery()`**.
5. Use the **`getter`** methods such as **`getInt()`**, **`getString()`**, etc., to retrieve the result returned by the stored procedure.

Let us understand how to code for **`CallableStatement`** to call **`procedure1`** in different cases:

1. **Without IN or OUT parameter**:

```
CallableStatement callstmt = con.prepareCall("{call procedure1}");
callstmt.execute();
```

   This approach is typically used when the stored procedure performs an action such as logging or batch processing and does not accept or return any values.

2. **With the IN parameter but no OUT parameter**:

```
CallableStatement callstmt = con.prepareCall("{call procedure1(?,?)}");
callstmt.setInt(1,10);
callstmt.setString(2,"name1");
callstmt.execute();
```

This approach is typically used when the application sends some input parameter to the stored procedure, but the procedure does not return any value back to the application.

3. **With both IN and OUT parameters**:

```
CallableStatement callstmt =
                    con.prepareCall("{call procedure1(?,?,?)}");
callstmt.setInt(1,10);
callstmt.setString(2, "name1");
callstmt.registerOutParameter(3, Types.VARCHAR);
callstmt.execute();
String address = cstmt.getString(3);
```

In this approach, the stored procedure takes the input parameter from the application and also returns the value back to the application, which is retrieved by the application when needed.

4. **With IN and INOUT parameters**:

```
CallableStatement callstmt = con.prepareCall("{call procedure1(?,?)}");
callstmt.setInt(1,10);
callstmt.setString(2, "name1");
callstmt.registerOutParameter(2, Types.VARCHAR);
callstmt.execute();
String address = cstmt.getString(2);
```

An **INOUT** parameter accepts an initial value from the application and returns a modified value after procedure execution. The same parameter index is used for both setting and retrieving the value.

What is ResultSet? How to obtain ResultSet?

The **ResultSet** refers to the data in the form of rows and columns, which is achieved as a result of a select query execution. **ResultSet** maintains a cursor that initially points before the first row. This cursor can be moved forward or even backward using the navigation methods like **next()**, **previous()**, etc.

We can obtain **ResultSet** by executing the select query with **Statement** as follows:

```
Statement st=con.createStatement();
ResultSet rs=st.executeQuery("select * from employee") ;
```

We can also use a parameterized query, or **PreparedStatement**, to obtain the **ResultSet** object.

What functionalities does ResultSet provide? Which of the functionalities of ResultSet have you worked with?

`ResultSet` provides the methods to obtain the data, navigate through the data, and to update the data. The following are some of the methods of **`ResultSet`**:

- **getXXX(int)**: Returns data from the column, the index of which is declared in the method. XXX represents the type of data that you are interested in retrieving. For example, if you wish to retrieve the String data from the second column, the method will be invoked as **`getString(2)`**.
- **getXXX(String)**: This method is exactly similar to the earlier method. The only difference is that instead of the column index number, you need to provide the column name as an argument. For example, if you wish to retrieve the String data from the **`first_name`** column, the method will be invoked as **`getString("first_name")`**.
- **next()**: Moves the cursor to the next row of the **`ResultSet`**.
- **previous()**: Moves the cursor to the previous row of the **`ResultSet`**.
- **first()**: Move the cursor to the first row of the **`ResultSet`**.

Note: **These are not all the methods. However, given the scope of the question, these are sufficient to demonstrate a clear understanding of the concept. The interviewer can effectively assess the depth of your knowledge if you can enlist and explain even these methods.**

How to find out if a ResultSet has data or is empty?

The cursor returned by the **`ResultSet`** always points to the beginning of the **`ResultSet`**. It means the cursor points even before the first row. This means the cursor does not initially point to the valid row. Even if no records are returned based on the query, the **`ResultSet object`** still generates; however, it will be empty. However, in such a case, when we invoke the **`next()`** method, the application throws an exception. In order to avoid this, we need to verify what the **`next()`** method returns before we process the returned result. The **`next()`** method returns **`false`** if there is no next record available in the **`ResultSet`**.

The following code snippet demonstrates the recommended approach:

```
Statement st = con.createStatement();
ResultSet rs = stmt.executeQuery("select * from Employee");
if (rs.next() == false) {
System.out.println("ResultSet in empty");
} else {
do {
String name = rs.getString(1);
System.out.println(name);
} while (rs.next());
}
```

In this example:

- The initial **`rs.next()`** call checks whether at least one record is present.
- If records exist, a do-while loop is used to process the current row and all subsequent rows efficiently.

This approach ensures safe and reliable handling of **`ResultSet`** data, even when the query returns no records.

What is scrollable ResultSet?

This can be rephrased as:

What is ResultSet.TYPE_SCROLL_INSENSITIVE and ResultSet.TYPE_SCROLL_SENSITIVE?

`ResultSet` holds the data. By default, **`ResultSet`** is not updatable. The cursor moves in the forward direction only. Moreover, the data in the **`ResultSet`** cannot be changed. However, the scrollable **`ResultSet`** is more flexible, and it is scrollable as well as updatable.

`ResultSet` is scrollable, which means we can traverse through records in both the forward and backward directions. The scrollable **`ResultSet`** has the ability to read the first record, the last record, the next record, and the previous record.

To generate the scrollable **`ResultSet`**, the **`Statement`** object must be provided by the scroll type constants as follows:

- **ResultSet.TYPE_FORWARD_ONLY**: The default type of **`ResultSet`**, which allows the **`ResultSet`** to move only in the forward direction.
- **ResultSet.TYPE_SCROLL_INSENSITIVE**: This constant enables scrolling of data in both the forward and backward direction, but it is insensitive to **`ResultSet`** updates.

- **ResultSet.TYPE_SCROLL_SENSITIVE**: This constant enables scrolling of data in both the forward and backward directions. Opposite to **ResultSet.TYPE_SCROLL_INSENSITIVE**, the data is sensitive to **ResultSet** updates.

In an updatable **ResultSet**, the changes will be immediately persisted in the database and reflected by the **ResultSet** object in real time.

The **ResultSet** concurrency type helps in finding whether the **ResultSet** is updatable or only readable. **ResultSet** has two concurrency levels:

- **ResultSet.CONCUR_READ_ONLY:** ResultSet is not updatable.
- **ResultSet.CONCUR_UPDATABLE:** ResultSet is readable as well as updatable.

The following code snippet shows how to create a scrollable **ResultSet**, which is insensitive and only readable:

```
Statement st = con.createStatement(ResultSet.TYPE_SCROLL_INSENSITIVE,
                ResultSet.CONCUR_READ_ONLY);
```

We can also use **PreparedStatement** instead of **Statement**. As mentioned earlier, to create an updatable **ResultSet**, you need to change the second argument of the **createStatement()** method to **ResultSet.CONCUR_UPDATABLE**.

We can execute a query using the Statement instance, so is it possible to insert a row in a database without using Statement or executing a query?

The Updatable **ResultSet** can be used to insert rows in the table using the method **insertRow()** of the **ResultSet** interface. To use the Updatable **ResultSet**, it must be created using **ResultSet.CONCUR_UPDATABLE**. The SQL query should select the data only from one table.

We also need to ensure that each column in the inserted row, which does not allow null values and also does not have a default value, must be given an explicit value. Before you invoke **insertRow()**, you must invoke the **updateXXX()** method, to modify the column data.

The following code snippet demonstrates the usage of the **insertRow()** method:

```
Statement st = con.createStatement(ResultSet.TYPE_FORWARD_ONLY,
                                            ResultSet.CONCUR_UPDATABLE);
ResultSet rs = stmt.executeQuery("SELECT  * FROM employee");
rs.moveToInsertRow();
rs.updateString("first_name", "Value of name");
rs.updateString("last_name", "Value of Last name");
```

```
rs.updateInt(„emp_id", 123);
rs.insertRow();
rs.moveToCurrentRow();
```

The following is an explanation:

- **`moveToInsertRow()`** positions the cursor on a special insert row
- **`updateXXX()`** methods assign values to the respective columns
- **`insertRow()`** persists the new row into the database
- **`moveToCurrentRow()`** returns the cursor to its original position

What happens if an attempt is made to update data using a ResultSet created with the default (read-only) configuration?

This will cause an exception, **`com.mysql.jdbc.NotUpdatable`**. This means that the **`ResultSet`** must be obtained from a **`Statement`** or **`PreparedStatement`**, which is created from the scrollable and updatable **`ResultSet`** type, such as:

- **`ResultSet.TYPE_SCROLL_INSENSITIVE or ResultSet.TYPE_SCROLL_SENSITIVE`**
- **`ResultSet.CONCUR_UPDATABLE`**

Only when these options are specified does the JDBC driver allow the **`ResultSet`** to perform data modification operations.

What kind of an exception would normally occur in JDBC, and how to handle it?

`java.sql.SQLException` is the most common exception that must be handled in a JDBC program. There is no difference in handling the traditional exception and an exception in JDBC. We can use the **`try-catch`**, **`try-multi catch`**, and even the **`finally`** block. Along with this, we can also use the **`AutoClosable`** interface to get rid of the **`finally`** block.

Additionally, we can also encounter other exceptions like **`SQLNonTransientException`**, **`SQLTransientException`**, **`SQLRecoverableException`**, **`BatchUpdateException`**, and **`SQLClientInfoException`**.

What is metadata? What are DatabaseMetaData and ResultSetMetaData?

Metadata is the data that provides a structured description of other data. JDBC provides different objects to provide information about the information, as follows:

- **DatabaseMetaData**: It provides information about the underlying database with which the application is communicating.

  We can use **`DatabaseMetaData`** to obtain database information, as follows:

  - o Database users, tables, views, and stored procedures
  - o Database schema and catalog information
  - o Information about PK and foreign key of a table

- **ResultSetMetaData**: It provides information about the **`ResultSet`** that is generated by the query.

  We can use **`ResultSetMetaData`** to obtain database information, as follows:

  - o Number of columns, name, type, and length
  - o Is the column readable/writable, searchable

What is Batch Update? How to perform batch processing?

In **Batch Update**, a batch of updates is grouped together and sent to the database in one batch instead of sending the updates one after another. The following are the advantages of Batch Update:

- Using a batch of updates helps to perform updates in one go, which is faster than sending the data one by one, and then to wait for each one to finish.
- Batch Update helps in reducing the network traffic.
- The speed is comparatively more than executing the updates one by one.
- We can use batch updates for SQL inserts, updates, as well as deletes.

The following code snippet describes how to use batch updates:

```
Statement st = null;
try{
    st = con.createStatement();
    st.addBatch("update employee set firstname='ABC' where id=1");
    st.addBatch("update employee set firstname='Eric' where id=4");
    st.addBatch("update employee set firstname='May'  where id=7");
    int[] affected = st.executeBatch();
} finally {
    if(st != null) st.close();
}
```

In this example, multiple update statements are added to the batch using the **addBatch()** method. The **executeBatch()** method sends all the statements to the database in a single request and returns an array indicating the number of rows affected by each statement.

Note: **We can also use PreparedStatement instead of Statement in the preceding code.**

What is SQLTimeoutException?

JDBC provides the **setQueryTimeout(int seconds)** method to set up the waiting time to capture the result from the statements. If the query does not return the result within the specified time given in the argument, the JDBC driver throws **SQLTimeoutException**. This mechanism helps prevent applications from waiting indefinitely for long-running or unresponsive database operations and enables better control over resource utilization and application responsiveness.

How can you optimize the JDBC performance?

The following approaches can be used to optimize the JDBC performance:

- Use connection pooling
- Prefer **PreparedStatement** over **Statement**
- Use batch processing
- Use forward-only **ResultSet** if scrolling is not required
- Use appropriate transaction management

Transaction management

Transaction represents a single unit of work to be performed on a database. In other words, a transaction can also be considered as a group of operations that perform a task.

When multiple operations are executed as a single unit of work, transaction management becomes more critical. If all operations are completed successfully, then the transaction becomes successful. If any operations fail, the transaction is rolled back, leading the transaction to reach a failure state.

This ensures data consistency, integrity, and reliability within the system.

What do you mean by ACID properties of transaction management?

ACID properties define the properties of transaction management. It is an acronym for **Atomicity, Consistency, Isolation, and Durability**. These are:

- **Atomicity**: Atomicity means either all fired queries will be successful or none of them.
- **Consistency**: Consistency ensures the consistent state of data.
- **Isolation**: Isolation makes sure one transaction is isolated from other transactions.
- **Durability**: Durability ensures that once the transaction is committed, it will remain committed, even if an event of errors occurs.

Why does the application need transaction management?

In JDBC, a transaction is auto-committed. This default behavior is acceptable in small applications. However, in the enterprise Java application, we may need to customize the behavior for the following reasons:

- **Improved application performance**: Grouping multiple database operations into a single transaction reduces the overhead of frequent commits, thereby improving overall system performance.
- **Maintaining business process integrity**: Enterprise applications often involve complex business workflows that span multiple database operations. Transaction management ensures that all operations either complete successfully together or are rolled back entirely in case of failure, preserving data consistency.
- **Support for distributed transactions**: Transaction management enables coordination across multiple transactional resources (such as multiple databases or messaging systems), making it possible to implement distributed transactions in enterprise systems.

Can you explain how transaction management improves the speed or performance of an application?

Sometimes, an application needs to perform bulky operations. It may happen that the user is inserting hundreds of rows into a database. Such insertions, if performed independently, can cause a performance hit. However, using a transaction, you will be able to commit all these insertions in a single go, which is obviously beneficial for the performance of the application.

What are the types of transactions?

Transactions can be categorized as:

- **Local transaction**: A local transaction ensures that all statements are executed on a single transactional resource, such as a JDBC connection. Local transactions are easier to implement, which is useful in a centralized computing environment. In a local transaction, the application components and resources are located at a single site, and it involves a local data manager running on a single machine.
- **Distributed transaction**: The **distributed transactions** span multiple transactional resources. In distributed transaction management, the transaction manager is responsible for all database-specific operations. We need to keep in mind that the distributed transaction must be synchronized and available at different locations.
- **Nested transaction**: The **nested transaction** occurs within the reference of some other transaction. Any changes made by the nested transaction are not visible to the existing or host transaction. All the changes that occurred in the nested transaction can be notified to the host transaction once it is committed. A nested transaction helps in managing the isolation of the transaction mechanism.

How to implement transaction management in JDBC?

By default, JDBC is in auto-commit mode. This means that every SQL statement is considered to be independent and is committed immediately after execution. To take control of transaction management, we need to perform the following steps:

1. **Disable auto-commit mode**: The first step is to disable the default auto-commit behavior of the `Connection` object. It facilitates the application to decide whether to commit the transaction or rollback.

   ```
   con.setAutoCommit(false);
   ```

2. Perform CRUD operations using the **`execute()`** or **`executeUpdate()`** methods and then invoke the **`commit()`** method:

   ```
   con.commit();
   ```

3. In case any operation in a transaction fails or an exception occurs, then invoke the **`rollback()`** method:

   ```
   catch(SQLException se){
   // Whenever exception occur
   con.rollback();
   }
   ```

By explicitly controlling commit and rollback operations, JDBC enables reliable transaction management, ensuring data consistency, fault tolerance, and integrity of business processes.

What are the commit() and rollback() methods?

The transaction initiated by an application may either be successful or fail due to an error or an exception. Based on the outcome, the application must decide whether the changes made by the executed operations should be permanently committed to the database or undone. To achieve this, transaction management provides two methods, which are as follows:

- **commit()**: Once the CRUD operation is performed and we want those changes to be reflected in the database permanently, we call the **`commit()`** method.
- **rollback()**: Whenever the CRUD operations are performed, there is a chance of getting an exception while executing one of the steps. There might be some already executed steps as well. So, to maintain consistency of the data, whatever changes are made till that point need to be rolled back. To undo these changes, we need to invoke the **`rollback()`** method.

What is Savepoint? How to use Savepoint?

Transaction is a concept of performing more than one operation one after the other. While performing these multiple operations, we may need an intermediate mark within the current transaction, which can be achieved by **`Savepoint`**. Once we set **`Savepoint`**, the transaction can be rolled back to that **`Savepoint`**, preserving all changes made prior to **`Savepoint`** while discarding the subsequent operations. The following code snippet elaborates on how to create and use **`Savepoint`**:

```
Savepoint savepoint = con.setSavepoint();
//intermediate operations
con.rollback(savepoint);   // rolling back till 'savepoint'
```

This approach provides finer control over transaction management, especially in complex business processes where selective rollback is required.

What is a cursor in JDBC?

A cursor is a pointer maintained by the **`ResultSet`** object that points to the current row in the **`ResultSet`**. When a **`ResultSet`** is initially instantiated, the cursor is positioned before the first row.

As the application processes the result set, the cursor moves from one row to another using navigation methods such as **`next()`**, **`previous()`**, **`first()`**, and **`last()`**, depending on the type of **`ResultSet`**. At any given time, the cursor determines which row's data is accessible to the application.

Connected and disconnected architecture in JDBC

Java provides different architectures to retrieve data from a database, such as:

- **Connected architecture**: The connection must be opened to access the data retrieved from the database.
- **Disconnected architecture**: The data retrieved from the database can be accessed even when the connection to the database is closed. In this architecture, the data is retrieved from the database and stored in an in-memory structure.

JDBC by default uses a connected architecture. However, a disconnected **RowSet** supports a disconnected architecture to deal with the database.

What is RowSet in JDBC?

The instance of **RowSet** is a Java bean component introduced in JDK 1.5. It is a wrapper of **ResultSet**, which holds tabular data in an easier and more flexible way than **ResultSet**. The **RowSet** object is scrollable and updatable by default.

What are the different types of RowSet?

RowSet is of two types:

- **Connected RowSet**: A connected **RowSet** object establishes a connection with the database to carry out the CRUD operations. The connection is maintained until the **RowSet** object is closed. **JdbcRowSet** is a wrapper over **RowSet** to provide the connected architecture.
- **Disconnected RowSet**: In a disconnected **RowSet** object, the connection is established to the database only while reading and writing the data to the DB. It does not hold a connection while processing the data. **CachedRowSet** is a wrapper over **RowSet** to provide the disconnected architecture.

Both connected and disconnected **RowSet** objects are almost the same, except in the following ways:

- Disconnected **RowSet** is lighter in weight compared to connected **RowSet** objects.
- Disconnected **RowSet** is by default **Serializable**.
- Disconnected **RowSet** can be used to send data to lightweight clients such as mobiles, etc.

RowSet is an interface. What are its types and implementation classes?

RowSet is a JDBC interface that extends the **ResultSet** interface and provides additional capabilities for connected and disconnected architectures. Since **RowSet** itself is an interface, it is further extended by some interfaces and implemented by some classes for concrete implementations.

The following are the different types of **RowSet** along with their implementations:

- **JdbcRowSet**: One of the extended interfaces of **RowSet** is **JdbcRowSet,** which is a wrapper around a **ResultSet** object. This enables the use of **ResultSet** as a **JavaBean** component. **JdbcRowSet** is a connected **RowSet**, which maintains its connection to a database using a JDBC technology-enabled driver. An instance of **JdbcRowSet** can simply take calls invoked on it, and then, in turn, that is invoked on its **ResultSet** object. The **JdbcRowSet** object is by default scrollable and updatable. When the driver and database do not support scrollable or updatable **ResultSet**, the application can populate a **JdbcRowSet** object with the data of a **ResultSet** object, and then we can operate on the **JdbcRowSet** object.

  The concrete implementation of **JbdcRowSet** is **JdbcRowSetImpl**.

  The following code snippet illustrates the usage of **JdbcRowSetImpl**:

```
JdbcRowSetImpl jdbcRowset= new JdbcRowSetImpl();
jdbcRowset.setCommand("SELECT * FROM employee WHERE empid = ?");
jdbcRowset.setURL("jdbc:mysql:mydb");
jdbcRowset.setUsername("mysql");
jdbcRowset.setPassword("mysql");
jdbcRowset.setInt(1, 100);
jdbcRowset.execute();
JdbcRowSetImpl jdbcRowset= new JdbcRowSetImpl();
jdbcRowset.setCommand("SELECT * FROM employee WHERE empid = ?");
jdbcRowset.setURL("jdbc:mysql:mydb");
jdbcRowset.setUsername("mysql");
jdbcRowset.setPassword("mysql");
jdbcRowset.setInt(1, 100);
jdbcRowset.execute();
```

  In this example, a parameterized SQL query is configured using **setCommand()**, database connection details are provided programmatically, and the query is executed using the **execute()** method. The parameter value is supplied using the **setInt()** method before execution.

- **CachedRowSet**: A **CachedRowSet** object is a disconnected **RowSet**. It is a container for rows of data, which caches its rows in memory, enabling it to operate without always being connected to a data source. A **CachedRowSet** object contains rows from **ResultSet**. However, it can also contain rows from any file with a tabular format like a spreadsheet. Whenever the data in **CachedRowSet** is modified, those modifications can be propagated to the source of the data. The implementation of this is **CachedRowSetImpl**.
- **WebRowSet**: **WebRowSet** is better for platform-independent communication. **WebRowSet** is an extension of **CachedRowSet**. Using this, **RowSet** provides the facility for reading and writing database query results into an XML file. The implementation of this is **WebRowSetImpl**.
- **JoinRowSet**: A **JoinRowSet** is an extension of **WebRowSet**, which consists of related data from different **RowSets**. **JoinRowSet** facilitates a standard way to establish an SQL JOIN between disconnected **RowSets** without connecting to the data source. Any number of **RowSet** objects, which implement the **Joinable** interface, can be added to a **JoinRowSet** object. The **Joinable** interface provides methods for specifying the columns based on which the JOIN action will be performed.
- **FilteredRowSet**: Sometimes, a **RowSet** object has to provide a degree of filtering to its contents. Here, we can provide a query language for all standard **RowSet** implementations. However, it is a complex and impractical approach for lightweight components. The **FilteredRowSet** supplies a lightweight solution for filtering the data.

Conclusion

In this chapter, we explored the types of JDBC-related questions commonly asked in a Java interview. While discussing this, we gained a deeper knowledge of how to connect with a database and how to retrieve information or data from a database to an application. We also examined different interfaces and their implementation, which form the core part of JDBC. Managing the transaction is most important when we work with the enterprise application development. In this chapter, we also gathered detailed knowledge about how to handle the transactions in JDBC. We explored different concepts like rollback and savepoints during this discussion. At the end of the chapter, we also discussed important concepts like cursors and batch updates. We are still on the first floor of the tower; there are still many advanced concepts to learn and explore to build strong interview readiness for a Java interview. In the next chapter, we will discuss the Collections Framework in detail.

CHAPTER 8
Collections

Introduction

Java is an object-oriented programming language. Software created using Java comprises a number of objects that interact with each other. In real-world applications, it is always essential to group these objects together so as to perform some common operations such as storage, retrieval, manipulation, and traversal. Normally, such operations need to be performed manually by a developer repetitively, which could be time-consuming and error-prone. To reduce such effort, Java introduced the Collection Framework, which consists of predefined data structures and algorithms, and these can be applied to a group of objects. The **Collections Framework** is essentially a unified set of interfaces and their implementation classes, which enables developers to group objects based on different scenarios. Each interface on its own facilitates different functionalities to a group of objects based on which objects are arranged or traversed. Such functionalities enable developers to use objects in an application to their full capacity to achieve the desired result. Sometimes, the developers are in need of objects that are ordered; other times, they want the same object group without duplicates, or sometimes, the same object group in some sorted order. The Collections Framework provides all such solutions to the developers.

Structure

We will be covering interview questions based on the following topics in this chapter:

- Overview of Collections Framework
- List interface
- Set interface
- Map interface
- Queue interface
- Collection utility interfaces and collections

Objectives

Every interface in Collection is defined to achieve a specific functionality. To remember such a big API is not an easy task. And, because of its importance in real-time projects, Collection is one of the most favorite topics in the Java interview process. As mentioned, the Collections Framework API is huge. Thus, covering each and every class is not possible or, in fact, not required as far as the interview process is concerned. Despite that, in this chapter, you will learn how to answer almost every important question, right from the concept to its implementation, so that you will succeed in the interview. You will be able to master the different collection types like List, Set, Queue, and Map, and their implementations.

Overview of Collection Framework

JDK 1.2 introduced the Collection Framework, which provides a comprehensive architecture that includes a unified set of collection interfaces, their implementations, and supporting algorithms. These APIs, which are a collection of classes and interfaces, are used to store, find, add, and manipulate the objects. The framework offers interfaces such as **`List`**, **`Set`**, **`Map`**, **`Queue`**, and their implementation classes like **`ArrayList`**, **`Vector`**, **`HashMap`**, **`Stack`**, and **`HashSet`**, and so on, for this purpose.

List the benefits of the Collections Framework

Java Collections is now equipped with Generics and Concurrent Collection classes for thread-safe operations. It includes blocking interfaces along with their implementations in the Java concurrent package.

The following are some of the benefits of the Collections Framework:

- The framework reduced the development effort with the help of core collection classes instead of implementing our own version of collection classes.
- The code quality is enhanced by the use of well-tested Collections classes.
- It reduces the effort for maintaining the code by using the collection classes offered in JDK.
- It helps in reusability and interoperability.

What are the key differences between arrays and collections?

Both arrays and collections support storing data. However, there are some differences amongst them, which are stated as follows:

- Arrays always have a fixed size. It means once the size of an array is defined, it cannot be modified at runtime. However, the collections are dynamic in size. It means the size of a collection can be modified dynamically.
- Arrays are designed to store the same type of data, making them homogeneous in nature. However, a collection can hold heterogeneous data or objects.
- Arrays do not have predefined methods for data manipulation, and the developer must provide their own logic for operations like sorting and searching. In contrast, the Collections Framework offers a rich set of predefined utility classes and methods for data manipulation tasks.

What are legacy classes?

The Collections Framework is not part of JDK from the beginning. It was added from JDK 2 onward. This means that prior to the Collections Framework, JDK relied on some classes and interfaces for storing and manipulating the collection of data, which were termed as legacy classes.

The major legacy classes are described as follows:

- **Vector**: **`Vector`** is similar to **`ArrayList`**, except that the methods of **`Vector`** are synchronized, while those of **`ArrayList`** are non-synchronized. This makes **`ArrayList`** the preferred approach in modern applications over Vectors.
- **Stack**: **`Stack`** is referred to as **last-in, first-out** (**LIFO**), which allows popping and pushing of the elements only from one end. It is an extension of the **`Vector`** class. This contributes to the developers' preference for the use of **`ArrayDeque`** over **`Stack`**.
- **Dictionary**: **`Dictionary`** is an abstract class that holds each element as a key-value pair. **`Hashtable`** is a subtype of the **`Dictionary`** class.
- **HashTable**: **`HashTable`** implements the Map interface and stores the data in key-value pairs. Similar to Vector, it is thread-safe, which makes it less reliable than **`HashMap`**.
- **Properties**: It is an extension to the **`Hashtable`** class. **`Properties`** is thread-safe, so it does not need any manual sync to hold the values in the key pair.

List the various interfaces used in the Collections Framework

The **`java.util`** package offers various interfaces and classes as a part of the Collections Framework. The following is the list of interfaces offered by the framework:

- Collection interface
- List interface

- Set interface
- Queue interface
- Map interface

These core interfaces define the fundamental data structures used to store and manipulate groups of objects in Java. Each interface provides specific behaviors and contracts, while multiple concrete classes implement them to offer different performance characteristics and ordering mechanisms based on application requirements.

What are the advantages of the generic collections in Java?

The following are some of the key advantages of using the generic collection:

- While fetching or iterating the elements, typecasting is not required.
- The generics are type-safe and checked at compile time. This results in reducing the type mismatch errors and runtime exceptions.
- The generic collection ensures the stability of the code by making it bug-detectable in the early stages of development.

What is type erasure in generics?

By default, the collection API allows for heterogeneous elements. This heterogeneity may create some issues while processing the data of the collection. To avoid such processing issues, generics were introduced in JDK 1.5. The use of generics assures type safety; it means the collection is allowed to hold the elements only of the same type, and heterogeneous elements cannot be allowed inside.

Though generic is powerful, it only enforces the type constraints at compile time, and the information about the type is not available at runtime. This process of erasing the type information at runtime is termed as **type erasure**.

What is the difference between Collection and Collections?

The **`Collection`** interface and the **`Collections`** class serve different purposes within the Java Collection Framework. The following are the key differences between them:

- **`Collection`** is an interface, whereas **`Collections`** is a utility class.
- The **`Collection`** interface offers standard functionalities of data structures to **`List`**, **`Set`**, and **`Queue`**. The **`Collections`** class is a general-purpose class that offers helper methods that can be invoked on collection objects.

- The **Collection** interface provides the methods that can be used to manipulate the elements stored in the respective data structure. The **Collections** class provides the static methods for various utility methods for collection objects.

What are the benefits of the Collections Framework?

The following are the key benefits of the Collection Framework:

- The framework reduces the programming efforts as it provides predefined interfaces, classes, and methods.
- Use of the framework increases the performance, as it offers the use of high-performance implementations of data structures and algorithms.
- It offers interoperability between unrelated APIs so that the collection can be changed from one to another.
- The framework is very easy to learn and implement functionalities even for developers who are new to Java.

Which classes from the Collections Framework are thread-safe?

Classes such as **Vector**, **Hashtable**, **Properties**, and **Stack** are synchronized; this means they are thread-safe and safe to use in a multi-threaded environment. In JDK 1.5, some concurrent APIs are included, which allow modification during the process of iteration. It is possible because they work on a clone of the collection, making them safe to use in a multi-threaded environment. These classes are available in the `java.util.concurrent` package. These classes are **CopyOnWriteArrayList**, **ConcurrentHashMap**, and **CopyOnWriteArraySet**, which allow modifying the collection while iterating.

Can we synchronize the collection interfaces? What are the ways by which we can synchronize the List, Set, and Map elements?

There are different ways in which the standard collection interfaces can be synchronized. The **Collections** utility class offers different methods to facilitate the conversion of **List**, **Set**, or **Map** elements, as synchronized.

The key methods include:

- **`public static List synchronizedList(List l)`**
- **`public static Set synchronizedSet(Set s)`**
- **`public static SortedSet synchronizedSortedSet(SortedSet s)`**

- `public static Map synchronizedMap(Map m){}`
- `public static SortedMap synchronizedSortedMap(SortedMap m)`

By using these methods, developers can safely share collection instances across multiple threads without manually implementing synchronization logic.

Which features are added to collection in JDK 8? What are the Collection-related features in Java 8?

The following features have been added to the Java 8 Collection API:

- The Stream API has been added to collection classes for processing the data sequentially as well as in parallel.
- The `Iterable` interface is now enhanced with the default `forEach()` method, which we can use to iterate over the elements in the collection.
- The `forEach()` method works seamlessly with lambda expressions accepting the Consumer interface as an argument.
- The `Iterator` interface now includes the `forEachRemaining` (Consumer action) method, allowing remaining elements in the iteration to be processed conveniently without explicit loops.

Why does Collection not extend the Cloneable and Serializable interfaces?

Collection is an interface that specifies a group of objects, known as elements. However, this does not dictate how these elements are stored or managed. This responsibility is delegated to concrete implementations like `List` and `Set`.

For example, `List` is extended from the Collection interface, which allows duplicate elements. In contrast, `Set`, which is another extension of `Collection`, does not allow duplicates. Adding `clone()` in **collection** is meaningless, as `Collection`, being an interface, is an abstract representation. Hence, it is all up to how we implement the `clone()` method. The concrete implementation should decide how it should be cloned or serialized.

Making the cloning or serialization implementation compulsory by adding it to the interface is less flexible and more restrictive. This means that it has to be the choice of the specific implementation class to decide whether it can be cloned, serialized, or both.

How can you create a new collection from the existing collection using the feature introduced in Java10?

Java10 provided the additional static method **`copyOf()`** in the collections API, which we can invoke on **`List`**, **`Set`**, and **`Map`**. This method creates a new collection from the existing collection. We must make a note that this method returns an unmodifiable collection. We cannot modify this collection once created. Additionally, the iteration order of this collection is maintained.

Are there any rules applied to use the copyOf() method from Java10?

When we work with the **`copyOf()`** method, we must consider the following points:

- The original collection should not be null or should not contain any null elements.
- If the original collection itself is modifiable, invoking the **`copyOf()`** method does not create a copy.
- If the original collection is modified after the invocation of the **`copyOf()`** method, then the newly created list is not updated.

What updates provided in Java9 to create the collections?

Java9 provided the static factory method **`of()`** to create collections of type **`List`**, **`Set`** and **`Map`**. The method **`of()`** can be applied to any of the collections to create empty collections or collections with some predefined elements in them. The collections created by this method are always unmodifiable. The following list represents different overloaded signatures of the method:

- **`of()`**
- **`of(element1,element2)`**
- **`of(elements…)`**

As discussed, these methods are static methods and can be invoked as **`List.of()`**, **`Set.of()`** or **`Map.of()`**.

What is the significance of the SequencedCollection interface introduced in Java21?

In Java 21 (JEP 431), **`SequencedCollection`** is a new interface introduced to provide a uniform way to work with ordered collections.

Before Java 21, some collections preserved order (like **`List`** or **`LinkedHashSet`**), but there was no common interface to access the *first* and *last* elements consistently.

`SequencedCollection` solves that problem. From this version, the collection classes implement the **`SequencedCollection`** interface additionally. This facilitates the collection to use methods like:

- **`E getFirst();`**
- **`E getLast();`**
- **`E removeFirst();`**
- **`E removeLast();`**
- **`void addFirst(E e);`**
- **`void addLast(E e);`**
- **`SequencedCollection<E> reversed();`**

As the names signify, these methods provide standardized ways to access, add, and remove elements at both ends of an ordered collection.

Do all the collections implement the SequencedCollection interface?

`SequencedCollection` is implemented only by collections that have a defined encounter order. This includes **`ArrayList`**, **`LinkedList`**, **`Vector`**, **`Stack`**, **`LinkedHashset`**, **`TreeSet`**, **`ArrayDeque`**, etc. Collections like **`HashSet`**, **`HashMap`**, and **`HashTable`**, which are typically unordered collections, do not implement the **`SequencedCollection`** interface.

What are the best practices related to the Java Collections Framework?

We have to make the right choice of the collection based on the needs of size. For example, if we need a fixed-size group of objects, we might use an array over **`ArrayList`**. If we need uniqueness, we need to go with **`Set`**. If we need to maintain the object in a sorted way, we need to use **`TreeSet`**. If we want to achieve uniqueness even for duplicate objects, we need to make use of the **`Map`** implementation. Some collections allow us to specify the initial capacity, so if we can estimate the number of elements that we want to store, we can use this feature to avoid rehashing or resizing.

Along with this, we also need to keep the following in mind:

- Always make use of interfaces, not implementations. This ensures the flexibility to change the implementation easily in the future.
- Always use generics that offer type safety to avoid **`ClassCastException`** at runtime.

- Use the immutable classes provided by JDK as keys in **Map** so that we do not need to implement the **hashCode()** and **equals()** methods for a custom class. It avoids coding overhead.
- Try to use the **Collections** utility class as much as possible for algorithms or to get read-only, synchronized, or empty collections, instead of writing your own implementation. Own implementation means rigorous testing.
- The use of predefined classes will reduce code reuse. Also, they have low maintainability.

List interface

The **java.util.List** interface extends the **Collection** interface and represents an ordered collection of elements, which are not necessarily sorted in their natural order. It allows duplicate elements and preserves insertion order. The interface also supports positional (index-based) access to elements, enabling random access and precise control over where elements are inserted, retrieved, updated, or removed.

Additionally, a **List** provides specific methods such as **add(int index, E element)**, **get(int index)**, **set(int index, E element)**, and **remove(int index)** for index-based operations. It also offers the **ListIterator**, which allows bidirectional traversal and modification of elements during iteration. Common implementations of the **List** interface include **ArrayList**, **LinkedList**, **Vector**, and **Stack**.

State the differences between ArrayList and Vector

Both **ArrayList** and **Vector** have **List** as the parent interface. It means both of these objects represent an indexed, ordered, unsorted collection. However, there are some major differences between them, which are stated as follows:

- **ArrayList** is not synchronized; however, **Vector** is synchronized, which makes it relatively slower than **ArrayList**.
- **ArrayList** is a part of the modern Java Collections Framework, but **Vector** is a legacy class as it was introduced in Java 1.0.
- Whenever an internal array size needs to grow, **ArrayList** increases its size by 50% of the array size. **Vector** increases its capacity by doubling the existing size.

What are the similarities between ArrayList and Vector?

Both **ArrayList** and **Vector** possess the following similarities:

- Both classes are indexed collections, allowing positional access to elements.
- Internally, both are backed up by a resizable array.

- Both classes are ordered collections. This means that the order in which we insert the elements is always maintained, and the elements are retrieved in the same order.
- The iterator implementation of both classes is fail-fast by design. This means they throw **ConcurrentModificationException** if the collection is structurally modified during iteration.
- Both collections allow null elements to be stored.
- Both allow random access to elements with the help of an index number.

What is the difference between ArrayList and LinkedList?

Both these classes implement the **List** interface. However, they differ significantly in their internal implementation. The following are the key differences between **ArrayList** and **LinkedList**:

- **ArrayList** is implemented using a dynamic array, and **LinkedList** is implemented as a doubly linked list.
- **ArrayList** is not efficient for manipulation as it requires the shifting of elements for insertions and deletions. On the other hand, **LinkedList** is more efficient in such operations as they need to only update the node references.
- **ArrayList** is better for scenarios involving frequent read and fetch operations. However, **LinkedList** is the best option for manipulating the data.
- **ArrayList** provides random access using the index positions, but **LinkedList** does not provide efficient random access as the elements are traversed sequentially.
- As **ArrayList** stores only objects, it takes less memory overhead, but **LinkedList** stores the object as well as the address of that object. So, it takes more memory overhead.

What are the key differences between Array and ArrayList?

Both array and **ArrayList** are indexed collections with the following differences:

- The array is always of fixed size, and it cannot be resized at runtime, while the size of **ArrayList** can be changed dynamically.
- The array is of a static size, and the **ArrayList** is of a dynamic size.
- The array allows storing primitives as well as objects; however, in **ArrayList**, we can store only objects.

Explain the difference between the length of an array and the size of ArrayList?

The length of an array represents the fixed number of elements the array can hold and is accessed using the length property. Once an array is created, its length cannot be changed.

In contrast, **`ArrayList`** does not support the length property. Instead, it provides the **`size()`** method, which returns the current number of elements present in the list. Since **`ArrayList`** is a dynamic collection, its size can grow or shrink as elements are added or removed.

Is it possible to convert between an array and ArrayList in Java? If so, what are the standard approaches to convert ArrayList to an array and an array to ArrayList?

We can convert **`ArrayList`** to an array and vice versa in the following manner:

- We can convert an array to **`ArrayList`** with the help of the **`asList()`** method of the **`Arrays`** class. The **`asList()`** method is the static method offered by the **`Arrays`** class that accepts the **`List`** object as an argument.
- In the same way, we can convert **`ArrayList`** to an array using the **`toArray()`** method of the **`ArrayList`** class.

How would you create an array of primitives from a list?

The **`toArray()`** method discussed in the earlier question creates an array of wrappers and not the primitives. If you try to generate an array of primitives using this method, it will throw an exception. To create an array of primitive types, the elements must be explicitly copied from the list into the primitive array. This is typically done by iterating over the list and retrieving elements using the **`get()`** method, followed by auto-unboxing into the corresponding primitive type.

ArrayList can be modified at runtime. What if we want a read-only ArrayList?

By default, **`ArrayList`** in Java is mutable. It means we can access, remove, or update the elements using the **`add()`**, **`remove()`**, or **`set()`** methods.

However, we can obtain a read-only **ArrayList** by invoking the **Collections.unmodifiableList()** method. When **ArrayList** is read-only, we cannot modify the collection using the **add()**, **remove()**, or **set()** methods.

The following code snippet demonstrates how to create a read-only **ArrayList** using this approach:

```
List<Integer> list = new ArrayList<Integer>();
        // populate the list
        list.add(10);
        list.add(20);

        // printing the list
        System.out.println("Initial list: " + list);

        // getting unmodifiable list
        // using unmodifiableList() method
        List<Integer> nonModifiableList = Collections
                                      .unmodifiableList(list);

        // Adding element to new list
        System.out.println("Trying to modify the list");
    nonModifiableList.add(30);
```

If you try to execute this code, you will end up with the exception **UnsupportedOperationException**, shown as follows:

```
Initial list: [10, 20]
Trying to modify the list
Exception in thread "main" java.lang.UnsupportedOperationException
    at java.util.Collections$UnmodifiableCollection.add(Unknown Source)
```

This behavior confirms that the list has been successfully converted into a read-only view, allowing only read operations while explicitly preventing any changes to its structure or elements.

Can ArrayList contain duplicate elements? What are the different ways to remove duplicate elements from ArrayList?

By default, **ArrayList** can contain duplicate elements. Using the following two ways, one can remove duplicates from **ArrayList**:

- **Using HashSet**: We can remove the duplicates from **`ArrayList`** using **`HashSet`**. This means that you need to convert **`ArrayList`** to **`HashSet`**. However, in that case, it will not preserve the insertion order.
- **Using LinkedHashSet**: The use of **`LinkedHashSet`** maintains the insertion order while removing the duplicates. It can be done using the following steps:
    1. First, copy all the elements of **`ArrayList`** to **`LinkedHashSet`**.
    2. Now, empty **`ArrayList`** with the help of the **`clear()`** method. The **`clear()`** method will remove all the elements from the list and make it empty.
    3. Finally, copy all the elements of **`LinkedHashset`** to **`ArrayList`**.

By default, ArrayList is ordered. Is there any way by which you can reverse or sort the elements in ArrayList?

By default, **`ArrayList`** does not provide any such functionality to reverse or sort the elements. However, using the utility methods from the **`java.util.Collections`** class, we can achieve this. The following code snippet shows how to achieve the same:

```
List<Integer> list = new ArrayList<Integer>();
// populate the list
list.add(10);
list.add(6);
list.add(20);
list.add(4);
list.add(15);
// printing the list
System.out.println("Initial list: " + list);
Collections.reverse(list);
System.out.println("Reversed list: "+list);
Collections.sort(list);
System.out.println("Sorted list: "+list);
```

The output of the preceding snippet would be as follows:

```
Initial list: [10, 6, 20, 4, 15]
Reversed list: [15, 4, 20, 6, 10]
Sorted list: [4, 6, 10, 15, 20]
```

In summary, although **`ArrayList`** itself does not provide explicit methods for reordering elements, the **`Collections`** utility class enables powerful operations such as reversing and sorting with minimal effort. Additionally, **`Collections.sort()`** can also accept a custom **`Comparator`**, allowing developers to define their own sorting logic based on specific business requirements.

What are the different ways to synchronize ArrayList?

`ArrayList` can be synchronized using the following two ways:

- **Using the Collections.synchronizedList() method**:
    - The method accepts a list and returns a synchronized list.
    - The method is useful when we do not want to synchronize the traversal, but needs to prevent interference among concurrent threads.
    - This is costly, as it needs a separate array copy with every write operation.
    - This mechanism is very efficient when we have a list, and we only need to traverse over its elements without modifying them frequently.
- **Using the CopyOnWriteArrayList() method**:

    While iterating over **`CopyOnWriteArrayList()`**, even if we try to modify the data while iterating over it, it does not throw **`ConcurrentModificationException`** because the iterator iterates over a separate copy of **`ArrayList`**. Also, the write operations will be performed on a copy of **`ArrayList`**.

Which are the most common methods from the Collections class that can be used to perform operations on List?

The following methods of the **`Collections`** class can be invoked to perform operations on **`List`** specifically:

- **`void reverse(List<?> list)`**
- **`void rotate(List<?>, int distance)`**
- **`void shuffle(List<?> list)`**
- **`void sort(List<T> list)`**
- **`void sort(List<T> list, comparator<? Super T> c)`**
- **`void swap(List<?> list, int i, int j)`**
- **`void copy(List<?> dest, List<?> src)`**
- **`void fill(List<? super T> list, T obj)`**
- **`void replaceAll(List<T> list, T oldVal, T newVal)`**

These methods provide powerful utility operations that simplify common list manipulations without requiring manual implementation. By using these predefined methods, developers can perform sorting, reordering, replacement, and bulk operations efficiently while improving code readability and maintainability.

Set interface

The **`java.util.Set`** interface represents a collection of unique elements and does not allow duplicate values. The elements are generally unordered and unsorted (depending on the implementation). The interface inherits methods from the **`Collection`** interface.

A **`Set`** ensures that no two elements are equal, based on the **`equals()`** method. It does not provide index-based access like a **`List`**. Common implementations such as **`HashSet`**, **`LinkedHashSet`**, and **`TreeSet`** differ in terms of ordering, performance, and sorting behavior.

Explain the difference between the List and Set interfaces

Both, **`List`** and **`Set`** interfaces are extended from the **`Collection`** interface. They have the following differences:

- **`List`** can contain duplicate elements, but **`Set`** can contain only unique elements.
- **`List`** is an ordered collection. It means it maintains the insertion order. However, **`Set`** is an unordered collection.
- The **`List`** interface allows any number of null values, but the **`Set`** interface only allows a single null value.
- The **`List`** interface contains **`Vector`** as a single legacy class. However, the **`Set`** interface does not have any legacy class.

What is the difference between HashSet and TreeSet?

Both **`HashSet`** and **`TreeSet`** are concrete implementations of the **`Set`** interface, but they have the following differences:

- **`HashSet`** is unordered, but **`TreeSet`** maintains the natural ascending order.
- **`HashSet`** is impended by hash table, whereas **`TreeSet`** is implemented by using a self-balancing tree structure.
- **`HashSet`** offers better performance as these operations typically execute in the constant time *O(1)*. **`TreeSet`**, due to its tree-based structure, performs these operations in logarithmic time *O(log n)*.
- Internally, **`HashSet`** is backed by **`HashMap`**, and **`TreeSet`** is backed by **`TreeMap`**.

How can we ensure that a Set correctly identifies and stores only unique objects according to their logical equality?

According to theoretical concept, **Set** interface allows only unique elements. When we add instances of the user-defined classes in the **Set** interface, the uniqueness is checked based on the implementation of **equals()** and **hashCode()** methods. In the absence of these two method implementations, **Set** interface uses the object references to check the equality of the object. As every object is stored in a different memory location, the references to the objects are different. Obviously, in this case, even though the objects are the same, the **Set** interface treats them as unique.

What will be the output of a given program? Could you justify your answer by explaining how TreeSet determines element ordering and handles duplicate objects?

Considering the following code snippet:

```
class Employee{
      private int empId;
      private String name;
    //default and parameterised constructor
    //getters and setters
   //compareTo method
  }
Class Test{
    public static void main(String[] args){
    Set<Employee> employees =new TreeSet<>();
    employees.add(new Employee(1,"abc"));
    employees.add(new Employee(2,"abc1"));
    employees.add(new Employee(1,"abc"));
    System.out.println("elements of set:-"+ employees);
  }
}
```

This code will generate the exception **java.lang.ClassCastException**. This occurs because a **TreeSet** in Java requires its elements to be naturally comparable (i.e., the elements must implement the **Comparable** interface) or a custom **Comparator** must be provided at the time of set creation. In the provided code, although the comment mentions a **compareTo()** method in the **Employee** class, it is unclear whether the class actually implements **Comparable<Employee>**. Without implementing **Comparable** or providing a **Comparator**, the **TreeSet** cannot determine the order of the objects and attempts to cast the elements internally, resulting in a **ClassCastException**.

Can you explain more about CopyOnWriteArraySet?

Introduced in JDK 1.5, it is a thread-safe version of **Set**. Internally, it uses **CopyOnWriteArrayList** for all the operations that are performed on the elements. Interestingly, this is backed by an immutable array. That means if you change any of the elements of **CopyOnWriteArraySet**, it creates an entirely new array behind the scenes. So, this **Set** implementation of **Set** is costlier if we are in a situation where we want to modify the elements often.

What is the purpose of the hashCode() method in Java, and how does it work?

The **hashCode()** method returns an integer value known as the hash code of an object. This value is used in the hash-based collection to determine the internal storage location (bucket) of the object. The **hashCode()** method for the different objects returns the same integer value if the keys are identical. Two objects are always considered equal if they are equal according to the **equals()** method and have the same hash code values. However, it is possible that hash code values are the same, but the objects are not equal. JVM always returns different hash code values internally if the objects are stored in different memory locations. The **hashCode()** method can be overridden to generate a custom hash code value based on the specific fields of a class. By providing a proper implementation, developers can ensure that the hash code is consistent with the logic defined in the **equals()** method.

When overriding **equals()**, it is essential to also override **hashCode()** so that equal objects produce the same hash code. This ensures correct behavior when the objects are stored in hash-based collections and allows equality comparisons to function reliably and efficiently.

What will be the output of a given code?

Considering the following code:

```
class Employee{
    private int empId;
    private String name;
  //default and parameterised constructor
  //getters and setters
```

```
    }
Class Test{
    public static void main(String[] args){
    Set<Employee> employees =new HashSet<>();
    employees.add(new Employee(1,"abc"));
    employees.add(new Employee(2,"abc1"));
    employees.add(new Employee(1,"abc"));
    System.out.println(“initial size:-“+ employees.size());
    employees.remove(new Employee(2,"abc1"));
    System.out.println(“ after removal the size:-“+ employees.size());
    }
}
```

The output of the code will indicate that the size of the **HashSet** remains the same even after invoking the **remove()** method. The **Employee** class does not override the **equals()** and **hashCode()** methods inherited from the **Object** class. Therefore, object comparison is based on **reference equality**, not on the values of **empId** and **name**. This causes the new object created in the argument of the **remove()** method to be not equal to the actual object already existing in the **HashSet**. As a result, that object will not be deleted, and the size of the **HashSet** remains unchanged.

What do you do so that the remove() method from the HashSet works properly??

To ensure that an object is successfully removed from a **HashSet**, you must override both the **equals()** and **hashCode()** methods in your Employee class. This is necessary because **HashSet** uses:

- **hashCode()** to locate the correct bucket
- **equals()** to identify the exact object within that bucket

If these methods are not overridden, Java uses the default implementations from **Object**, which compare memory references rather than object data. As a result, two objects with identical field values will not be considered equal.

Why is it necessary to override the equals() method in Java?

The **equals()** method is defined in the **Object** class and is used to determine whether two objects are considered equal. By default, the implementation provided by the **Object** class compares objects based on their memory reference (reference equality), not on their internal data. We need to override the **equals()** method if we wish to compare the object equality based on the state of the properties of objects rather than the memory reference.

What are the additional features provided by NavigableSet interface compared to the SortedSet interface?

NavigableSet was introduced in JDK 1.6, which is extended from the **SortedSet** interface. It provides more functionalities than **SortedSet** by providing richer navigation and retrieval operations based on element ordering. Unlike **SortedSet**, we can navigate in both forward and reverse directions in **NavigableSet**. Additionally, it provides some more methods like **headset()**, **tailSet()**, **subset()**, **ceiling()**, **floor()**, **pollFirst()**, **pollLast()**, and so on.

Map interface

The **java.util.Map** interface stores elements in a key-value pair structure. It does not extend the Collection interface. While keys must be unique, values can be duplicated. The elements are generally stored in an unordered and unsorted manner (depending on the implementation).

A Map provides fundamental operations such as **put()**, **get()**, **remove()**, and **containsKey()** to manage entries. It also offers different views of the data through **keySet()**, **values()**, and **entrySet()** methods. Various implementations, such as **HashMap**, **LinkedHashMap**, **TreeMap**, and **Hashtable**, differ in terms of ordering, synchronization, and performance characteristics.

What is the difference between HashMap and HashTable?

The **HashMap** and **Hashtable** classes are two important implementations of the Map interface in Java. Although both store data in key–value pairs and use hashing mechanisms for storage, they differ in terms of synchronization, performance, and handling of null values. The following are the key differences between them:

- **HashMap** is non-synchronized, meaning it cannot be used to share between threads directly, and it needs to implement a proper synchronization code, but **Hashtable** is synchronized, and it can be safely shared with many threads.
- **Hashtable** does not allow any null key or value, but **HashMap** allows one null key and multiple null values.
- **HashMap** is generally preferred over **Hashtable** if we do not need synchronization.

Does HashTable allow a null key or value? Can you explain the reason why HashTable does not permit null?

Each entry in the `HashTable` is in the form of a key-value pair. If we want to successfully store and retrieve elements from it, the objects that are used as keys must implement the `hashCode()` and `equals()` methods. Since null is not an object it cannot implement both the `hashCode()` and `equals()` methods. Allowing null keys or values would therefore lead to ambiguity and potential runtime errors during hashing and lookup operations. To avoid such issues and to maintain strict synchronization and legacy behavior, `HashTable` explicitly disallows null.

Why does HashMap allow null?

`HashMap` is an improvement over `Hashtable`. `HashMap` was launched as a part of the Java Collection Framework. When we put a null key into `HashMap`, the `hashcode()` method is not invoked on the null values; instead, it puts the key in a bucket with a value equal to 0 (zero). The bucket value is 0 (zero) because there is no hash value for null. If multiple entries are mapped with the same bucket, the `LinkedList` is used internally to manage the objects in that bucket. Thus, if there are already objects in a bucket having a value equal to 0, the null object will be appended to `LinkedList` in that bucket. When we try to retrieve the value stored at a null key from `HashMap`, the search is done for the value at the null key present in bucket 0. We must ensure that we store only one null key in the `HashMap`.

What is WeakHashMap?

This is also an implementation of `Map` similar to `HashMap`, with one important change in terms of how it interacts with the garbage collector. In the case of `HashMap`, if the key that we declared is of object type, then `HashMap` maintains a strong reference for that key. It means the `HashMap` takes over the garbage collector, because of which garbage collection cannot delete the key, even if there are no live references attached to that key in an application. In the case of `WeakHashMap`, the same `HashMap` gives up the power of deleting the used keys of type objects to the garbage collector, which makes `HashMap` weak; thus, the reason it is termed as `WeakHashMap`.

Can you explain the concept of WeakHashMap with the help of some code?

Sure. The following code snippet shows how the garbage collector can take an active role in deleting the unused keys that are of the object type:

```
Map hashMap= new HashMap();
Map weakHashMap = new WeakHashMap();
```

```

String keyHashMap = new String("HashMapKey");
String keyWeakHashMap = new String("WeakHashMapKey");

hashMap.put(keyHashMap, "MyHashMap");
weakHashMap.put(keyWeakHashMap, "MyWeakHashMap");
System.out.println("Values before GC :");
System.out.println(hashMap.get("HashMapKey")+" "+weakHashMap.
get("WeakHashMapKey"));

keyHashMap = null;
keyWeakHashMap = null;

System.gc();
System.out.println("Values after GC :");
System.out.println(hashMap.get("HashMapKey")+" "
                    +weakHashMap.get("WeakHashMapKey"));
```

As shown, the keys associated with the objects are set to null. However, even after that, the **HashMap** key survives and points to the actual object, which is not the case with **WeakHashMap**.

The following is the output of this code snippet:

```
Values before GC :
MyHashMap MyWeakHashMap
Values after GC :
MyHashMap null
```

Note: **You can also use a user-defined object as a key instead of a String and implement the finalize() method to prove that the garbage collector is actually working in WeakHashMap.**

What are the differences between the Set and Map interfaces?

The differences between the **Set** and **Map** interfaces are as follows:

- **Set** contains only elements, but **Map** contains the key and values (elements) both.
- **Set** contains all unique values. However, **Map** can contain duplicate values associated with the unique key.

- `Set` can have a single null value; `Map` allows a single null key but can have any number of null values.

What are the differences between HashMap and HashSet?

The differences between `HashSet` and `HashMap` are as follows:

- `HashSet` implements the `Set` interface, and `HashMap` implements the `Map` interface.
- `HashSet` contains only values, whereas `HashMap` includes key and value as one entry.
- `HashSet` can be iterated directly. However, to iterate over `HashMap`, we need to convert it into `Set` first.
- `HashSet` cannot contain duplicate values. `HashMap` can contain duplicates, which will be associated with unique keys.
- `HashSet` can contain a single null value, but `HashMap` can have only a single null key. `HashMap` allows any number of null values.

What are the differences between HashMap and TreeMap?

The differences between `HashMap` and `TreeMap` are as follows:

- `HashMap` is unordered. However, `TreeMap` is sorted in ascending order.
- `HashMap` implements a hash table by default, and `TreeMap` implements a tree structure.
- We can sort `HashMap` using key or value, but `TreeMap` can be sorted by keys only.
- `HashMap` allows a null key with multiple null values, but `TreeMap` does not allow any null key but can contain multiple null values.
- Search operation is faster in `HashMap` as compared to `TreeMap`.

Since HashMap does not maintain any ordering of its elements, how can you sort a HashMap by its values?

We can perform the following steps to sort `HashMap` by its values:

1. **Convert** HashMap **entries into** LinkedList: Invoke the **`entrySet()`** method to obtain a set of key–value mappings, and pass this set to the constructor of a LinkedList.
2. **Sort the** LinkedList: Use the **`Collections.sort(arg1, arg2)`** method and pass **`LinkedList`** as the first parameter. The second parameter of this invocation would

be the **Comparator** implementation, which provides the business logic for the value-based sorting.

3. **Convert LinkedList to HashMap**: Iterate over the sorted list and insert the entries into a new **HashMap** (or preferably a **LinkedHashMap** if you want to preserve the sorted order).

What is IdentityHashMap? How is it different from a normal HashMap?

IdentityHashMap was added in Java 1.4. This class is also the implementation of **Map**, but it does not use the **equals()** and **hashCode()** methods for object comparison internally. Instead of that, it uses the equality (**==**) operator to check the equality of objects. Thus, this **Map** implementation is faster than **HashMap**. Another difference is in terms of key, which is stored in **HashMap** and **IdentityHashMap**. In **HashMap**, the key has to be immutable, but in the case of **IdentityHashMap**, the key is not required to be immutable.

What are the differences between HashMap and Hashtable?

The following are the differences between **HashMap** and **HashTable**:

- **HashMap** is unsynchronized, while **HashTable** is synchronized.
- **HashMap** allows one null key and multiple null values. However, **HashTable** does not allow any null key or null value.
- **HashMap** is not read-safe and can be useful for non-threaded applications. On the other hand, **HashTable** is thread-safe, and it can be shared between various threads.
- **HashMap** inherited from the **AbstractMap** class and **HashTable** is inherited from the **Dictionary** class.

What is hash-collision in HashTable, and how to handle it?

When we have two different keys with the same hash value, the scenario is termed hash-collision. In such cases, both objects are kept in a single hash bucket to resolve the conflicts.

We have the following two ways to avoid hash-collision:

- **Separate chaining**: Separate chaining is simple to implement. In this approach, the arrangement is made in such a way that each cell of hash table will point to a linked list of records that have same hash function value.

- **Open addressing**: In this approach, all the elements are stored in the hash table itself. This means the size of the table must be greater than or equal to the total number of keys. Open addressing is achieved by performing linear probing, quadratic probing, or double hashing.

Explain the purpose of the initial capacity and load factor parameters of a HashMap? What are their default values?

A HashMap in Java uses two important parameters—initial capacity and load factor—to manage its internal storage efficiently. These parameters influence performance, memory usage, and resizing behavior.

- **Initial capacity**:
    - This defines the number of buckets in the internal array when the **`HashMap`** is created.
    - We can pass the value for the initial capacity as an argument to the constructor while creating an instance of **`HashMap`**. The initial capacity affects the size of the internal data structure of **`HashMap`**. **`HashMap`** maintains the internal data structure as an array. This array has the power of two. This means the initial capacity argument value is increased to the next power of two to optimize the hashing efficiency.
    - The default initial capacity is 16.
- **Load factor**:
    - The load factor of **`HashMap`** is the ratio of the number of elements divided by the number of buckets.
    - For example, if we have 16 buckets containing 12 elements, then its load factor is 12/16 = 0.75. A higher load factor denotes multiple collisions. When the load factor is high, the map should be resized to the next power of two. It means the load factor argument is the maximum value of the load factor of a map. When the map achieves this load factor value, it will resize its internal array to the next power of two value.
    - The default load factor value is 0.75; this means we can add 12 elements in **`HashMap`** when the initial capacity is not mentioned.
    - The same is true for **`HashSet`**, as it is internally backed by **`HashMap`**.

What is the default size of load factor in any hash-based collection, and how is the threshold capacity calculated?

- The default load factor of hash-based collections, such as HashMap and HashSet is **`0.75`**.
- The threshold capacity can be computed as the initial capacity multiplied by the load factor.
- For example, 16 * 0.75 = 12, which means 12 is the default capacity of Map.

What is the meaning of fail-fast in the context of Java collections?

Whenever we try to modify the internal structure of a collection while we iterate through its elements, the iterator throws a **`ConcurrentmodificationException`** exception. This is termed as **fail-fast**. This is usually implemented to prevent unpredictable behavior. All the standard implementations of **`Iterator`** in the collection classes are fail-fast, except the concurrent collection classes, such as **`ConcurrentHashMap`** and **`CopyOnWriteArrayList`** which allows the safe modifications during iteration.

What are the differences between fail-fast and fail-safe?

In Java, iterators can exhibit different behaviors when a collection is modified during iteration. Understanding these behaviors is important for writing thread-safe and efficient code. Broadly, iterators fall into two categories: fail-safe and fail-fast.

- **Fail-safe**: The classes in **`java.util.concurrent`** are fail-safe. This means that they are not affected by any modification made to collections while iterating. In such classes, the Iterator never throws **`ConcurrentModificationException`**. The Iterator fail-safe property works with the clone of the underlying collection. Yet, of course, to achieve this, there is a requirement for additional memory to maintain a copy of the collection.
- **Fail-fast**: By contrast, all the collection classes in the **`java.util`** package are fail-fast. This does not allow collection modification while iterating. When we try to modify the element while iteration, the fail-fast iterator throws **`ConcurrentModificationException`**. It uses the original collection to traverse the elements. There is no requirement for any additional memory.

Why does the Map interface not extend the Collection interface?

The **Map** interface and all of its implementations are the part of the Collections Framework. However, **Map** does not extend **Collection** because all of the interfaces that extend **Collection** operates on the individual element. However, **Map** contains every entry in it as a key and value pair. **Collection** offers the methods to retrieve the elements. However, the **Map** methods offer retrieving the list of keys or list of values that do not fit in handling the elements paradigm.

How does HashMap work in Java?

HashMap stores every entry as key-value pair in the **Map.Entry** static nested class implementation. It works on the hashing algorithm. It uses the **hashCode()** and **equals()** methods to perform efficient insertion and retrieval operations. When we invoke the **put()** method by passing an entry as key-value pair, the **HashMap** uses the **hashCode()** of the key to find out the index where to store the key-value pair. The entry is stored in **LinkedList** format. It uses the **equals()** method to check the duplicate key existence. If it exists, then it overwrites the value associated with the existing key, and if it does not find any matching key, then it creates a new entry and stores this key-value entry. When we invoke the **get()** method by passing the key as an argument, **HashMap** again uses **hashCode()** to find the index in the array, and after that, it uses the **equals()** method to find the correct entry and return its value.

HashMap is governed by internal parameters such as initial capacity, load factor, and resizing threshold, which together determine how entries are stored and when the internal table is expanded to maintain optimal performance. The initial default capacity of **HashMap** is **16**, and the load factor is **0.75**. The threshold is calculated by multiplying the capacity with the load factor. Whenever we try to add an entry, the map size is checked. If the map size is greater than the threshold, then the **HashMap** rehashes the contents of the map into a new array having the larger capacity. The capacity of the **HashMap** is always the power of **2**. Thus, if we know that we need to store a large number of key-value pairs, then it is a good idea to initialize **HashMap** having the correct capacity and load factor.

Can we use the instance of any class as a key in a Map?

Yes, we can use an instance of a user-defined class as key of the map. However, we need to consider the following criteria before using the given instance as a key:

- If that class overrides the **equals()** method, it must also override the **hashCode()** method to maintain the general contract between the two methods
- The class must follow the rules associated with **equals()** and **hashCode()** for all instances.

- The class field if is not used in **`equals()`**, should not be used in the **`hashCode()`** computation as well.
- The best practice for a user-defined key class is to make it immutable. If we make the key class immutable, it ensures that **`hashCode()`** and **`equals()`** will not change in future, which solves any issue with mutability. It also prevents the lookup failures and improving performance.

How to iterate over each entry in the collection of type Map?

The **`Map`** interface provides the following ways or methods to access the elements:

- **Set<K> keySet()**:
    - The **`keyset()`** method returns a **`Set`** that contains the keys in the map. This set is backed by map. This means any changes to the map are reflected in the set, or if changes happen in the set, they will be reflected to map.
    - If the map is modified in the process of iteration over the set, the result of the iteration is undefined.
    - The set supports element removal, which removes the corresponding mapping from the map. This removal can be done via the **`remove()`**, **`Set.remove()`**, **`removeAll()`**, **`retainAll()`**, and **`clear()`** operations of **`Iterator`**. It does not support the **`add()`** or **`addAll()`** operations.
- **Collection<V> values()**:
    - The method returns a collection that contains the values from the map.
    - The collection is backed by the map, and any changes to the map are reflected in the collection or vice-versa.
    - If the map is modified in the process of iteration over the collection is in progress, the results of the iteration are undefined.
    - The collection supports removal of an element that removes the corresponding mapping from the map via the **`remove()`**, **`Collection.remove()`**, **`removeAll()`**, **`retainAll()`**, and **`clear()`** methods of Iterator. It does not support the **`add()`** or **`addAll()`** operations.
- **Set<Map.Entry<K, V>> entrySet()**:
    - The method returns a set of the mappings contained in the map.
    - The set is backed by the map, so changes to the map are reflected in the set or vice-versa.
    - If the map is modified while iteration over the set, the results of the iteration are undefined.

- The set allows removal of an element that actually removes the corresponding mapping from the map via the **Iterator.remove()**, **Set.remove()**, **removeAll()**, **retainAll()**, and **clear()** operations, but it does not support the **add()** or **addAll()** operations.

Queue interface

The **java.util.Queue** interface defines a queue data structure that stores elements in **first-in, first-out** (**FIFO**) order. It provides specific methods such as **offer()**, **poll()**, and **peek()** to insert, remove, and examine elements in a controlled manner without necessarily throwing exceptions. The **Queue** interface is commonly implemented by classes like **LinkedList**, **PriorityQueue**, and **ArrayDeque**, each offering different ordering mechanisms and performance characteristics based on use cases.

What are the differences between Queue and Stack?

Queue and **Stack** are used to store data before processing the data, with the following key differences:

- **Queue** is an interface; however, **Stack** is a class that is extended from **Vector**.
- **Queue** allows retrieval of elements in the FIFO order, while **Stack** allows elements to be retrieved in the LIFO order.
- **Stack** offers the **push()** and **pop()** operations, and **Queue** offers the **offer()** for insertion and **poll()** for removal of elements.
- The **Stack** data structure is naturally a recursive data structure, which has well-suited well-recursive operations such as implementing pre-order, post-order, and in-order traversal of the binary tree. **Queue**, on the other hand, is a sequential data structure that can be used to process data in order.

What is the PriorityQueue class, and how does it work?

PriorityQueue is the concrete implementation of **Queue** interface, and as the name indicates, it works on the basis of the priorities of elements. It pushes the sorted element to the head, which can be pooled out. Internally, it also uses the **Comparator** and **Comparable** interfaces for sorting to decide the priority of the elements.

How does PriorityQueue differ from TreeSet and TreeMap, given that all three use the same Comparator or Comparable interfaces to maintain ordering?

Though `TreeSet`, `TreeMap`, and `PriorityQueue` all use the `Comparator` or `Comparable` interface, there is a fundamental difference between them. Both `TreeSet` and `TreeMap` provide sorting and iteration over the elements. However, in case of `PriorityQueue`, the elements are not traversed. The primary objective of `PriorityQueue` is to determine the priority of the elements and push that element to the head according to priority configuration (highest or lowest).

What is Dequeue? Can you explain its working?

On a very simple note, `Dequeue` is a double-ended `Queue`. In Queue, the elements are inserted at the tail and removed from the head. In `Dequeue`, you can perform these operations from both the ends. It is in fact a combination of Queue and Stack. It means it works on both the FIFO and LIFO algorithms. The classes `ArrayDeque` and `LinkedList` are implementation classes of the `Dequeue` interface. To facilitate addition and removal of elements from both sides, it provides different methods from `Queue` like `addFirst()`, `addLast()`, `offerFirst()`, `removeFirst()`, `removeLast()`, and so on.

Out of the different Queue implementations, how do you decide which one to use?

It is often confusing as to which implementation of `Queue` is to be used, but if you are sure about your functional requirement along with the need for concurrency, your selection will be easier.

If you are interested in getting the elements in the FIFO order, then the obvious choice is `ArrayDeque`, but if you are more interested in elements based on priority, you need to choose `PriorityQueue`. This selection is based on the assumption that you do not expect the concurrent access for elements. If you intend to get concurrent access, then you can go for `PriorityBlockingQueue` or `DelayQueue`. In the situation in which you do not want to go for blocking approach for the `Queue`, then you can go for `ConcurrentLinkedQueue`.

What is a BlockingQueue in Java?

The `BlockingQueue` is an interface that extends the Queue. It offers concurrency in the operations such as retrieving, inserting, and deleting the data. While retrieving any element, it waits for the queue to be non-empty. While storing the collection, it waits for the available space. It is a thread-safe collection that cannot contain null elements.

Implementations of **BlockingQueue** include classes such as **ArrayBlockingQueue**, **LinkedBlockingQueue**, and **PriorityBlockingQueue**.

Collection utility interfaces and collections

The Collection Framework in Java also provides several utility interfaces and classes that enhance the functionality of data structures. The Java Collections Framework includes utility classes such as **Collections** and **Arrays**, which offer static methods for sorting, searching, synchronization, and other common operations on collections and arrays. These utility classes help developers perform complex operations efficiently without implementing the logic manually.

What are the differences between Collection and Collections?

The following are the key differences between **Collection** and **Collections**:

- **Collection** is an interface, and **Collections** is a utility class.
- The **Collection** interface provides the standard functionality of data structures to **List**, **Set**, and **Queue**. On the other hand, the **Collections** class offers methods to sort and synchronize the collection elements.
- **Collection<E>** defines a generic container capable of holding elements of type **E**. On the other hand, **Collections** works on already-created generic collections and does not define element storage.

What is the use of properties file in Java?

Sometimes, in application development, we may need certain configuration values to be used, which may change in the future as per the client's requirements or development scenarios. If we hardcode these values in the code, we need to recompile the class along with redeployment to get the updated configuration values. The properties file can contain such entries in the key-value pair. Instead of hardcoding, if these values are fetched from the properties file, the recompilation of the class is not required, even though the values in the properties file are updated at runtime. Using the properties file makes the application more manageable, scalable, and maintainable across different environments. The values, such as driver name, username, and password for database connectivity, are a very common way to store the values in the properties file.

What does Comparable do?

The **Comparable** interface is used to sort the objects of the class using **compareTo(Object)**. A class implements **Comparable** and overrides **compareTo(T obj)** method to specify how the objects should be compared. However, it offers only a single sorting algorithm to sort the objects. Proper implementation ensures consistency with **`equals()`** and helps maintain predictable sorting behavior.

What is the difference between Comparable and Comparator?

Both the **`Comparable`** and **`Comparator`** interfaces are used to sort the elements in a collection, but there are a few differences as follows:

- The **`Comparable`** interface allows sorting of a collection only in a single way. However, **`Comparator`** allows a collection to be sorted in multiple ways.
- **`Comparable`** is included in the **`java.lang`** package, and **`Comparator`** is included in the **`java.util`** package.
- **`Comparable`** provides **`compareTo()`** for comparing the data, and **`Comparator`** provides the **`compare()`** method for sorting.
- The **Plain Old Java Object** (**POJO**) class needs to implement the **`Comparable`** interface for sorting the data of the collection. However, there is no compulsion to implement **`Comparator`**.

What is an Iterator interface in Java, and what is its purpose?

`Iterator` is an interface that offers the standard mechanism to iterate over a collection. We can obtain the **`Iterator`** instance using the **`iterator()`** method of that particular collection. Using the iterator, we can also safely remove the elements from the underlying collection during iteration. **`Iterator`** implements the iterator design pattern to offer a generic way for traversing through the elements of the collection. This abstraction decouples the traversal logic from the collection's internal structure.

Why does Iterator not offer a method for adding elements to the collection?

The contract by which the iteration over the elements happens is unclear. So, if we try to add the element to the list, which is an ordered collection, due to the unclear semantics of the iterator, it will not guarantee the addition of the element to the last position. In contrast, the special iterator **`ListIterator`** provides an operation to add the elements, as it guarantees the order of the iteration.

Is it possible to retrieve the next element using the next() method without advancing the iterator's cursor?

The object is stored in the memory, which has a reference address. Now, to retrieve the value of any object, you need to provide this reference information. According to the API, the cursor in the **Iterator** is always positioned between the elements. Therefore, it is important to move that cursor to the current position. The call to the **next()** method moves the cursor to the current position.

State the differences between the Iterator and ListIterator interface

Both **Iterator** and **ListIterator** are used for iteration, with the following differences:

- **Iterator** can be used to traverse over the **List** and **Set** collections. On the other hand, **ListIterator** can be used for traversing over the **List** only.
- **Iterator** can traverse in the forward direction only. However, **ListIterator** can be used to traverse in both the forward and reverse directions.
- **ListIterator** is inherited from the **Iterator** interface. It offers extra functionalities such as adding, replacing, and fetching using the index position for both previous and next elements.

What are the different ways available to iterate over a list?

Both the **Iterator** and **enhanced for-each** loop can be used for iterating over the elements in the list. However, **Iterator** is more thread-safe because whenever the underlying list elements are modified during iteration, it throws **ConcurrentModificationException**.

Both these ways can be used as shown in the following code snippet:

- **Using an Iterator**:

```
List<String>list = new ArrayList<>();
Iterator<String> it = list.iterator();
while(it.hasNext()){
    String data = it.next();
    System.out.println(data);
}
```

The **iterator()** method returns an Iterator object that maintains a cursor pointing to the current element. The **hasNext()** method checks whether more elements are available and retrieves the next element while advancing the cursor. This approach is useful when elements may need to be removed safely during iteration using the **remove()** method.

- **Using enhanced for-each loop**:

```
List<String> list = new ArrayList<>();
for(String data : list){
    System.out.println(data);
}
```

The for-each loop internally uses an Iterator, but hides its complexity and improves readability. However, it does not allow direct modification (such as removal) of the collection while iterating, as doing so will result in a **ConcurrentModificationException**.

Use the for-each loop for simple read-only traversal, and prefer the Iterator when controlled modification of the collection is required.

What is UnsupportedOperationException, and under what circumstances is it thrown during program execution?

UnsupportedOperationException is a runtime exception that indicates that the requested operation is not supported by a particular collection. When we work with read only collections, this exception is raised if we try to add or remove the elements.

For example, consider the following code:

```
List<String> fruits= Arrays.asList("Mango", "Kiwi", "Orange", "Papaya");
```

The **Arrays.asList()** method returns a **fixed-size list** backed by the original array. Since its size cannot be changed, any structural modification is not permitted. If we try to add another fruit to the list as:

```
Fruits.add("Strawberry");
```

Then the JVM will throw **UnsupportedOperationException** as discussed. The same exception will occur while removing the elements from the obtained list.

What is the difference between two given code snippets?

Consider the given code:

```
1. List<String> fruits= Arrays.asList("Mango", "Kiwi", "Orange", "Papaya");
                                  and
2. String [] fruits= {"Mango", "Kiwi", "Orange", "Papaya"};
3. List<String> fruitList= new ArrayList<>(Arrays.asList(fruits));
```

The first statement provides a non-mutable list backed by an underlying array. If we try to add or remove the element from the list, JVM throws **UnsupportedOperationException**.

The second set of statements provides a mutable list, which means we can add as well as remove the elements from the list without any restrictions.

What are the differences between Iterator and ListIterator?

The following are the key differences between **Iterator** and **ListIterator**:

- **Iterator** is useful for traversing the elements in the forward direction only. **ListIterator** is useful for traversing the elements both in the forward and backward directions.
- **Iterator** can be used in most of the collections such as **List**, **Set**, and **Queue**. The **ListIterator** use is limited to **List** only.
- **Iterator** offers only removal operation while traversing the collection. **ListIterator** offers adding, updating, and removing the elements while traversing the collection.

State the differences between Iterator and Enumeration

The following are the key differences between **Iterator** and **Enumeration**:

- **Iterator** can traverse through both legacy and non-legacy collections, but **Enumeration** can traverse only legacy collections.
- **Iterator** is fail-fast, and **Enumeration** is not fail-fast and does not detect concurrent modifications.
- **Iterator** is slower than Enumeration because of the additional safety checks.

- **`Iterator`** offers removal operation while traversing the collection. However, **`Enumeration`** can only traverse through the collection, it does not facilitate the removal operation while traversal.

How can we check the equality of the partial arrays using the updated equals() method in Java9?

Java9 provides the static overloaded **`equals()`** method using which we can check the equality of the partial arrays. Unlike the predefined **`equals()`** method which checks the entire array for equality, this overloaded method can check the slices of array for the equality.

The syntax of the method is:

```
public static boolean equals(int[] a, int index1, int index2,
    int[] b, int index3, int index 4)
```

In this case, both the array slices are checked for equality, and the slices are generated by **`index1`**, **`index2`**, **`index3`**, and **`index4`**).

What is the use of Collectors.teeing() method, introduced in Java12?

`Collectors.teeing()` was introduced in Java 12 to allow performing two independent collector operations on the same stream and then merging their results into a single final result.

It is useful when you need to compute multiple aggregates (for example, count and average) in a single stream pipeline without traversing the stream twice. This method is works only with the **`collect()`** method of the Stream API. The method takes three arguments; **`collector1`**, **`collector2`** and a merger function to merge the result.

Conclusion

You have just completed one of the most important and complicated chapters for a Java interview. In this chapter, we discussed about the Collection Framework in Java. We discussed in detail different interfaces and classes from this powerful API. We talked about the different types of collections like List, Set, Queue, and Map along with their significance. During this, we covered different implementation classes from this interface. Along with these classes, we also discussed the utility classes like Arrays and Collections and how they enhance the behavior of collections. Additionally, we also discussed improvements in Collection API that had been introduced in different Java versions.

In the next chapter, we will discuss some miscellaneous concepts of Java like String, StringBuffer, inner classes, reflection, and so on.

Join our Discord space

Join our Discord workspace for latest updates, offers, tech happenings around the world, new releases, and sessions with the authors:

https://discord.bpbonline.com

CHAPTER 9
Miscellaneous

Introduction

Till now, we have seen many concepts in Java that will help you to crack a Java interview. We started right from the architecture of Java and discussed how Java is internally built. We also discussed in detail how to implement the object-oriented approach and how to deal with exception handling, concurrency, file handling, JDBC, etc. However, Java is very vast. Apart from all these, there are many other components that really make application development more flexible and maintainable. In this chapter, we will talk about such miscellaneous concepts, and we will discuss them via different interview questions that you may face.

Structure

This chapter covers the following concepts:

- String, StringBuffer, and StringBuilder
- Reflection API
- Optional class
- Inner class
- Var keyword
- Compact Number Formatting
- RandomGenerator interface
- Hidden class
- Unit testing
- Internationalization
- Updates in switch-case
- Java Platform Module System

Objectives

At the end of this chapter, you will be able to answer interview questions based on different concepts like String, StringBuffer, StringBuilder, inner classes, Reflection API, Optional class, Internationalization, Unit testing, and so on. This chapter will also give you some basic knowledge about how to implement all these concepts through some code snippets.

String, StringBuffer, and StringBuilder

In Java, strings are fundamental objects used to represent textual data. Understanding the difference between **String** and **StringBuffer** is essential for writing efficient and thread-safe applications, especially when working with frequently modified text. While String objects are immutable, meaning their values cannot be changed once created, **StringBuffer** provides a mutable and synchronized alternative, allowing modifications without creating new objects. This section explores their design, behavior, performance implications, and appropriate use cases.

Are the two given statements the same or different?

Considering the following:

```
String emptyLiteral = "";
String emptyNewString = new String("");
```

In the above code, **emptyLiteral** will be added to the String pool, while **emptyNewString** will be pushed directly onto the heap. Although both objects represent an empty string (**""**) and their contents are equal, they are not necessarily the same reference in memory. Therefore, using the **==** operator may return false when comparing them, whereas the **equals()** method will return **true** because it compares the actual content of the given strings.

What is String Constant Pool?

It is a special memory block in JVM. If the two Strings have the same literals, then they share the same memory block of the String Constant Pool. This makes the usage of an immutable String more memory efficient, as multiple references can point to the same **String** object in the String Constant Pool.

Are the two given statements the same or different?

Considering the given statements:

```
String nullValue = null;
```

and

```
String emptyLiteral = "";
```

These are two different statements. If we try to invoke any method on a String having a null value, we will get **NullPointerException**. The first statement will not raise **NullPointerException**, as creating such a String is not invalid. Invoking any String API method on that reference will generate **NullPointerException**. The second statement is also valid. However, it does not throw **NullPointerException**, even if we invoke any String API method on the given string reference.

What are the differences between StringBuffer and StringBuilder?

The following are the key differences between **StringBuffer** and **StringBuilder**:

- **StringBuffer** is synchronized, and **StringBuilder** is non-synchronized.
- **StringBuffer** is less efficient because of the synchronization overhead as compared to the **StringBuilder**.

What are the differences between StringBuffer and String?

The following are the differences between **StringBuffer** and **String**:

- **String** class is immutable, **StringBuffer** is mutable.
- **String** consumes more memory because a new instance will be created on each modification operation performed on it. On the other hand, **StringBuffer** consumes less memory when you update strings, as it does not create a new instance upon modification.
- The **String** class overrides the **equals()** method of the **Object** class. However, the **StringBuffer** class does not override the **equals()** method of the **Object**; rather, it compares the object reference for equality instead of the actual content of the strings.

Could you explain the difference between the two given statements?

Considering the following statements:

```
String s="Java"
String s=new String("Java")
```

In layman's language, both statements might look the same, but there is a fundamental difference in the way they occupy the memory. The first statement, i.e., **`String s="Java"`**, creates and stores the **`new String`** object in the String Constant Pool. Meanwhile, the second statement, i.e., **`String s=new String("Java")`**, creates and stores the new **`String`** object in the JVM, even if a similar literal is present in the String Constant Pool.

Does the String always get created in the String Constant Pool?

No, it does not. As discussed in the previous question, it depends on how you create the Strings. However, the concept of the memory occupation of the String changes when you create the String dynamically.

Consider the statements:

```
String s1="Learn";  //statement 1
String s2="Java";   //statement 2
String s3=s1+s2;    //statement 3
```

Here, the third statement creates a **`String`** object at runtime. Although we are creating this **`String`** without using the **`new`** keyword, the internal workings of this are a bit different. In this case, the concatenation of **`s1`** and **`s2`** generates the **`StringBuilder`** object, and then the **`StringBuilder`** object is converted to a **`String`**.

Why does the compiler not consider String instead of StringBuilder in the previous question?

This is because we are performing the operations at runtime. The compiler does not know whether the operands in the operations are String literals or some dynamic values. Thus, it considers them as **`StringBuilder`** to optimize the operation and internally uses the **`append()`** method of **`StringBuilder`** to concatenate. This approach is also used when we perform the bulk of **`String`** operations in sequence:

For example, consider the code snippet:

```
String s = "";
for (int i = 0; i < 1000; i++) {
    s = s + i;
}
```

With the theoretical concept of String manipulation, this code would create 1000 **`Strings`**, and this would create significant memory overhead and reduce performance. To mitigate this issue, the compiler internally converts it to **`StringBuilder`** or **`StringBuffer`**.

What is the constant folding approach in Strings?

When we try to concatenate the **String** at runtime, one of the approaches followed by the JVM is to convert the **String** variables to **StringBuilder**. Yet, consider the case where we are concatenating the String literals directly as:

```
String s="Java" +" Learning";
```

Then, the compiler handles it differently. Since both operands are compile-time constants, the expression is evaluated during compilation itself. The compiler optimizes the statement by converting it into:

```
String s="Java Learning";
```

This optimization technique is known as the **Constant Folding** approach in String. It reduces runtime overhead by resolving constant expressions at compile time, thereby improving performance and avoiding unnecessary object creation.

How does the strip() method introduced in Java 11 differ from the trim() method of the String class in terms of whitespace handling and overall behavior?

Both **strip()** and **trim()** methods are used to strip off the leading and trailing spaces of the given string, but there are a couple of differences between them:

- The **trim()** method uses the ASCII value for identifying white spaces, but the **strip()** method uses Unicode values for identifying white spaces.
- The **trim()** method removes the characters with the ASCII values less than or equal to 'U +0020' or '32'. On the other hand, the **strip()** method removes all the white spaces according to Unicode.

As a result, **strip()** provides more accurate and consistent whitespace handling, especially when working with Unicode text.

How does the isBlank() method introduced in Java 11 differ from the existing isEmpty() method of the String class?

The method **isEmpty()** was introduced in Java6, while the **isBlank()** method was introduced in version 11 to enhance the white space handling of the string. One of the key differences between these two methods is that **isEmpty()** does not ignore the white spaces while it checks the String, but **isBlank()** ignores the white spaces by providing a more meaningful approach to the String evaluation. Interestingly, the **isEmpty()** method can efficiently check for the zero length of the string. The **`isBlank()`** method returns false if the String does not contain any characters but contains only white spaces, as it cannot ignore the white spaces.

What is the significance of the lines() method of String in Java11?

The **`lines()`** method returns the number of lines extracted from the given string. This method returns the stream of lines where each element of the stream is represented by String, which is generated from the given string. The **`lines()`** method uses the line terminator present within the given String.

Which characters are considered line separators in the lines() method of String?

The **`lines()`** method of the **`String`** class recognizes specific line terminators to determine line boundaries. The following character sequences are treated as line separators:

- **`\n`** as a line feed character
- **`\r`** as a carriage return character
- **`\n\r`** as a combination of line feed and carriage return character

These line terminators enable the **`lines()`** method to correctly split the String into a stream of individual lines.

How is the split() method different than the lines() method of String?

The **`split()`** method works similarly to the **`lines()`** method, i.e., it generates the lines from the given String. The key difference is that the **`split()`** method returns an array of Strings, while the **`lines()`** method returns a stream of lines. The **`lines()`** method is considered to be faster than the **`split()`** method as it supplies the elements lazily separating them by searching the new line terminator more efficiently.

What is the functionality of the repeat() method introduced in Java 11, and how does it operate?

The **`repeat(int)`** method is used to repeat the given String. It creates copies of String equal to the argument provided in the method. If the provided argument is negative, then the method throws **`IllegalArgumentException`**.

Can you explain the transform() method of String introduced in Java12?

As the method name indicates, the **`transform()`** method is used to transform the given String to some other format.

The syntax of the method is as follows:

```
public <R> transform(Function<? super String, ? extends R> fn)
```

Here:

- **`R`** represents the type of the result produced after applying the function.
- **`fn`** is a functional interface (**`Function`**) that defines the operation to be performed on the given String.

The **`transform()`** method applies the specified function to the current **`String`** instance and returns the result produced by that function. The provided function accepts **`String`** as input and generates an output based on the logic defined within the functional implementation.

Could you explain the working of transform() with a working example?

Consider the following code:

```
String str1="Life is beautiful"
String str2=str1.transform(input->input.concat(“ have fun"))
```

In this example, **`str1`** is concatenated with **“`have fun`"** using the transform function. We can also do the chaining of the transform as:

```
String str2=str1.transform(input->
input.concat(“ have fun")).transform(String::toUpperCase)
```

In the chained version, the result of the first **`transform()`** operation is further processed using **`String::toUpperCase`**, demonstrating how multiple transformations can be applied sequentially.

What is the use of the indent() method of String in Java12?

The **`indent()`** method is used to adjust the indentation of the String. It takes an argument in an integer that decides the number of leading white-space characters to be added or removed.

The syntax of the **indent()** method is:

```
String indent(int i)
```

Here:

- If n > 0, the specified number of whitespace characters is inserted at the beginning of each line.
- If n < 0, up to the specified number of leading whitespace characters is removed from each line (if present).

This method provides a convenient way to programmatically adjust the formatting and alignment of multi-line strings.

What are textblocks in Java?

Textblocks are introduced as a preview feature in Java13 and added as a standard feature in Java15. A textblock is considered a multiline String literal, which avoids the need for most escape sequences and automatically formats the string in a predictable way. It also provides control over the formatting whenever desired. In Java, when we need to embed an HTML, XML, SQL, or JSON in a String literal enclosed in double-quotes (" "), it requires a significant amount of editing with a lot of escape sequences along with concatenation. This embedding makes the snippet often difficult to read and maintain.

Reflection API

The Reflection API in Java provides the ability to inspect and manipulate classes, interfaces, fields, methods, and constructors at runtime. It allows programs to analyze their own structure and behavior dynamically, even when the details are not known at compile time.

Primarily located in the **java.lang.reflect** package, the Reflection API is widely used in frameworks, Dependency Injection containers, testing tools, and serialization mechanisms. This section explores its core concepts, capabilities, and practical use cases.

What do you mean by reflection?

Reflection is a process that enables examining the class and modifying its behavior at runtime. Using this, we can also examine the different components of a Java application, like interfaces, fields, and methods, at runtime, making it particularly useful in frameworks, Dependency Injection containers, and tools that require dynamic class loading or runtime configuration.

Can you explain how to use reflection?

The class **java.lang.Class** offers various methods that can be used to get metadata of a class, examining and changing the runtime behavior of a class.

The following code demonstrates one of the ways to achieve reflection:

```
Class c=Class.forName("Employee");
System.out.println(c.getName());
```

In this code, the **`Class.forName("Employee")`** method dynamically loads the **`Employee`** class at runtime and returns its corresponding **`Class`** object. The **`getName()`** method then retrieves and prints the fully qualified name of the class. This illustrates how reflection can be used to identify and inspect class metadata during execution.

How to create an object of a class in Java without directly using the new operator?

There are three ways to generate an object of a class, as shown:

- **The forName() method of the Class class**:
  - The method is used to load the class dynamically.
  - It should be used if you know the fully qualified name of the class. This cannot be used for primitive types.

  Note: **The code snippet for this is already shown in the previous question.**

- **getClass() method of the Object class**:
  - The method returns an instance of the **`Class`** class. It should be used if we know the type. It can be used with primitives as well.

    Consider the following code:

    ```
    Simple s=new Simple();
    Class c=s.getClass();
    System.out.println(c.getName());
    ```

    In this example, the **`getClass()`** method returns the runtime **`Class`** object associated with the **`Simple`** instance. The **`getName()`** method then retrieves and prints the fully qualified name of the class, demonstrating how reflection can be used to obtain class metadata dynamically.

- **The .class syntax:**
  - If there is no instance but we know the type, it is possible to obtain a class by appending **.class** to the name of the type. The syntax can be used for primitive data types as well. Consider the following code:

    ```
    Class c = MyClass.class;
    System.out.println(c.getName());
    ```

    In this example, the **.class** literal is used to obtain the corresponding **Class** object when the type is known at compile time. The **getName()** method then retrieves and prints the fully qualified name of the class. This approach is straightforward and type-safe, and it can also be applied to primitive data types such as **int.class** or **double.class**.

Could you list out the different methods of the Reflection API with their usage?

The following table lists some of the important methods of the Reflection API:

Method	Description
`public String getName()`	Returns the class name
`public Class getSuperclass()`	Returns the super class
`public Class[] getInterfaces`	Returns the array for different interfaces implemented by the class
`public Method[] getDeclaredMethods()`	Returns the array of methods declared in the class
`public Field[] getDeclaredFields()`	Returns the array of the field declared in the class
`public Constructor[] getDeclaredConstructors()`	Returns the array of constructors declared in the class

Table 9.1: Important methods of the Reflection API

Can we access the private field of another class using reflection?

Private field members are normally not accessed outside of a class, but using reflection, we can do so. The Reflection API provides a method **getDeclaredField()**, using which you can get a reference to that field, and then you can access that field in your class. The following code snippet shows how to access the private field **personId** declared in the **Person** class from some other class:

```
Field personData= Person.class.getDeclaredField("personId");
personData.setAccessible(true);
String personValue= (String) personData.get(Person);
System.out.println("personValue= " + personValue);
```

In this example, **getDeclaredField("personId")** retrieves the **Field** object representing the private member. The **setAccessible(true)** call bypasses Java's access control checks, allowing the field value to be accessed. This demonstrates how reflection can be used to inspect and manipulate private members at runtime, though it should be used cautiously to avoid violating encapsulation and security constraints.

Optional class

The **Optional** class, introduced in Java8, is a container object designed to represent the presence or absence of a value. It provides a structured and expressive way to handle null values, thereby reducing the risk of **NullPointerException**.

By encouraging explicit handling of missing values through methods such as **isPresent()**, **orElse()**, and **ifPresent()**, **Optional** promotes more readable and robust code.

What is the use of the Optional class?

This class was introduced in Java8 as a part of the **java.util** package. This class is used to represent the presence or the absence of a value and helps to avoid **NullPointerException**. The class consists of the following methods to handle the optional values safely:

- **isPresent()**
- **ifPresent()**
- **orElse()**
- **orElseGet()**

Additionally, the **Optional** class also provides **orElseThrow()**, which allows developers to explicitly throw an exception when a value is absent, and **map()** and **flatMap()**, which enable functional-style transformations of the contained value.

How does the Optional class avoid NullPointerException?

This class provides an approach that returns **Optional<T>** instead of returning null if the value is not found. As a result, developers do not need to handle null values directly. This also eliminates the need for chained null checks, which would otherwise require multiple if conditions, leading to cleaner and more readable code. Then we can invoke different methods on the **Optional** object to use the return value if generated, or else we can use other default values by using methods like **isPresent()** and **orElse()**.

How does the ifPresentOrElse() method work in the Optional class? (Java 9 update)

Java 9 introduced several enhancements to the **Optional** class. One such method is **ifPresentOrElse()**. This method is a combination of the **isPresent()** and **orElse()** methods, which were available in the Java8 API.

This method allows the developers to define two actions. It executes one action if the value is present and another action if the value is absent. Internally, it uses the functional approach as shown in the following code:

```
optional.ifPresentOrElse(
        value -> System.out.println(value),
                () -> System.out.println("Value not present")
);
```

This method provides a more concise and expressive way to handle both scenarios, presence and absence of a value, without writing explicit conditional statements. It improves code readability by clearly separating the success and fallback logic using lambda expressions.

Inner class

In Java, an inner class is a class defined within another class. It is used to logically group classes that are closely related and to increase encapsulation by restricting access to the outer class's internal members.

Inner classes can access all members of the enclosing class, including private variables and methods. This feature makes them particularly useful when implementing helper classes, event handling mechanisms, or when modeling relationships that are tightly bound to the outer class.

What is an inner class, and what are its types?

The **inner class** is a class nested inside another class. We have four flavors of inner class as follows:

- A class inside another class
- A class declared inside the function of a class
- An anonymous class
- Static inner class

What is the need for inner classes, or why do we use inner classes?

Inner classes are used when we want to group classes together logically. More specifically, if we want only one class to utilize the services of another class, then instead of creating the class separately, we would create it as an inner class.

Can a static nested class have access to any other members from an enclosing class?

The static nested class does not have access to any other members of the enclosing class. This ensures the data, which is common to all the objects, is being accessed by the static nested class.

Can an inner class be declared as private?

Yes, the nested class can be declared with any specifier. As the outer classes have restrictions on using the access specification, the inner classes do not have such restrictions and can even be declared as private. This offers the flexibility for the nested class and also allows it to be used only by the enclosed class.

What is shadowing?

When a declaration of a member in the inner class has the same name as that in the outer class, the inner class will have more preference for its local members than for the enclosed members. It means it will shadow the member of the enclosed class. This process is known as **shadowing**.

Var keyword

The **var** keyword was introduced in **Java10** as part of local variable type inference. It allows the compiler to automatically determine the type of a local variable based on the assigned expression. By reducing repetitive type declarations, var improves code readability while maintaining strong static typing. However, it can only be used for local variables with an initializer and not for method parameters, return types, or instance variables.

Can you explain the use of the var keyword introduced in Java10?

From Java10 onwards, Java developers do not need to mention the data types while declaring the variable. The data type of the variable can be declared as **var**. The data type of the identifier will be generated dynamically based on the value passed to that variable. This concept is termed the local variable type inference.

Can the var keyword be used in scenarios involving polymorphism in Java?

Yes, the **var** keyword can be used in polymorphic contexts, provided that the compiler can infer the target type from the initializer. Since var relies on type inference at compile time, the declared variable will assume the static type of the expression assigned to it.

What are some rules that you must follow in Java10 when you declare an identifier using the var keyword?

The following rules must be followed when we use the **var** keyword:

- Variables or members declared with **var** must be initialized while declaring them.
- The initialization cannot be null, as the type inference cannot be identified with null.
- The **var** keyword cannot be followed by multiple variables.
- If **var** is used to refer to any array, we cannot initiate it without the data type.
- The **var** keyword cannot be followed by **[]**, which defines the array dimension.
- The **var** keyword cannot be directly used to point to the lambda expression because the lambda expression needs a target type to infer its types.
- The **var** keyword cannot be used with **static** keywords and instance variables.
- We cannot use the **var** keyword in the lambda expression.

Compact Number Formatting

Compact Number Formatting was introduced in **Java 12** to display large numbers in a short, human-readable form. It allows numbers like 1,000 to be formatted as 1K or 1,000,000 as 1M based on locale. This feature is supported through the **NumberFormat** class using the **getCompactNumberInstance()** method. It is especially useful for dashboards, reports, and user interfaces where space-efficient number representation is required.

What is the Compact Number Formatting concept introduced in Java 12?

For years, the **NumberFormat** class was used to format the numeric data generated in Java.

From Java 12 onwards, we have the Compact Number Formatting to handle data like percentages and currency. The new class **CompactNumberFormat** is a subclass of **NumberFormat** class. To use this class, you need to use the static method **getCompactNumberInstance()** of the **NumberFormat** class.

This method takes two parameters:

- Locale
- NumberFormatStyle

The method throws **NullPointerException**, if either locale or **numberformatstyle** is null.

Once you get the **NumberFormat**, you can use the **format()** method to format your numeric data.

How can you use the plural support for the Compact Number Format?

From Java14 onwards, we can also get plural support in Compact Number Format. To use this concept, you must connect your Compact Number Format to the Locale. The plural support will be implemented for the language denoted by the Locale object. This means the formatted output will adapt according to the singular and plural rules of the selected language. For example, certain languages have multiple plural forms depending on the numeric value, and the Compact Number Format handles this internally using the locale-specific **Common Locale Data Repository** (**CLDR**) rules.

As a result, developers do not need to manually implement pluralization logic; the **NumberFormat** API ensures that the compact representation remains grammatically accurate and culturally appropriate for the target audience.

RandomGenerator interface

The **RandomGenerator** interface was introduced in **Java17** as part of the enhanced random number generation framework. It provides a common abstraction for various random number generator algorithms, offering better flexibility and extensibility. This interface standardizes methods for generating primitive random values, streams, and bounded numbers. It enables developers to choose and switch between different generator implementations more easily and efficiently.

What is the use of the RandomGenerator interface?

This interface is introduced in Java17. It is designed to provide a common protocol for objects that generate random numbers, a pseudorandom sequence of numbers, or even boolean values. You can also specify a particular range of values for random number generation. In addition, this interface serves as a foundation for the enhanced random number generator framework introduced in Java17, offering better extensibility and consistency compared to the traditional **Random** class.

What are the main implementations of the RandomGenerator interface, and how are they instantiated and used in Java?

The **RandomGenerator** interface has a static method **of()**. This takes a **String** as an argument, which specifies the implementor class. For example, you can generate an object of the Random class as:

```
RandomGenerator generator=RandomGenerator.of("Random")
```

This approach allows you to dynamically select the desired random number generation algorithm at runtime without directly instantiating a specific class using the **new** keyword.

Why do we need the RandomGenerator interface even though we have the legacy class Random?

Random numbers play a very important role in many business algorithms. Java has introduced the **Random** class since its inception, i.e., from JDK 1.0, to generate random numbers. Yet this class has certain weaknesses, such as:

- It has a poor randomness quality.
- It has often been observed that this approach may produce predictable output under certain conditions.
- It is not well-suited for modern computational use cases such as machine learning and advanced statistical simulations.
- The **Random** class does not provide support for splittable random algorithms, which are essential for certain concurrent and parallel computations.
- The Random class was not originally designed with parallelism in mind, making it less efficient in multi-threaded environments.

RandomGenerator interface provides a solution to all these issues through the implementor classes like **Random**, **SecureRandom**, **SplittableRandom**, and many more.

Java17 also has RandomGeneratorFactory. How is it different than the RandomGenerator interface?

Both interfaces work almost similarly. However, there is a difference in the way they choose the implementor classes. **RandomGenerator** has only the **of()** method, where you can directly choose which concrete class you wish to instantiate.

The **of()** method does not talk about:

- Whether the algorithm supports splittable behavior for parallel computations.
- Whether the algorithm offers jumpable capabilities, allowing the sequence to advance deterministically by large steps.
- Whether the algorithm provides cryptographically secure properties suitable for security-sensitive applications.

In simple words, the **RandomGenerator** only provides a way to create the *PRNG by name. On the other hand, **RandomGeneratorFactory** provides a more advanced, metadata-aware, and capability-driven factory. You may call it an introspective factory. The **RandomGeneratorFactory** gives you the ability to filter the concrete classes based on their properties and then create them.

How do you instantiate the concrete Random algorithm using the RandomGeneratorFactory?

RandomGeneratorFactory can instantiate the concrete implementation in two different ways:

- It has the **of()** method similar to **RandomGenerator** interface, which can be chained with the **create()** method as:

```
RandomGenerator generator=
            RandomGeneratorFactory.of(“SplittableRandom").create();
```

- We can also filter the concrete classes based on their meta information and invoke the **create()** method as:

```
RandomGenerator generator =
    RandomGeneratorFactory.all()
        .filter(RandomGeneratorFactory::isJumpable)
        .filter(f -> f.stateBits() > 128)
        .findFirst()
        .orElseThrow().create();
```

In summary, **RandomGeneratorFactory** provides a flexible and extensible mechanism for creating random number generator implementations. You can either instantiate a specific algorithm directly by name using the **of()** method, or dynamically discover and select an implementation based on its capabilities and metadata.

Hidden class

Hidden classes were introduced in Java15 to support frameworks that dynamically generate classes at runtime. These classes are not discoverable through normal class-loading mechanisms and cannot be referenced directly by name. They are primarily used by frameworks such as proxies, lambdas, and runtime bytecode generation tools. Hidden classes improve performance and security by allowing temporary, non-discoverable class definitions.

What is the need for a hidden class, and how does it work?

Sometimes frameworks use the services of another class. Normally, such a class is imported into the consumer class. Though there is no harm in importing a class, it exposes the definition of the entire class to the consumer. Using the Reflection API, we can discover the details of the class. The hidden class is the concept that controls the discovery of classes in the consumer class. When we do not want to expose the source code or the class in the class path, we can store the class file in some other location. Then, we can encode and decode the class and use the **MethodHandle** object to use the services from that class.

How do hidden classes differ from anonymous inner classes in Java?

When we look at the definition, which talks about hiding the code from other parts of the program or restricting the reusability of the implementation of the code from other parts of the program, both the anonymous inner class and the hidden class look similar.

There are some key differences. Anonymous inner classes have a reference name by which we can refer to them. Such classes are mostly used by application developers and often take an active part in the business logic. The classical usage of anonymous classes is in event handling, classbacks, etc. On the other hand, the hidden class is meant for frameworks, the internals of JVM, and bytecode generators. They are not typically intended for business logic written by an application developer. Hidden classes are always invisible outside of the context where they are defined. Anonymous classes are normally loaded as normal classes, while the hidden classes are unloadable. Anonymous classes persist as long as the classloader is live. On the other hand, hidden classes are short-lived in nature.

How do you define the hidden class object?

To define the hidden class, we have to use the **defineHiddenClass()** method from **Methodhandles.lookup()**, which returns the **MethodHandles.Lookup** object, which represents the access right used by JVM. The **defineHiddenClass()** method takes three arguments, which are:

- **bytes**: These are the bytes that make up the class data.
- **Initiate**: This decides if the class will be initialized or not. If set to true, the class will be initialized.
- **Options**: It had the following two options:
    - **NESTMATE**: This specifies that a hidden class can be added to the nest of the lookup class as a nestmate.
    - **STRONG**: This specifies that a hidden class has a strong relationship with the class loader.

Overall, **defineHiddenClass()** provides fine-grained control over dynamically generated classes, making it particularly useful for frameworks that rely on runtime bytecode generation and enhanced encapsulation.

How to invoke the static method from a hidden class?

To invoke a static method declared in a hidden class, you must first obtain a **MethodHandle** representing that method. This is achieved using the **findStatic()** method of the **MethodHandles.Lookup** API.

The **findStatic()** method requires the following arguments:

- Proxy of the hidden class
- Method name
- Method signature(including the return type and parameter types)

Once we get the handler, we can invoke the **invokeExact()** method on the handler. The following code depicts the working of the static method invocation, where we have invoked the static method **greet()** of the hidden class:

```
MethodHandle handler=MethodHandles.lookup()
                                .findStatic(proxyClass,
                                “greet",MethodType.methodType(String.class));
String s=(String)handler.invokeExact();
```

After obtaining the **MethodHandle**, the **invokeExact()** method performs a strongly typed invocation, meaning the method signature must match exactly with the declared **MethodType**. Any mismatch in return type or parameter types will result in a **WrongMethodTypeException**.

How to invoke the non-static method from a hidden class?

To invoke the non-static or an instant method of the hidden class, we need to first create an instance of the hidden class using the **newInstance()** method. Once we get the instance, we have to use the Reflection API and use **getDeclaredMethod** of the class. Finally, we need to use the **invoke()** method shown as follows:

```
1. Object object=proxyClass.getConstructor().newInstance();
2. Method method=object.getClass().getDeclaredMethod("doTask",String.class);
3. String s=method.invoke(object,"All about the hidden class")
```

Note that you do not have to provide any method name to the **invoke()** method, as the method reference is already linked to the **doTask()** method.

Unit testing

Unit testing is a software testing technique in which individual units or components of an application are tested independently to verify that they function as expected. A *unit* typically refers to the smallest testable part of an application, such as a method or a class. The primary goal of unit testing is to ensure code correctness, improve reliability, and detect defects at an early stage of development. By writing automated test cases, developers can confidently refactor code, enhance maintainability, and support continuous integration practices.

What is JUnit?

JUnit is the testing framework that is used for unit testing of Java code. It provides annotations, assertions, and test runners that help developers write and execute repeatable automated tests efficiently. With versions such as JUnit 4 and JUnit 5, JUnit has evolved to support more flexible and powerful testing features, including parameterized tests and improved extension models.

What is unit testing?

The process of testing individual functionality (known as a unit) of the application is termed **unit testing**. Each unit is tested in isolation to ensure that it behaves as expected under various conditions, including edge cases and invalid inputs. This approach helps in identifying defects early in the development cycle and improves the overall quality and stability of the software application.

How do you test a unit of your application?

JUnit provides different annotations that you can use to test your application. One of the important annotations we can use is **@Test**. This annotation can be applied to the method that is under test. The method under test can use methods like `assertEquals()`, `assertTrue()`, and `assertFalse()` to check the expected result against the generated result. If the assertion conditions are satisfied, the test passes; otherwise, it fails.

What are the useful JUnit extensions?

The following are some of the extensions of JUnit:

- **JWebUnit**: Used for testing web applications by simulating browser interactions.
- **XMLUnit**: Helps in validating and comparing XML documents in test cases.
- **Cactus**: Designed for in-container testing of server-side Java components such as Servlets and EJBs.
- **MockObject**: Provides support for creating mock objects to isolate dependencies during unit testing.

These extensions enhance the capabilities of **JUnit** by enabling specialized testing scenarios such as web-layer validation, XML comparison, and container-based testing.

What are the important JUnit annotations?

JUnit provides several annotations that help define the structure and lifecycle of test execution. Some of the most important annotations in **JUnit** include:

- **@Test**: Marks the method as a test case
- **@BeforeAll**: Executes once before all the test methods
- **@BeforeEach**: Runs before each test method
- **@AfterEach**: Executes after each test method
- **@AfterAll**: Executes after all the test methods

These annotations help organize test execution, manage setup and teardown logic, and ensure consistency and maintainability in unit testing practices.

What is the use of @BeforeEach and @AfterEach annotations?

When we execute any test case, we might need to execute some business logic before and after that test. The `@BeforeEach` annotation is applied to a method to inform that before every test, the method should be executed. On similar lines, the `@AfterEach` annotation is used to inform that the method will be executed after each test case.

What is the use of the JUnitCore class?

Using the **`@Test`** annotation, we can test different methods individually.

If we want to test multiple methods of application at the same time, we can use the **`JUnitCore`** class. This class has a method **`runClasses()`**, which will run all the test cases and return the information in a bundle.

How is the testing of the private method done?

There is no direct way to test the private method as it is not accessible outside its declaring class; hence, manual testing is to be performed. Sometimes the method is changed to a *protected* method temporarily. Though this approach is discouraged as it breaks the encapsulation concept.

Internationalization

Internationalization, which is also termed i18N, is a concept where we create an application that can be adapted globally and display the messages or currencies, and so on, in the language corresponding to a specific country or region. This is typically achieved by externalizing user-facing text into resource bundles, using locale-aware APIs for formatting, and avoiding hard-coded cultural assumptions in the codebase.

What is localization?

Localization is the process of adding a resource to an application so that the application can support a particular language. To achieve this, we can take the help of the **`Locale`** class, which represents languages and other settings like time zone, and so on, for that region. The object of the **`Locale`** class can be created by passing the language and the country as arguments.

How to change the format of a number using the Locale class?

The following code snippet shows how to change the format of a number using the **`Locale`** class:

```
double d=123.456
NumberFormat nf=NumberFormat.getInstance(Locale.ITALY);
System.out.println(" number in ITALY format is :"+nf.format(d));
```

This example demonstrates how the **`Locale`** class influences the formatting conventions of numbers based on regional standards. In the case of **`Locale.ITALY`**, the decimal separator and grouping symbols follow Italian formatting rules.

By simply changing the **`Locale`** instance (for example, to **`Locale.US`** or **`Locale.FRANCE`**), the same numeric value can be displayed according to different country-specific formats. This feature is particularly useful when developing internationalized applications that must present data appropriately for users in different regions.

Updates in switch-case

With the release of Java14, significant enhancements were introduced to the traditional switch statement, making it more expressive, concise, and less error-prone. These improvements include features such as switch expressions and the use of arrow labels, which simplify control flow and reduce boilerplate code.

Which new features were added to the switch-case in Java 14?

Java14 modified the switch-case statement drastically. The following are the different modifications added in this version:

- **Multiple labels**: In this feature, multiple cases can be declared by separating them with a comma (**`,`**) in a single case. Here, similar to a traditional switch case, the break statement is compulsory; otherwise, all the switch cases will be executed, which are followed after the matching case.
- **Arrow operators**: You can now use the arrow operator (**`->`**) instead of the colon (**`:`**) to denote the cases. The advantage is that with the use of the arrow operator, you do not have to use the break statement, unlike the traditional switch-case block.
- **Expressions in the case**: The modified switch-case now allows you to write the expression in the case body. You may either initiate the variable in each case and use it later, or assign the entire switch-case block to a variable that will store the expression values from the matching case.
- **Yield statement**: The yield statement is used to return the value from the switch case body.

How does using a switch expression differ from using the yield keyword within a switch construct?

Ideally, both return values. The expression is the single statement that follows the arrow operator in a case label. When you have more than one statement in the case, i.e., you have a body in the case, and you wish to return the value from that block, you will need the **`yield`** keyword to return the value.

Java Platform Module System

The **Java Platform Module System** (**JPMS**) was introduced in Java SE 9 as part of *Project Jigsaw*. It was officially launched in September 2017 to address issues related to scalability, maintainability, and strong encapsulation in large Java applications.

JPMS allows developers to organize code into modules, where each module explicitly declares its dependencies and controls which packages are accessible to other modules. This improves application structure, enhances security through strong encapsulation, and enables the creation of smaller, customized runtime images using tools like **jlink**.

What is a module in Java? How is it different from a package?

A module is a named, self-describing collection of packages and resources. It contains a special file termed as **`module-info.java`**, which declares:

- The module name
- Required dependencies (requires)
- Exported packages (exports)
- Services used or provided

What is the significance of module-info.java?

The module-info.java is the descriptor file of a module. It defines:

- The modules this module depends on
- The packages accessible to other modules
- Service usage and implementation

It acts as a contract between modules and enables compile-time and runtime checks.

What is the difference between exports and opens in a module?

The following are the key differences between exports and opens:

- **`exports`** allows other modules to access public types of a package at compile time and runtime.
- **`opens`** allows access only at runtime, mainly for reflection (e.g., frameworks like Hibernate or Spring).
- **`opens`** is commonly used when deep reflection is required.

What is the unnamed module in Java?

The unnamed module represents all classes and JARs placed on the classpath (instead of the module path). If an application does not define module-info.java, it automatically becomes part of the unnamed module.

What happens if both classpath and module path are used in the same application?

In real-world enterprise applications, especially during migration to the module system introduced in Java SE 9, it is common to use both the classpath and the module path together. This hybrid approach allows gradual modularization without rewriting the entire application at once:

- Classes on the module path belong to named modules.
- Classes on the classpath belong to the unnamed module.
- The unnamed module can read named modules.
- Named modules cannot formally depend on the unnamed module.

This setup is commonly used during migration from classpath to modules.

What are unnamed variables in Java 22?

Unnamed variables are variables declared using a single underscore (_) when the variable is required syntactically but is intentionally not used in the code. This feature improves readability and makes the developer's intent explicit that the variable is deliberately ignored. We only need to take care that we cannot initialize it with any value, like normal named variables.

The unnamed variables can be used in:

- Catch blocks
- Lambda parameters
- Pattern matching
- Record patterns

Similar to normal local variables, can we use the unnamed variables multiple times in the same scope?

Unlike a normal local variable, we can use the unnamed variables multiple times in the same scope. Since unnamed variables do not create the named binding in the scope where they are declared.

What are unnamed patterns in Java 22?

Unnamed patterns are used in pattern matching when we want to match a type or structure but do not need to bind the matched value to a variable.

The following code snippet shows how to utilize the unnamed patterns:

```
if (obj instanceof String _) {
    System.out.println("Yes, It is a String");
}
```

Here, the code checks whether **obj** is of type **String**, but the matched value is not stored or used.

Conclusion

In this chapter, we explored a comprehensive set of Java concepts that are frequently discussed in technical interviews and widely used in real-world applications. Starting with foundational topics such as String, StringBuffer, and StringBuilder, we examined immutability, mutability, and performance considerations. We then strengthened our understanding of advanced concepts like the Reflection API, inner classes, and the Optional class—features that improve flexibility, readability, and robustness in modern Java applications. We also covered language enhancements introduced in recent Java versions, including the var keyword for local variable type inference, Compact Number Formatting for improved localization support, and the RandomGenerator interface for better random number generation strategies. These additions reflect Java's evolution toward cleaner syntax and more expressive APIs. We also discussed powerful modern capabilities such as hidden class, internationalization, and the updates in the switch-case in the new versions of Java.

Finally, we examined the JPMS, a significant architectural enhancement that promotes strong encapsulation and modular design, helping developers build scalable and maintainable applications.

In the next chapter, we will explore the powerful paradigm of functional programming in Java, which has significantly influenced modern Java development since Java 8. We will dive into core concepts such as lambda expressions, functional interfaces, method references, and the Stream API, understanding how they enable a more declarative and concise coding style.

CHAPTER 10
Functional Interfaces, Lambda Expressions, and Streams

Introduction

Interfaces always provide the loose coupling or flexibility to your application. They facilitate the subclasses to implement their own version of business logic as and when required. Yet often, when interfaces contain only one method, the developer feels that the implementation code they are writing is getting messy unnecessarily. For implementing a single method, they may have to write a complete class, which is sometimes bulkier than the actual business logic, which is written in the overridden method from the interface. To overcome this complexity, Java introduced the concept of closure in the form of an anonymous inner class. Though an anonymous inner class avoids the usage of a class, it still lacks in reducing the bulkiness of the code. Normally, it is said that the anonymous inner classes have a *vertical problem*, as we need to stack some lines of code to just incorporate a single line of business logic. The main objective of functional programming is to avoid such ceremonial code, which replaces a block of structural code in the declarative approach. This has certainly improved the approach of developers to handle the functional interfaces and collections.

Structure

We will be covering interview questions based on the following topics in this chapter:

- Functional interfaces
- Lambda expression
- Stream API

Objectives

Though functional programming adds significant flexibility to developers in understanding how to implement, it is always a challenge for a beginner. It is not difficult, but shifting the mindset of a developer from traditional programming to functional programming is a point of concern. In this chapter, you will not only learn how to implement functional programming but also about different concepts like lambdas, streams, etc. We will walk through the basics of lambda and streams. We will discuss different interview questions based on lambdas and streams, which form a very important part of your Java interview, if the interview is based on Java 8.

Functional interfaces

Functional interfaces were introduced in Java SE 8 as part of Java's move toward functional programming. A functional interface is an interface that contains exactly one abstract method, which makes it suitable for implementation using lambda expressions and method references.

They serve as the foundation for features such as lambda expressions and the Stream API, enabling developers to write more concise, readable, and expressive code. By allowing behavior to be passed as an argument, functional interfaces help Java support a more declarative programming style while maintaining backward compatibility with existing object-oriented principles.

What is a functional interface, and how to create it? Is it mandatory to declare a functional interface with @FunctionInterface annotation?

Java 8 introduced functional interfaces. The functional interface is an interface having only one abstract method. Java 8 provides many functional interfaces such as `Supplier`, `Consumer`, `Function`, and so on. It is also possible to declare a user-defined functional interface whenever required. We can develop the functional interface either by declaring an interface with a single abstract method. We can also annotate such an interface with `@FunctionalInterface`, which contains a single abstract method. It is not compulsory to annotate the interface using `@FunctionInterface`. However, it is a preferred way, as the annotation makes sure that the interface will not contain any other abstract method, and if we try to add one, an error will occur.

Did we have any functional interfaces prior to Java 8 as well?

Yes. In pre-Java 8.0 versions, some interfaces behave like functional interfaces. In other words, they have only a single abstract method to implement. The only difference is that they are not annotated with `@FunctionalInterface`. The following are examples of such interfaces:

- `java.lang.Runnable`
- `java.util.Comparator`

- `java.util.concurrent.Callable`
- `java.io.FileFilter`
- `java.nio.file.PathMatcher`
- `java.lang.reflect.InvocationHandler`
- `java.awt.event.ActionListener`
- `javax.swing.event.ChangeListener`

What is a SAM Interface?

Java 8 has introduced the functional interface, an interface that can have only one abstract method. As these interfaces contain only one abstract method, they are also termed SAM interfaces. **SAM** means **Single Abstract Method** interface.

Which guidelines are to be followed while defining a functional interface?

The following guidelines should be followed while defining a functional interface:

- A functional interface must contain only one abstract method. This facilitates the implementation of methods using lambda expressions.
- To make sure that the interface does not contain more than one abstract method, the interface can be annotated by **`@Functionalinterface`**. However, the use of this annotation is not mandatory.
- A functional interface may contain a number of default or static methods.

What are the default methods?

Default methods are the methods of the interface that have an implementation. These methods, as the name suggests, use the **`default`** keyword. The use of these default methods is to support *backward compatibility*, which means if JDK modifies any interface (without the default method), then the classes that implement this interface will break.

On the other hand, if you add the default method in an interface, then you will be able to provide the default implementation. This will not affect the implementing classes, as the class does not have the responsibility to implement its own version of that method.

What is a Predicate functional interface?

The **`Predicate`** interface was introduced in Java SE 8 as part of the **`java.util.function`** package to support functional programming in Java. It represents a functional interface with a single method, **`test(T t)`**, that takes a single input argument and returns a boolean value.

Could you explain the difference between the Predicate and Function interfaces?

The following are the key differences between the **Predicate** and **Function** interfaces:

- **Predicate** and **Function** are pre-defined functional interfaces in Java 8 under the **java.util.function** package.
- **Predicate** returns a Boolean; however, Function returns an object.
- **Predicate** is written in the form of **Predicate<T>**, which accepts a single argument. However, **Function** is written in the form of **Function<T, R>**, accepting a single argument of type **T** and returns a result of type **R**.
- **Predicate** is used to verify a condition. However, **Function** is used to perform some action on the argument and then return the modified value.

What is a Consumer functional interface?

Consumer is a functional interface that accepts a single argument and processes it to produce a result without returning the generated result.

The core abstract method of the **Consumer** interface is **accept(T t)**, which defines the operation to be performed. It is commonly used in scenarios such as iterating over collections with **forEach()**, where the primary purpose is to process or act upon the data rather than compute and return a value.

What is a Supplier functional interface?

Supplier is a functional interface. It does not accept any input parameters but supplies the elements. The returned value from **Supplier** can be grabbed using the **get()** method. The functional method defined in this interface is **get()**, which returns a value of the specified type. The **Supplier** interface is commonly used in scenarios involving lazy generation of values, object creation, or deferred execution, such as supplying default values in **Optional** or generating random data on demand.

What is a method reference?

Method reference is one more feature introduced in Java 8. Method reference refers to the method of a functional interface. A method reference can be used to replace a lambda expression while referring to a method.

The following line depicts the lambda expression:

```
name ->System.out.println(name)
```

The same expression can be converted to a method reference as:

```
System.out::println
```

Here, `::` is an operator used to distinguish between the name of the class and the method name.

What is the meaning of String::valueOf?

It is an example of method reference or, more precisely, it is a static method reference. The expression creates a static method reference to the **`valueOf()`** method of the **`String`** class. The expression can be used to return the string representation of the argument that is passed of type **`Character`**, **`Integer`**, **`Boolean`**, and so on.

Lambda expression

Lambda expressions were introduced in Java SE 8 to bring functional programming capabilities into Java. A lambda expression is a concise way to represent an anonymous function that can be passed as an argument or assigned to a functional interface.

They eliminate the need for verbose anonymous inner classes and make the code more readable and expressive, especially when working with collections and the Stream API.

What are the different characteristics of the lambda function?

The main characteristics of the lambda function are as follows:

- Lambda expression can be passed as a parameter to another function.
- A function exists standalone without belonging to any class. It does not require a separate class declaration.
- We can skip declaring the parameter type as the compiler can fetch the type from the target functional interface.
- We can skip writing parentheses if the function has no parameters or a single parameter. However, if we have multiple parameters, then the parentheses are mandatory.
- Whenever the body of the expression has a single statement, we can skip the use of curly braces to declare the function body. We can also skip the **`return`** statement in such a case. However, if the body contains multiple statements, curly braces are required, and an explicit **`return`** statement must be used when returning a value.

Can you explain the different parts of a lambda expression, or how to write a lambda expression?

A typical lambda expression can take the form as follows:

```
(value1, value2) → {body of function}
```

It consists of the following components:

- Parameter List, to be passed to that function depending upon the declaration of the function.
- Arrow operator, which points to the function body.
- Function body, which may contain one or more than one lines of code.

Can you show how you can implement a lambda expression with some real code?

A **lambda expression** is essentially connected with the functional interface and the anonymous inner class concept. Let us consider the following functional interface:

MyInterface.java:

```
@FunctionalInterface
interface MyInterface{
  public void doSomething();
}
```

The `@FunctionalInterface` annotation in the preceding code is absolutely optional.

Traditionally, to implement this interface, we can either write a concrete class that overrides the abstract method. However, instead of that, we can also go for the following lambda expression as shown in the following class:

TestLambda.java:

```
public class TestLambda {
    public static void main(String[] args) {
          MyInterface m=()->{
            System.out.println("Task is done");
        };
        m.doSomething();
    }
}
```

In this example, the lambda expression provides the implementation of the single abstract method defined in **MyInterface**. The JVM internally treats the lambda expression as an instance of the functional interface and binds the provided behavior to its abstract method.

What is the significance of using the var keyword as lambda expression parameters? (Java11)

The **var** keyword was introduced in Java10, but its role was limited to declaring normal variables only. From Java11 onwards, we can use the **var** keyword as a datatype for the parameters used in the lambda expression as follows:

```
(var parameter1, var parameter2)-> {body of the lambda expression}
```

The use of **var** keyword in the lambda parameter is useful because:

- It applies the uniformity between the lambda variables and local variables.
- It facilitates the usage of the modifiers or annotations like **@Nonnull**, which we cannot apply if we do not declare a datatype for the parameters.

Are there any rules to follow to use the var keyword in the lambda expression parameters? (Java11)

The following rules are to be followed while we use the var keyword in the lambda expression parameters:

- If the lambda expression uses multiple parameters, then we have to apply the **var** keyword to all the parameters.
- Mixing the **var** keyword with the normal data type is not permitted.
- The parameters for the lambda expression signature with the **var** keyword are not optional, unlike the normal lambda expression.

Stream API

Java Streams were introduced in Java SE 8 to provide a modern and declarative approach for processing collections of data. A stream represents a sequence of elements that can be processed through operations such as filtering, mapping, and reduction.

Streams enable functional-style programming in Java, allowing developers to write concise, readable, and efficient code, especially when working with large datasets or performing parallel operations.

Can you explain the difference between the Collection API and Stream API?

The following points give an idea about the differences between the collection API and the Stream API:

- The Stream API is introduced in Java 8 Standard Edition, while the collection API is introduced in Java 1.2.
- The Stream API is used to compute data. However, the Collection API can be used to store as well as compute the data.
- Stream API does not make use of an **`Iterator`**. To iterate through the different elements, it simply uses **`forEach`**.
- Using the Stream API, we can consume and iterate through the elements only once; however, using the collection API, it can be done as and when required.

What is Stream API? Why do we require the Stream API?

The **Stream API** has been added in Java 8, which includes the APIs for processing objects from a source such as a collection.

It facilitates:

- Functional-style programming
- Aggregate operations making simplified processing
- Faster processing leading to better performance
- Parallel operations taking advantage of multithreading

What is the difference between limit() and skip()?

The **`limit()`** method is used to specify the number of elements to be returned. The following code snippet illustrates the working of the **`limit()`** method:

```
Stream.of(1,2,3,4,5,6,7,8,9,10,11,12,13,14,15,16).limit(10)
```

This statement creates a stream of integers from 1 to 16 using **`Stream.of()`**.

The **`limit(10)`** method is an intermediate operation that restricts the stream to the **first 10 elements.**

As a result, the stream will contain only the first 10 elements. The remaining elements (11 to 16) are not processed because **`limit()`** short-circuits the stream after reaching the specified number of elements.

The **skip()** method skips the number of elements till the specified index number.

The following code snippet illustrates the working of the **skip()** method:

```
Stream.of(1,2,3,4,5,6,7,8,9,10,11,12,13,14,15,16).skip(5)
```

This statement creates a stream of integers from 1 to 16 using **Stream.of()**.

The **skip(5)** method is an intermediate operation that discards the first 5 elements of the stream.

How would you write a program to print 5 random numbers using forEach in Java 8?

The following code will generate 5 random numbers and print the generated values with the help of the **forEach** function:

```
Random random = new Random();
random.ints().forEach(System.out::println);
```

In this example, the **ints()** method returns an infinite stream of random integer values, and the **forEach()** terminal operation consumes each generated element by printing it to the console. Since the stream produced is unbounded, it will continue generating values indefinitely unless a limiting operation such as **limit()** is applied.

What is the use of the takeWhile() method in Stream API?(Java9)

The **takeWhile()** method, introduced in Java 9, is an intermediate operation in the Stream API that returns elements from the stream as long as the specified condition evaluates to true. Once the predicate returns false, the processing stops, and no further elements are considered.

What is the use of the dropWhile() method in Stream API? (Java9)

The **dropWhile()** method, introduced in Java 9, is an intermediate operation in the Stream API that discards elements from the stream as long as the specified predicate evaluates to true. Once the condition becomes false, it returns the remaining elements of the stream without further dropping. It is particularly useful with ordered streams when you intend to skip a sequence of elements at the beginning based on a condition and then process the rest of the stream normally.

What is the use of the iterate() method in the Stream API? (Java9)

The `iterate()` method in the Java Stream API is a static factory method used to create an infinite sequential stream by repeatedly applying a function to an initial seed value. It is useful for generating repetitive sequences.

In Java 9, an overloaded version of `iterate()` was introduced that accepts a predicate, allowing the stream to terminate when the specified condition becomes false, thereby preventing infinite processing.

What is the significance of toList() method of Stream API? How is it different than the collect() method? (Java16)

The `toList()` method, introduced in Java 16, is a terminal operation in the Stream API that collects stream elements into a `List`. It is considered to be simpler as it eliminates the usage of a collector. Importantly, it returns an unmodifiable `List`, which makes it safer for immutable data handling.

What is Gatherer interface provided in Java? (Java24)

Gatherer interface is introduced in Java24. It is used to perform the intermediate operation that transforms the input elements into a stream of output elements. Sometimes, it facilitates the final action or operation when the end of the upstream is reached. The transformation of the input elements obtained from the Gatherer may be stateless or stateful.

Gatherer can be used in the following scenarios:

- To group the elements in the batches
- De-duplicating the consecutive similar items
- Incremental accumulation functions
- Incremental reordering functions

What is the Gatherers class and its significance? (Java24)

The `Gatherers` class is a utility class provided by Stream API which facilitates the instance creation the `Gatherer` interface.

It provides the following static methods which returns the instance of the Gatherer interface:

- **scan()**: Performs a running accumulation and emits every intermediate result.
- **fold()**: Performs accumulation but emits only the final result.
- **windowFixed(int size)**: Creates the fixed-sized windows (batches) from a stream of elements.
- **windowSliding(int size)**: Creates sliding windows over elements.

Apart from these predefined gatherers, developers can use their customized gatherers using the methods **`Gatheres.of(…)`** and **`Gatherers.ofSequential(…)`** to perform custom batching and transformation, etc.

Can you explain the working of any gathered of Stream API using some code? (Java24)

The following code shows how to use the **`scan()`** method of gatherer to accumulate the data:

```
List<String> generatedStrings =
    Stream.of(1,2,3,4,5)
          .gather(
              scan(() -> "", (string, data) -> string + data)
          )
          .toList();
System.out.println(generatedStrings)
```

This code generates the output as:

```
["1", "12", "123", "1234", "12345"]
```

This code creates a stream of numbers from 1 to 5 and applies the **`scan()`** gatherer to perform a running string accumulation. Starting with an empty string (""), each number is appended to the previous result, and every intermediate value is emitted into the stream.

What are intermediate and terminal operations? What is the difference between intermediate and terminal operations in Stream?

All Stream operations are categorized into terminal and intermediate operations.

- **Intermediate operations**: These are the operations that return the Stream on which some other operations can be carried out. The **intermediate operations** are termed **lazy operations,** as they do not process the Stream unless any terminal operation is carried out on it. Some of the intermediate operational functions are **map()**, **filter()**, **distinct()**, **sorted()**, **limit()**, and **skip()**.

- **Terminal operations**: The terminal operations initiate processing of the Stream. When a **terminal operation** is invoked, the Stream undergoes all the intermediate operations. Some of the terminal operational functions are **forEach()**, **toArray()**, **reduce()**, **collect()**, **min()**, **max()**, and **count()**.

Can you explain the reduce operation in Stream?

Often when we work with a group of data, that is a collection, we need to perform different operations. Some of these operations may require generating a single value based on the elements present in that stream. It may be counting the elements or calculating the average or sum. In such cases, we can use the **reduce()** function of streams.

The following is the syntax of the **reduce()** function:

```
T reduce(T identity, BinaryOperator<T> accumulator);
```

Here:

- `T` is the identity of the initial value
- Accumulator is the function or process that we would like to perform on elements

For example, the following code snippet uses the **reduce()** function, which calculates the total of all elements from the stream:

```
int total= data.stream().reduce(0,
                        (value1, value2) -> value1+ value2);
```

In this example, the **reduce()** method performs a terminal operation that combines all elements of the stream into a single result. The value 0 acts as the identity element, and the lambda expression specifies how two elements are combined during each step of the reduction process.

What is stream pipelining?

The **stream pipelining** is the concept of chaining operations together to produce the desired result. The stream operations are categorized as intermediate operations and terminal operations. Each of the intermediate operations returns an instance of **Stream** itself when it runs. We can perform any number of intermediate operations to process data. All these operations form a processing pipeline.

The pipeline must have a terminal operation, which terminates the pipeline and returns a final value.

What does it mean when we say that Java Streams are lazily evaluated?

Stream is lazy, because no action in the chain of intermediate operations will take place unless the terminal operation is used. Usually, when we use the function, the movement, the flow control comes on that line, the function will be invoked, and the action will take place. In Stream, however, that is not true. The intermediate operation will work only when a call to the terminal method on the Stream is given.

Can you demonstrate, with an example, how Java Streams exhibit lazy evaluation?

Let us consider the following code snippet where we would like to search the first occurrence of element whose value is greater than 5:

```
List<Integer> data= Arrays.asList(1,2,15,2,2);
Integer a = data.stream()
                .peek(num -> System.out.println("Filtered element: " + num))
                .filter(x -> x > 5)
                .findFirst()
                .orElse(null);
System.out.println(a);
```

The output of this code snippet is as follows:

```
Filtered element: 1
Filtered element: 2
Filtered element: 15
15
```

As we can observe, we have used the **findFirst()** method of streams, and the moment the first matched element is found, the further elements are not checked. This approach makes the streams *lazy streams*.

Could you list and explain different intermediate and terminal operations?

The following table lists different intermediate operations:

Method	Description
`filter()`	Returns a stream of elements that satisfy the given condition via the predicate
`map()`	Returns a stream that consists of the result after applying some function to each element of the stream
`sorted()`	Returns a stream that consists of elements in a naturally sorted order
`distinct()`	Returns a Stream of unique elements
`forEach()`	Performs the given action on all the elements of a stream
`limit()`	Returns a stream with the first n elements of the collection
`skip()`	Returns a stream by skipping the first *n* elements

***Table 10.1**: Intermediate operations*

The following table lists different terminal operations:

Method	Description
`toArray()`	An array containing an array of a stream
`Reduce()`	Performs a reduction operation on the elements of a stream using some initial value and a binary operation
`Collect()`	Return a mutable result as a container of a List or a Set
`Min()`	Returns the minimum element in a stream wrapped in an element of type Optional
`Max()`	Returns the maximum element in a stream wrapped in an element of type Optional
`Count()`	The total number of elements in a stream
`anyMatch()`	Returns true if any one of the elements of the stream matches the given predicate
`allMatch()`	Returns true if all of the elements of the stream match the given predicate
`noneMatch()`	Returns true if all of the elements of the stream do not match the given predicate
`findFirst()`	Returns the first element of the stream wrapped in an object of type Optional
`findAny()`	Returns any one of the elements of the stream

***Table 10.2**: Terminal operations*

What is the difference between the findFirst() and findAny() methods?

The following are the differences between **`findFirst()`** and **`findAny()`** method:

- The **`findFirst()`** method returns the first element meeting the specified condition using the predicate.
- The **`findAny()`** method returns any element matching the specified condition. The **`findAny()`** method is very useful while working with a parallel stream.

What is the difference between Iterator and Spliterator?

The following are the key differences between Iterator and Spliterator:

- **`Iterator`** was introduced in JDK 1.2, and **`Spliterator`** was introduced between JDK 1.8
- Iterators are used for iterating the Collection API. However, **`Spliterator`** used for the Stream API.
- **`Iterator`** has the methods **`next()`** and **`hasNext()`** for the iteration of the elements. **`Spliterator`** has method **`tryAdvance()`**.
- We need to invoke the **`iterator()`** method on collection object for the iteration. However, for spliterate, we need to invoke the **`spliterator()`** method on the Stream Object.
- **`Iterator`** can iterate only in sequential order. However, **`SplitIterator`** iterates in parallel and sequential order too.

What does the map() function do? Why do you use it?

The **`map()`** function of Stream API performs a mapping operation. It allows the transformation of one type of object into another object by applying some logic. It means we can take a list of strings and transform it into a List containing the length of each string using map.

This is used when we intend to convert one object to another object.

Explain the difference between map() and flatMap()?

When we use the Stream function **`map()`**, it gives one output value per input value. However, when we use the **`flatMap()`** operation, it gives zero or more output values per input value.

Let us take an example.

Using **map()**, we will create a list as follows:

```
List<String>fruits =
        Arrays.asList("orange", "banana", "papaya", "mango");
List<String>fruits_updates =
        fruits.stream()
        .map(String::toUpperCase).collect(Collectors.toList());
```

In this example, the **map()** method transforms each element of the stream individually. Here, every fruit name is converted to its uppercase representation, and the transformed elements are collected into a new list.

Let us use **flatMap()**:

```
List<List<Integer>>listOfList=
    Arrays.asList(Arrays.asList(1, 2, 3),Arrays.asList(4, 5),
    Arrays.asList(6, 7, 8) );
List<Integer>list_flatten =
    listOfList.flatMap(list ->list.stream())
    .collect(Collectors.toList());
```

In this example, the **flatMap()** method is used to flatten a nested structure.

The original list contains multiple lists of integers (a list of lists). The **flatMap()** operation converts each inner list into a stream and then merges them into a single continuous stream of integers.

What does the filter() method do? When to use it?

The **filter()** method of the Stream is used to filter elements. The filtering condition is specified using a **Predicate** function.

For example, if you have a list of integers and want only the integers that are divisible by 3, then we can use the **filter()** function. We will supply a function to check if a number is divisible by 3 or not using a **Predicate**, and **filter()** will apply this to each element of the stream.

Why should we use the peek() function? What does the peek() method do? When should you use it?

The **peek()** method of the **Stream** class enables one to see through a stream pipeline. Here, we can peek through each step of the processing done and then print meaningful messages on the console. The main purpose of **peek()** is debugging the issues related to the lambda expression and the Stream processing.

What are the different ways to create a Stream?

The following are the different ways to create a stream:

- **Using collection**: The Collection API has a stream method that enables the creation of a stream from a collection as:

  ```
  Stream<String> stream= list.stream();
  ```

- **From specified values**: We can create a stream from some specified values as:

  ```
  Stream<String> stream= Stream.of("mango","papaya","banana");
  ```

- **Creating an empty stream**: The **empty()** method allows the creation of stream to avoid returning null for streams with no elements. This can be achieved as shown:

  ```
  Stream<String> stream= Stream.empty();
  ```

- **Create a stream from an array**: The Stream has an **of()** method, and the **stream()** method of arrays can also be used to get the stream sequential stream from a specified array. Both these methods return a Stream when invoked with a non-primitive type **T** as:

  ```
  String[]fruits ={ ("mango","papaya","banana"};
  Stream<T>stream  =Arrays.stream(fruits);
  ```

  And:

  ```
  Stream<T> stream = Stream.of(fruits);
  ```

Can you create a stream for primitives? What are its different types?

Yes, we can also create streams from a group of primitives. The Stream API provides different types of Streams to deal with primitives like **int**, **long**, and **double**. **IntStream** handles **int**, **DoubleStream** handles double, and **LongStream** handles long type of data. The following code snippet shows how to handle the **int** data type with **IntStream** and print it:

```
IntStream.range(1, 5)
    .forEach(System.out::println);
```

The **range()** method generates a sequential stream of integers starting from the inclusive lower bound (1) to the exclusive upper bound (5). In this case, it produces the values 1, 2, 3, and 4.

Can you re-use the stream once the terminal operation is invoked? Can you give any real-time example?

As the word itself explains, the terminal operation terminates the stream. You cannot perform any further action once the terminal operation is performed, as the stream is closed after that.

Consider the following code snippet:

```
Stream<String> mystream =
     Stream.of("d", "a2", "ab1", "ab3", "dce")
          .filter(s -> s.startsWith("ab"));
mystream.anyMatch(s -> true);     // ok
mystream.noneMatch(s -> true);    // exception
```

In the preceding code, after **anyMatch()**, the stream is closed, because of which we cannot use any other methods on stream. So, invoking of **noneMatch()** after that will result in **IllegalStateException**.

Is there any way to reuse the stream after the terminal operation?

Though there is no direct method available for this, we can make use of the **Supplier** stream. This type of streams can store the original stream, which processes all the intermediate operations.

Consider the following code snippet:

```
Supplier<Stream<String>> mystreamSupplier =
     () -> Stream.of"d", "a2", "ab1", "ab3", "dce")
           .filter(s -> s.startsWith("ab"));
mystreamSupplier.get().anyMatch(s -> true);    // ok
mystreamSupplier.get().noneMatch(s -> true);  // ok
```

In this example, a **Supplier** is used to provide a fresh **Stream** instance each time the **get()** method is invoked. As we are using the **Supplier**, the JVM does not throw any exception and generates the new stream as requested.

Can you explain how you would use streams to collect the object of students whose names start with an S?

Assume that we have a **Student** class with data members as name and age. It also has a **toString()** method that returns a name.

The following code snippet uses the list, *students*, to create a stream and perform the operations to generate the list **studentList**, which starts with **S**:

```
List<Student> studentList=
     students
          .stream()
          .filter(s -> s.name.startsWith("S"))
          .collect(Collectors.toList());
System.out.println(studentList);
```

In this example, the **stream()** method converts the students' collection into a sequential stream. The **filter()** intermediate operation applies the given predicate to retain only those Student objects whose names begin with the letter **S**.

Finally, the **collect()** terminal operation gathers the filtered results into a new **List** using **Collectors.toList()**. This demonstrates how the Stream API enables declarative and readable data processing without modifying the original collection.

How would you group students by age using the Stream API?

The following code snippet can group the students by age:

```
Map<Integer, List<Person>> studentsByAge= students
     .stream()
     .collect(Collectors.groupingBy(s -> s.age));
```

In the above example, the **groupingBy()** collector classifies the stream elements based on the provided key extractor function; in this case, the age field. As a result, students are grouped into a **Map** where the key represents the age, and the value is a list of students belonging to that age group.

Can you explain Stateless and Stateful operations in Java streams?

Intermediate operations of streams are classified as:

- **Stateless operation**: Some of the intermediate operations do not require retaining the information about the previous elements. It is processed independently of earlier elements. Some examples of stateless operations are **map()** and **filter()**.
- **Stateful operation**: Some operations require a reference to earlier elements or the state of earlier elements. Such operations are termed stateful operations. Some examples of stateful operations are **sorted()** and **distinct()**.

What is the parallel stream?

A **parallel stream** can execute in parallel for processing tasks. It enables the faster processing of the elements, which leads to the enhancement of application performance.

For example, if a stream contains one million elements and a filtering operation is applied, a parallel stream can distribute the filtering task across multiple threads. After processing, the results from each thread are merged to form the final filtered collection.

Can you explain how to create a parallel stream?

The following code snippet shows how to create parallel streams for a list:

```
List<Integer> data= Arrays.asList(1,2,15,2,2,7,12);
data.parallelStream().forEach(System.out::println);
```

The output of this program is shown as follows:

```
2 12 2 2 1 15 7
```

As you can observe, the sequence of the list is not maintained, though we know that the list is ordered. This is because of the fact that the parallel stream creates multiple threads to do the task of iteration and printing. Thus, where you are keen to keep the sequence of elements maintained, it is not advisable to use parallel streams.

Can we define the number of threads to generate parallel streams?

Yes, we can. Though there is no direct API in the stream to do that, we can take the help of the **Fork/Join** framework to achieve this. You can create the fork and join object and wrap your stream operations within that.

The following code snippet shows how you can achieve that:

```
List<Integer> data= Arrays.asList(1,2,15,2,2,7,12);
ForkJoinPool customThreadPool = new ForkJoinPool(4);
int actualTotal = customThreadPool.submit(() ->
                   data.parallelStream().reduce(0, Integer::sum)).get();
System.out.println(actualTotal);
```

The preceding code creates a custom **Fork/Join Pool** with 4 worker threads and submits a task that executes a parallel stream reduction. The **parallelStream()** divides the data into smaller chunks, and the **Fork/Join** framework distributes these chunks among the available threads for concurrent processing.

Conclusion

Throughout this chapter, we have discussed some updates in Java 8. Specifically, we talked about functional programming. We discussed the implementations of lambda and streams. We discussed what lambda is and how to form lambda expressions. We also discussed streams, which give more flexibility to iterate and operate on a collection of data. During this, we also talked about the different methods that are provided by the Stream API, like intermediate and terminal operations. At the end, we also discussed parallel streams. Additionally, we discussed the updates in the Stream API in different Java versions from version 9 to version 24. In the next chapter, we will cover different design patterns that play a vital role in software architecture.

Chapter 11
Design Patterns

Introduction

We often find ourselves reiterating the statement that software design is complex. Each time we engage in designing software, we are reminded of this rather unwelcome reality. This naturally leads to an important question: what factors contribute to the complexity of software? Furthermore, when considering object-oriented programming, the level of complexity tends to increase even further. When we design software, we need to think about different objects for which we design different classes and interfaces. The behavior of objects is dependent on how effectively the developer has defined the classes and interfaces. Many times, we need to change the initial design of a class so as to achieve more flexibility and extensibility of the system. Sometimes, the client changes the requirement in terms of the process or structure of software, because of which we might have to design the complete structure from scratch. If you want to achieve that, a design pattern is to your rescue. A design pattern provides you with a way to design your classes and interface in a more flexible way.

Structure

We will be covering interview questions based on the following topics in this chapter:

- Understanding the design pattern
- Creational design patterns
- Structural design patterns
- Behavior design patterns
- J2EE design patterns

Objectives

This chapter will cover the most important design patterns that are useful for creating applications more effectively. Along with this, the chapter aims to make you aware of different interview questions that can be asked based on design patterns and how Java implements them.

Understanding design pattern

A **design pattern** is the extension code, which is a language-independent strategy to solve common object-oriented design problems, solutions to repetitive coding, or writing code from scratch. They define the techniques for making the application more flexible and reducing the coupling. The design pattern describes how to structure the classes to meet a given requirement of the system to save time and effort and increase efficiency.

What are the different categories of Java design patterns?

Based on the problem analysis, one can categorize the design patterns as:

- **Creational patterns**: These patterns are used to define and describe the ways of creating objects. They describe in depth how objects are created at class instantiation time. The following are the different implementations of this pattern:
  - Factory Method design pattern
  - Abstract Factory design pattern
  - Builder design pattern
  - Prototype design pattern
  - Singleton design pattern
  - Service Locator design pattern
- **Structural patterns**: The Structural design patterns are concerned with how the classes and objects can be composed together to form a larger structure. They offer an efficient solution for the class compositions and object structures. The patterns are dependent on the concept of inheritance, which allows multiple classes or objects to work together as a single working unit. They simplify the structure by identifying the relationships between them. These patterns focus on how the classes are inherited from each other and how they are composed from other classes. The following are the different implementations of this pattern:
  - Adapter design pattern
  - Bridge design pattern
  - Filter design pattern

- Composite design pattern
- Decorator design pattern
- Façade design pattern
- Flyweight design pattern
- Proxy design pattern

- **Behavioral patterns**: The Behavioral design patterns care about the interaction and responsibility of objects. The patterns focus on the ease in the interaction between the objects. However, the patterns make sure the communicating objects will be loosely coupled in order to avoid hardcoding. The following are the different implementations of this pattern:
    - Interpreter design pattern
    - Template Method design pattern
    - Chain-of-Responsibility design pattern
    - Command design pattern
    - Iterator design pattern
    - Strategy design pattern
    - Visitor design pattern
- **J2EE patterns**: The patterns used in designing J2EE applications. The following are the different implementations of this pattern:
    - MVC design pattern
    - Data Access Object design pattern
    - Front Controller design pattern
    - Intercepting Filter design pattern
    - Transfer Object design pattern

What are the advantages of the Java design pattern?

The following are the advantages of the Java design pattern:

- The design patterns provide a templated, reusable solution that can be used in multiple projects.
- The design pattern helps in defining a solution that helps in defining the system architecture and customizing it, instead of coding everything manually.
- The design pattern is a way of capturing the reflection of the expert and experienced software engineers or developers. They provide a well-proven solution.
- The design patterns enable transparency in the application design.

Could you explain the disadvantages of design patterns?

The following are the disadvantages of design patterns:

- The patterns do not lead to any direct code re-use.
- The patterns are deceptively simple.
- The teams using patterns in the application may suffer from pattern overload.
- When the teams are working together, integrating patterns into an application development requires highly intense human activity.

Which design pattern can be used to sequentially access the elements of a collection object easily?

The iterator pattern is used to sequentially access the elements of a collection object easily. It provides a standard way to traverse through a collection without exposing its internal representation, thereby maintaining encapsulation. This pattern also allows different types of collections to be iterated in a uniform manner, making the code more flexible and easier to maintain.

Can you name a few design patterns used in the standard JDK library?

The following are some of the examples of design pattern implementations in the JDK library:

- **Decorator design pattern**: It is used in various Java IO classes.
- **Singleton pattern**: It is used in the `Runtime`, `Calendar` class.
- **Factory pattern**: It is used with immutable classes like `Long`. For example, the `Long.valueOf()` method.
- **Observer pattern**: It is used in Swing programming and many of the event listener frameworks.

To decouple an abstraction from its implementation, one can use the **bridge pattern**. Here, the implementation can vary independently. To achieve this independent modification, an interface is used as a bridge between abstraction and implementation. This facilitates the use of implementation by multiple objects without concerning the changes at the abstraction level.

Which design pattern will be helpful when we wish to add a new functionality to an existing object?

The **decorator pattern** is the best choice when the developers wish to add new functionality to an existing object without changing its structure. It works by wrapping the original object with a new object that contains the additional behavior, following the same interface. This approach promotes flexibility and adheres to the Open/Closed Principle, allowing functionality to be extended without modifying existing code.

Which design pattern is useful in case of passing data with multiple attributes from the client to the server in one shot?

The **transfer object pattern** is useful in case one has to pass the data with multiple attributes from the client to the server in one shot.

When should you use the Intercepting design pattern?

The **Intercepting design pattern** can be used when we intend to perform pre- or post-processing of data in a request-response flow. This is also termed the intercepting filter pattern.

Creational design pattern

As the name indicates, this design pattern deals with object creation mechanisms. One of the main approaches this design pattern works with is to promote loose coupling and flexibility. Though this pattern facilitates the creation of the object, it does not promote the object creation directly by using constructors. Rather, this pattern abstracts the instantiation process, making the system more independent of how its objects are created, composed, and represented.

When is the Service Locator design pattern used?

We can use the Service Locator design pattern to locate various services. Normally, this pattern uses the central registry, which is responsible for returning the necessary service to the invoker. You may consider this central registry as JNDI. The important point to note here is that this pattern does not instantiate the services directly, so it is not tightly coupled. However, it registers the services with some servers and provides a way to locate them.

Which technologies use the Service Locator design pattern?

EJB and JMS are two examples that use the Service Locator design pattern internally. In **Enterprise JavaBeans (EJB)**, clients typically perform a lookup using **Java Naming and Directory Interface (JNDI)** to obtain references to enterprise beans. The lookup mechanism acts as a service locator by abstracting the process of locating and retrieving the required service object.

Similarly, in **Java Message Service (JMS)**, clients use JNDI to look up resources such as **`ConnectionFactory`** and **`Destination`** objects. The JNDI context functions as a centralized registry, providing access to messaging services without exposing their creation details.

In both cases, the Service Locator pattern helps decouple the client from the service creation logic and centralizes resource lookup, improving maintainability and flexibility in enterprise applications.

What is a Factory design pattern? When can the Factory design pattern be used?

The **Factory design pattern** is a creational pattern that offers the best way to create an object. It is also known as a **virtual constructor**. In this pattern, we do not expose the logic of creating objects to the client, and a standard interface for using the created object. It enables the subclasses to choose the type of objects to create.

We can use the factory pattern when we have to create an object of the parent or any one of the subclasses depending on the given data. The Factory design pattern can be used in the following situations:

- When a class is not aware of which type of objects needs to be created
- When the class specifies its subclasses to specify which objects are to be created

What are the benefits of the Factory design pattern?

The key benefits of the Factory design pattern are as follows:

- It increases the level of encapsulation while creating the objects.
- It allows replacing the original implementation of classes with a more advanced and high-performance functional implementation, that too without making any changes to the client-side code.
- The factory pattern makes the code more robust. The code is less coupled, so it is easy to extend.

When should one use the setter and constructor injection in the Dependency Injection design pattern?

The **setter injection** is used to provide the optional dependencies of an object, and the constructor is used to provide a mandatory dependency of an object.

The Spring Framework provides an IOC container, which provides ways to use the setter methods or constructors for the injection of dependencies.

Could you explain the Dependency Injection design pattern and the Service Locator design pattern?

In the **Dependency Injection design pattern**, the class that has dependencies is not aware of them, and it also does not care where they came from. The **Service Locator design pattern** is used to create class dependencies. The class is still responsible for creating its dependencies irrespective of whether it is using a **Service Locator design pattern** or not. The Service Locators can also be used to hide dependencies. We cannot determine from an object's signature whether it connects with a database or not while obtaining the connections from a locator.

What are the differences between the Dependency Injection design pattern and the Service Locator design pattern?

The **Dependency Injection** (**DI**) and **Service Locator** patterns both aim to manage object dependencies. However, they differ fundamentally in how those dependencies are obtained and controlled. In Dependency Injection, a class does not create or look up its dependencies; instead, they are provided externally, typically through a constructor, setter, or field injection. This promotes the principle of **inversion of control** (**IoC**), where the responsibility of creating and managing dependencies is delegated to a container or framework such as Spring Framework or Google Guice. As a result, dependencies are explicit, clearly visible in the class design, and easier to test and maintain.

In contrast, the Service Locator pattern requires the class to actively retrieve its dependencies from a central registry or locator. This means the class depends on the Service Locator to obtain required services, effectively pulling dependencies rather than receiving them. While this approach may simplify certain configurations, it hides actual dependencies within method invocations, reducing transparency and increasing coupling. Consequently, testing becomes more complex because dependency lookup logic is embedded inside the class.

What is the Builder design pattern in Java?

The **Builder design pattern** is a Creational design pattern. Whenever we are in need of creating a complex object, which is the result of different processes, this pattern achieves it by building simpler, smaller objects.

What are the advantages of the Builder design pattern?

The advantages of the Builder design pattern are:

- The pattern supports enhanced control over the construction process.
- The pattern facilitates a clear separation between the construction of an object and its representation.
- In this pattern, the object is always instantiated in its complete state.
- It facilitates the objects of immutable objects to be created quickly in the object building process.

Could you give examples from JDK that implement the Builder design pattern?

Some examples from the JDK that implement or resemble the Builder design pattern include:

- `java.lang.StringBuilder`
- `java.lang.StringBuffer`
- `java.nio.ByteBuffer`
- `java.nio.FloatBuffer`
- `java.nio.IntBuffer`

These classes allow step-by-step modification of internal state before producing the final result. For example, `StringBuilder` enables appending data incrementally before converting it into a String. Similarly, the NIO buffer classes allow controlled construction and manipulation of data buffers.

What is the difference between the Factory Method design pattern and the Abstract Factory design pattern?

The **Abstract Factory design pattern** provides an interface for creating families of dependent objects, and the **Factory Method design pattern** creates the objects by defining an interface for object creation, but allows the subclasses to decide which concrete class to instantiate.

Why use a factory class to instantiate a class when we can use a new operator?

The factory classes provide design flexibility with the following benefits:

- The use of this pattern results in more decoupled code, as it enables hiding the creational logic from the dependent code.
- The pattern enables the introduction of an inversion-of-control through a container.
- It provides more flexibility in case we need to change the underlying implementation, as the creational logic is hidden from the dependent code.

Can you give some examples of the Factory Method design pattern implementation in JDK?

Some examples of the Factory method pattern implementation in the JDK include:

- `java.util.Calendar`
- `java.util.ResourceBundle`
- `java.text.NumberFormat`

These classes typically expose static factory methods such as **`getInstance()`** or **`getBundle()`**, which return objects of concrete subclasses without exposing the actual implementation classes to the client. For example, **`Calendar.getInstance()`** may return a **`GregorianCalendar`** depending on the locale and configuration.

What is an Abstract Factory design pattern?

The **Abstract Factory pattern** provides an interface for creating families of related objects without specifying their concrete subclasses. It operates at a higher level of abstraction than the **Factory Method pattern**. While the Factory Method focuses on creating a single product, the Abstract Factory coordinates the creation of multiple related products that are designed to work together.

Could you explain the Singleton design pattern?

The **Singleton design pattern** offers a single instance creation within an application. JDK class **`java.lang.Runtime`** is based on the singleton pattern. The Singleton design pattern enables defining a class that has only one instance and provides a global point of access to that instance. It means that it is the responsibility of the class to offer a mechanism that should create a single instance, and all other classes can use that single object.

How to implement the Singleton design pattern?

The two ways of creating a **Singleton design pattern** are as follows:

- **Early instantiation**: In early instantiation, the instance will be created when the class is loaded by the JVM, before it is accessed for the first time. The following code represents how to implement the Singleton design pattern for early instantiation:

```
public class EarlySingleton
{
  private static EarlySingleton earlySingleton = new EarlySingleton();
  private EarlySingleton() {}
  public static EarlySingleton getInstance()
  {
    return earlySingleton;
  }
}
```

  This implementation ensures that only one instance of the class is created and shared throughout the application. The private constructor prevents external classes from creating new objects, while the static **getInstance()** method provides global access to the single instance.

- **Lazy instantiation**: In lazy initialization, the instance is created only when it is requested instead of at class loading time. The following code represents how to implement the Singleton design pattern for lazy instantiation:

```
public class LazySingleton
{
  private static LazySingleton lazySingleton;
  private LazySingleton() {}
  public static LazySingleton getInstance()
  {
    if (lazySingleton==null)
      lazySingleton = new LazySingleton();
    return lazySingleton;
  }
}
```

  This implementation creates the object only when it is needed for the first time, which helps in saving memory if the instance is never used. It follows the principle of delaying object creation until it is actually required.

What are the limitations and disadvantages of the Singleton design pattern?

The limitation of the Singleton design pattern: The Singleton design pattern ensures the class has only one instance, along with providing a global point of access to it. This single instance becomes the limitation because most of the classes in the application might need to create multiple instances.

The disadvantages of the Singleton design pattern are:

- The pattern does not follow the single repository principle as it controls its own logic of creating an instance and how to manage the object lifecycle.
- As it will have a shared global instance, it stops the de-allocation of the objects and the resources accessed by the global instance.

Can you give some examples of the implementation of the Singleton design pattern by JDK?

The following are some of the Singleton design pattern implementations from JDK:

- The **`getRuntime()`** method of **`java.lnag.Runtime,`** which returns the runtime object that is associated with the current Java application.
- The **`getSecurityManager()`** method of **`java.lang.System`** class. The method returns **`SecurityManager`**.
- The **`getDesktop()`** method of **`java.awt.Desktop`** class. The method **getDesktop()** returns the **`Desktop`** instance, which is associated with the current desktop context.

These examples demonstrate how the JDK uses the Singleton concept to control object creation and provide centralized access. However, it is important to note that not all of them strictly follow the classic **Gang of Four** (**GoF**) Singleton implementation; some exhibit contextual or controlled single-instance behavior rather than a rigid Singleton structure.

Can you implement a thread-safe Singleton design pattern? Why do we need that?

Even if we implement the private constructor for the implementation of the Singleton design pattern, there are a few situations in which multiple threads can access the class to create an object. In such cases, even if the singleton pattern is implemented, multiple objects can be created. To control this, we can create a synchronized or thread-safe singleton object.

There are many ways to implement a thread-safe Singleton design pattern as follows:

- The most straightforward way is by using the **enum** to create a thread-safe singleton.
- By implementing the Singleton design pattern with the help of double-checked locking.
- By using a static Singleton instance, which is initialized during class loading.

You can make the following change to the **getInstance()** method to make it thread-safe:

```
public static synchronized LazySingleton getInstance()
{
  if (lazySingleton==null)
    lazySingleton = new LazySingleton();
  return lazySingleton;
}
```

By adding the **synchronized** keyword, only one thread can execute the **getInstance()** method at a time. This ensures that multiple threads cannot create separate instances simultaneously, making the Singleton implementation thread-safe.

Can we create a clone of a Singleton object?

Yes, it is possible to create a clone of a **Singleton** object. If the class implements the **Cloneable** interface, then we can invoke the **clone()** method and create a new instance, thereby violating the Singleton principle.

Structural design patterns

Structural design patterns deal with the composition of classes and objects to form larger, well-organized structures. They emphasize how individual components can be combined to create flexible and efficient systems while preserving clarity and maintainability.

These patterns facilitate better design by promoting loose coupling, improved scalability, and seamless integration between different parts of an application. They are particularly useful when designing systems that need to evolve without requiring significant changes to existing code.

What is the Adapter design pattern?

In the **Adapter design pattern**, based on the requirements, we convert the interface of one class into another interface. It means the pattern allows the developers to convert the interface according to the requirement while using the class service with a different interface. The pattern is also termed a **wrapper pattern**. Using such a pattern, we can create an object that will be a hybrid object that can use the services from two interfaces at a time as and when needed.

How is the Bridge design pattern different from the Adapter design pattern?

The **Bridge design pattern** is designed for the isolation of an implementation of the interface from the class. It allows us to change the implementation without changing the client code.

On the other hand, the **Adapter design pattern** allows removing the need of having two class implementations so as to work with incompatible interfaces.

Under which scenarios can we use the Adapter design pattern?

We can use the Adapter design pattern when we need to make two classes work with incompatible interfaces. The pattern can be used to encapsulate the third-party code in such a way that your application only depends on the adapter. The adapter can adapt itself when the third-party code changes or when we move to a different third-party library.

Could you differentiate between the Strategy design pattern and State design pattern in Java?

Both the **Strategy design pattern** and **State design pattern** have the same structure. The UML class diagram of both looks the same, but their intent is very different. The **State design pattern** allows managing and defining the state of an object. On the other hand, the **Strategy design pattern** allows describing a set of interchangeable algorithms.

What is a Proxy design pattern?

The **Proxy design pattern** is a Structural design pattern. As the name itself indicates, it serves as a proxy for some other class, which in turn accesses the functionality of another class. So, instead of talking to the object directly, the client talks to the proxy object, which wraps the actual object inside to provide the functionality.

What is the difference between the Decorator design pattern and Proxy design pattern?

Both the **Decorator design pattern** and **Proxy design pattern** implement the interface of an object they decorate or encapsulate, which is very similar. However, the **Decorator design pattern** is used to implement the functionality on an object that is already created. And, the **Proxy design pattern** is used to control access to an object.

What is the difference between Proxy object and Adapter object?

The Proxy object has the same interface and input as that of the actual object. In contrast, the Adapter object has a different interface from the actual object.

Could you state the advantages of the Composite design pattern in Java?

The following are the advantages of the composite design pattern:

- The **Composite design pattern** allows the clients to operate collectively on a bunch of objects that may or may not represent the same hierarchy.
- The pattern provides an easy way to add new kinds of components.
- The pattern provides the flexibility of structure, which will have a manageable class or interface.

What are the uses of the Composite design pattern? When to use the Composite design pattern in Java?

The **Composite design pattern** allows us to treat the container and the object similarly. The best example of the Composite design pattern from JDK is the `JPanel` class. `JPanel` is a class that works as both a component and a container. Whenever some modification in the presentation of the panel is required, we invoke its `paint()` method. The `paint()` method internally will invoke individual components' `paint()` and allow them to draw themselves.

The **Composite design pattern** is used when in the application we need to represent a partial or full hierarchy of objects. We can also use this pattern when we need to add the responsibilities dynamically to the individual object, without affecting other objects.

What is the Decorator design pattern? Could you give some examples from JDK that implement the Decorator design pattern?

The **Decorator design pattern** is one of the most popular design patterns. It facilitates modifying the behavior of an existing object, which changes the code. This pattern creates a new class, which is termed a `Decorator` class. This `Decorator` class wraps the original class within it with additional methods. Obviously, this keeps the original class as it is, but along with that, because of the `Decorator`, you will be able to use the new features as well.

JDK's **java.io** package makes heavy use of it. The **Decorator design pattern** uses composition instead of inheritance to extend the functionality of an object at runtime.

The examples of the Decorator design pattern are as follows:

- **java.io.InputStream**, **java.io.OutputStream**, **java.io.Reader** and **java.io.Writer**
- **java.io.BufferedReader**
- **java.io.BufferedWriter**
- **synchronizedXXX()** from **java.util.Collections**
- **unmodifiableXXX()** from **java.util.Collections**

These classes and methods demonstrate the core idea of the Decorator design pattern, dynamically adding additional behavior to an object without modifying its original structure. For example, **BufferedReader** wraps a **Reader** object and enhances it with buffering capabilities, while still conforming to the same interface.

Behavioral design patterns

Behavioral design patterns address the assignment of responsibilities and the orchestration of communication among objects within a system. They formalize interaction patterns, encapsulate varying behavior, and define clear protocols for collaboration, thereby promoting high cohesion and loose coupling.

By abstracting control flow and delegating responsibilities effectively, these patterns enhance extensibility, improve maintainability, and enable systems to evolve with minimal impact on existing components.

When should one use the Template Method design pattern in Java?

The **Template Method design pattern** is also one of the most popular design patterns. The template method is written in super class, which declares the structure and sequence in which the operations can be performed. The subclass extends this super class and uses this template method to follow the sequence strictly declared in the super class. One of the most important aspects of this pattern is to ensure that the template method must be declared as final. This ensures that the child class will not be able to override this method to change the steps or sequence for algorithm implementation. At the same time, some individual steps can be abstract, so the child classes can implement them in their own way.

When should one use the Strategy design pattern in Java?

The **Strategy design pattern** is useful for implementing a set of related algorithms such as compression algorithms, filtering strategies, and so on. The pattern enables the creation of context classes that use the implementation of the strategy in order to apply the business rules. The `sort()` method of collections and comparator has a strategy of sorting, and the comparator interface provides a way of comparing objects. Due to the strategy, the `sort()` method does not need modification. At the same time, we can define the comparing strategy by overriding the `compare()` method of the `Comparator` interface. The `Strategy pattern` is a good example of the open–closed principle. We override the method of `Comparator`. So, it is open for implementation, but no need to override the `sort()` method as it does not change.

What is the Null Object design pattern?

The **Null Object design** pattern is a behavioral pattern in which the null object replaces the NULL check for the instance variable. Instead of checking for a *null* value, the *null* object provides a do-nothing implementation that safely handles the method invocation. It can also be used to provide default behavior when the real data is not available.

What is the Observer design pattern in Java? When do you use the Observer design pattern in Java?

The **Observer design pattern** is based on the concept of observation and notification. Our objects always collaborate with other objects in the application, and these objects are interested in knowing if any change occurs in the component they are connected with. In such cases, we can use the Observer design pattern, in which a notification is given to an object if there is a change in the component state to which they are connected to.

Can you give a typical example of the Observer design pattern?

One of the most common real-time examples of the Observer design pattern is the publisher–subscriber model. Let us assume that you have subscribed to a new channel that releases news updates. Thus, the news channel acts as a publisher, and you act as a subscriber. Any new update that is released by the news channel will reach you as you are a subscriber.

What is the Proxy design pattern, and what are its different types?

Proxy means a dummy, an object that represents some other object. The **Proxy design pattern** offers a substitute for some other purpose to control access to it.

According to GOF, the Proxy design pattern offers control for accessing the original object.

It allows performing security operations by hiding the information of the original object. It also allows on-demand loading of objects.

There are different types of proxies, which are as follows:

- **Protection proxy**: The protection proxy controls access to the original object depending on some condition.
- **Caching proxies**: The caching proxies prefer to cache the expensive invocation of the real object to enhance performance. These caching strategies are read-through, write-through, cache-aside, and time-based.
- **Virtual proxies**: The virtual proxies are used for instantiating the expensive object by managing the lifetime of the real object in the implementation. It optimizes performance by deciding the need for instance creation and when to reuse
- **Remote proxies**: The remote proxies are used under the distributed object communication. The remote proxy invokes a local object method to make an execution of the remote object.
- **Smart proxies**: The smart proxies are used for implementing log calls and reference counting for the object.

What are the use cases of the Proxy design pattern?

The Proxy design pattern can be used under the scenarios in which we want to provide the following services:

- Lazy initialization
- Implementation of logging
- Facilitation of the network connection
- A way to count references to an object

What is the Chain-of-Responsibility design pattern, and what are its advantages?

In the **Chain-of-Responsibility design pattern**, the sender sends a request to a chain of objects. Then any object in the chain can handle this request.

A **Chain-of-Responsibility design pattern** avoids the coupling of the sender of a request to the request receiver. Let us consider an example of an ATM service. The ATM service uses the pattern in monetary transactions. Each receiver contains the reference of another receiver. When one object fails to handle the request, it sends it to the next receiver, and the process continues.

The following are the advantages of this pattern:

- The pattern minimizes the coupling.
- The pattern provides the flexibility in assigning the responsibilities to objects.
- The pattern permits a set of classes to act as one unit. The events produced in one of the classes can be sent to the other handler classes with the help of composition.

J2EE design patterns

J2EE design patterns are proven solutions for recurring problems in enterprise-level Java applications. They provide standardized approaches for managing complexity in multi-tiered architectures, including presentation, business, and data layers, ensuring scalability, maintainability, and reusability.

These patterns, such as Business Delegate, Front Controller, **Data Access Object** (**DAO**), and Session Facade, help developers streamline communication between layers, optimize resource management, and simplify development of robust enterprise applications.

What is the MVC design pattern?

This is one of the most-used design patterns in J2EE Design. In MVC, *M stands for model, V stands for view,* and *C stands for controller*. Furthermore:

- The models are the objects used as the blueprints for all of the objects that will be used in the application.
- The views are the presentational aspect of the data, mostly to the user.
- The controllers are the control point. The controller acts as the connection between the model and view. The controller accepts the incoming requests and then may forward them to the next point, which might be the business logic layer or the view layer.

What is the Intercepting Filter design pattern?

The **Intercepting Filter design pattern** is used to intercept and manipulate the response before and after processing the request. Such filters can perform the security check using the authentication and authorization of the request, logging the requests, tracking the request, and, after logging or tracking, forwarding the requests to the corresponding handlers. These handlers can be another filter in the chain or a controller.

The components involved are the filter, filter chain, target, filter manager, and client:

- **Filter**: The filter is a unit that is involved in performing a certain task before or after the execution of a request by the request handler.
- **Filter chain**: A filter chain plays a very important role. Under certain circumstances, a single controller might not be able to perform the desired task, or sometimes, more than one task is divided into multiple steps performed in different filters. The filter chain contains multiple filters, which will be executed in a defined order on the target.
- **Target**: The target is the request handler.
- **Filter manager**: The filter manager manages the filters and filter chain.
- **Client**: The client is an object that sends a request to the target object.

What are the benefits of the Intercepting Filter design pattern?

The following are some of the key benefits of the **Intercepting Filter design pattern**:

- The pattern offers a central control over the request with loosely coupled handlers.
- It enables and expands reusability.
- Any time a new filter can be added without affecting the client code.
- The selection of the filters can be made dynamically during the program execution.

What is the Data Access Object design pattern?

The **DAO** design pattern is used to isolate the high-level business services from the low-level data accessing APIs or the actions. The DAO has the following components:

- **Data access interface**: The DAO interface describes the standard actions that can be performed on a model object.
- **The data access implementation or the concrete class**: This class is the implementation of the DAO interface. This class is responsible for getting the data from the data source. This data source can be an XML file, a database, or any other storage mechanism.
- **The model object**: The model object is a POJO containing the getters and setter methods, which allows the storage of data retrieved from the data source using the DAO class.

What is a Front Controller design pattern?

The **Front Controller** design pattern provides a centralized request handling mechanism in which all the requests are handled by a central handler. This centralized handler can be used for authentication, authorization, logging, and tracking requests. Once it is done, the Front Controller forwards the requests to the corresponding handlers.

The following are the entities involved in the Front Controller pattern:

- **Front Controller**: A single handler for all kinds of requests to be attended by the application.
- **Dispatcher**: A Front Controller may use a dispatcher object that can dispatch the request to the corresponding specific handler.
- **View**: The views are the objects for which the requests are made.

Can you give an example of a Front Controller design pattern?

An example of the Front Controller design pattern can be seen in web applications that use a single centralized servlet or controller to handle all incoming requests.

For instance, in a Java web application using Spring MVC, the `DispatcherServlet` acts as a Front Controller. It intercepts all HTTP requests, performs common processing like logging, authentication, or authorization, and then dispatches the requests to the appropriate handler (controller) based on the URL or request parameters.

This centralization provides consistent request handling, reduces code duplication, and simplifies maintenance by having a single point for common pre- and post-processing logic.

What are the SOLID design principles? Can you give an example of the SOLID design principles?

The SOLID design principles are actually a short form that is made up of taking the first letter of the actual principle as:

- Single Responsibility principle or SRP
- Open–Closed design principle or OCD
- Liskov Substitution principle
- Interface Segregation principle
- Dependency Inversion principle

What is the Open–Closed design principle?

The **Open–Closed design principle** is one of the SOLID principles defined by *Robert C. Martin* in his most popular book, *Clean Code*. This principle states that the code should be open for extension but closed for modification. Once we begin coding, we explore the power of polymorphism, and we will find the patterns that can provide the stability and flexibility of this principle. The **State design pattern** and **Strategy design pattern** are the critical examples of patterns where the context class is closed for modification, and we can add new functionalities by implementing a new state or strategy.

Conclusion

In this chapter, we discussed the different design patterns and their importance in the overall software development approach. We discussed many questions that could be asked on these patterns, which will help you to clear your Java interview. Though one may feel that the design patterns may not be that important as far as Java is concerned, knowledge of this is surely going to be one of the added flavors to your profile. In the next chapter, we will enter the world of web and will learn the basics of web application development.

CHAPTER 12
Spring and Spring Boot

Introduction

Application development is becoming complex day by day. Expectations of clients are increasing, and business scenarios are also becoming challenging. Apart from writing only business logic, a developer needs to think of other perspectives of the application, like the flow of application data and other cross-cutting concerns. While servicing all these needs, a developer also has to make sure that they deliver the software in the given timeframe. Traditionally, a developer was solely responsible for developing everything that was time-consuming, and it was difficult to maintain the software as well. Thus, to make things simpler for the developer, frameworks were introduced. Frameworks are semi-complete applications, with some ready-made code or configurations, which can be customized by developers to create customized applications as per the need.

There are different frameworks for different tasks. The Spring Framework is one such framework, which is known for its concepts like Dependency Injection and the **inversion-of-control** (**IoC**) technique. In this chapter, we will walk through all the common questions that might be asked based on the Spring and Spring Boot Frameworks.

The Spring Framework is one of the most demanding frameworks in the industry. Typically, if you are targeting financial institutions, Spring is the most preferred framework because of its high performance. The Spring Framework is a particularly well-regarded skill in the industry, and its presence on a candidate's profile often draws considerable attention from interviewers.

Structure

We will be covering interview questions based on the following topics in this chapter:

- Overview of Spring Framework
- Spring modules

- Dependency Injection and inversion-of-control in Spring
- Spring MVC framework
- Aspect-oriented programming
- Spring Boot Framework

Objectives

At the end of this chapter, you will be able to learn the Spring Framework and Spring Boot. You will also be able to answer different interview questions based on this framework, which has become an integral part of the interview process.

Overview of Spring Framework

The Spring Framework is a powerful, lightweight, and comprehensive framework for building enterprise-level Java applications. It provides core features such as **Dependency Injection** (**DI**), **aspect-oriented programming** (**AOP**), transaction management, and integration support for various technologies. Spring simplifies application development by promoting loose coupling and making applications easier to test and maintain.

The current stable version of the Spring Framework is 6.1.x (released under the Spring 6 generation), which requires Java 17 or higher and is fully aligned with Jakarta EE 9+.

Many times, we have seen blogs, books, or references claiming that the Spring Framework makes development easy. Can you explain how?

The following are the main features implemented by the Spring Framework to enable rapid or easy application development:

- **Easy configuration**: Spring provides both XML- and annotation-based configuration. Both of these ways are easy and self-explanatory.
- **Focus on development**: The main concern of a developer is to provide a solution to a problem using some business logic, algorithm, etc. However, in reality, many times, while developing Java enterprise applications, the developer needs to think about and code for configuration, logging, along with the logic. These configurations and loggings are time-consuming and repetitive. The framework manages beans and provides AOPs for the developers, which allows them to focus on the logical aspects of an application.
- **Reduces the plumbing code**: Spring handles low-level infrastructure concerns such as resource management, transaction handling, exception translation, and dependency

wiring. By delegating these responsibilities to the framework, developers are relieved from writing repetitive setup and integration code, allowing them to concentrate primarily on implementing business logic.

- **Reduces boiler-plated code**: In the process of development, the developers have to write similar kinds of code again and again, which is termed boiler-plated code. Spring provides templates such as `JdbcTemplate`, `JMSTemplate`, and `RestTemplate` components to get rid of the boilerplate code.

What do you mean by boiler-plated code?

In a process of development, in multiple situations, we need to write similar code again and again, and we cannot get rid of that easily. Let us take an example of fetching data from the tables. We know `ResultSet` is a collection of objects, but we cannot obtain an object or a list of objects directly. When we get a `ResultSet`, we need to write the code to convert each row from the `ResultSet` to an object. However, the way we get an `Employee` object from `ResultSet` is similar to the way we get an object of `Book` from `ResultSet`. The only difference in this process is that each of them has different data members or data types. This kind of code is considered boilerplate code.

Can you provide some examples of boilerplate code?

Yes. As already mentioned, the JDBC code is the best example of boilerplate code. Along with that, when we do exception handling, transaction management, and logging, we need to write boilerplate code.

Spring modules

Spring provides around 20 modules, as shown in *Figure 12.1*, which support different features. The Spring Framework is organized into several well-defined modules, each responsible for a specific layer of application development. The **Core Container** module provides fundamental features such as IoC and Dependency Injection. The **AOP and Aspects** module enables aspect-oriented programming for handling cross-cutting concerns. The **Data Access/Integration** module supports JDBC, ORM, and transaction management. The **Web** module provides support for building web and RESTful applications, while the **Test** module offers utilities for unit and integration testing of Spring applications.

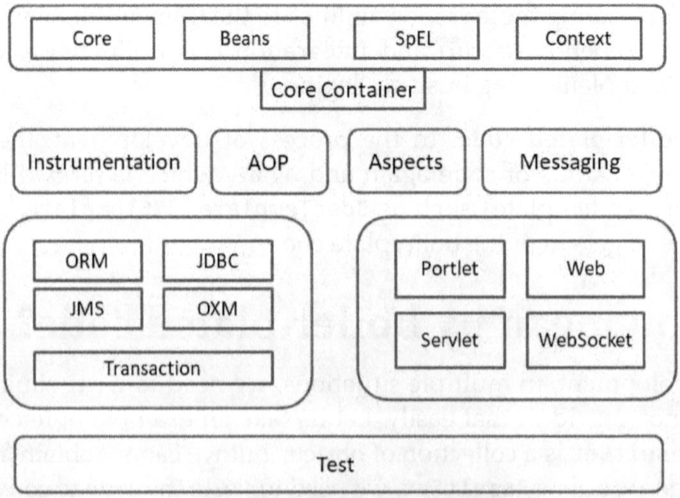

Figure 12.1: Spring modules

Could you explain the Core Container module of the Spring Framework?

The core container consists of the modules for **`spring-beans`**, **`spring-core`**, **`spring-context`**, and Spring Expression Language. Features such as Dependency Injection and IoC are supported by the **`spring-core`** and **`spring-beans`** modules. The **`spring-context`** module provides the means to access objects from the container.

The **`spring-expression`** module provides a way for querying and manipulating an object graph.

Could you explain the Spring AOP and instrumentation module of the Spring Framework?

The **Spring AOP** module supports integration of the aspect-oriented programming approach. By using AOP, cross-cutting concerns can be integrated into the application. The **Spring Aspects** module provides the integration of **AspectJ** in the application.

What is the data access or integration module of the Spring Framework?

This layer includes modules such as **`spring-jdbc`** for JDBC abstraction, **`spring-orm`** for integration with ORM frameworks like Hibernate and JPA, **`spring-tx`** for declarative and programmatic transaction management, **`spring-oxm`** for Object-XML Mapping, and **`spring-jms`** for messaging support.

What is the ORM module of the Spring Framework?

The **spring-orm** module provides integration support for popular **Object-Relational Mapping** (**ORM**) frameworks such as Hibernate, JPA, and others. It simplifies ORM usage by offering consistent exception translation, declarative transaction management integration, and seamless configuration within the Spring container.

The ORM module works closely with the **spring-tx** module to provide both programmatic and declarative transaction management. It helps developers integrate ORM frameworks into Spring applications in a clean, consistent, and maintainable manner.

What is the Messaging module of the Spring Framework?

The **Spring-Messaging** module has been included in Spring 4. The module provides support for integrating **Message**, **MessageChannel**, and **MessageHandler** in messaging applications.

Could you explain the Web module of the Spring Framework?

The Web Module layer consists of Spring-Web, Spring-Web MVC, and Spring-WebSocket.

The **Spring-Web Module** supports web-oriented development.

Spring-Web MVC supports application development for Spring MVC and REST-based Web services. The **spring-websocket** module provides support for WebSocket-based, real-time, bidirectional communication between the client and the server.

Could you explain the Test module of the Spring Framework?

The support for integrating unit testing and integration testing in the application with *JUnit* or *TestNG* is provided by the **Spring-Test module**.

Dependency Injection and inversion-of-control in Spring

Spring uses Dependency Injection for managing the dependencies of a bean. Instead of a class creating its dependent objects manually using the *new* keyword, the Spring container provides those dependencies at runtime. This promotes loose coupling between components, making the application easier to test, maintain, and extend.

What is Dependency Injection?

Dependency Injection is a process by which the values of data members are injected into an object by the container.

In simple terms, the object does not create its own dependencies; instead, they are provided externally by the container at runtime. This reduces tight coupling between classes and improves the modularity and testability of the application.

What are the ways of Dependency Injection in Spring?

Spring provides two ways for Dependency Injection:

- **Setter injection**: When the setter functions are used to set the values for data members, it is termed a setter injection. In XML, we can use the **`<property>`** tag, which is an instruction to the container to use setters/ setter functions for setting values.
- **Constructor injection**: When a parameterized constructor is used to push values for the data members, it is termed constructor injection. The **`<constructor-arg>`** tag is used for generating a constructor injection.

Could you expltain Dependency Injection with a relevant example?

Let us take an example of database communication for DI. If we are not using Spring, we need to obtain a **`Connection`** object with the **`Singleton`** or **`Factory design pattern`** implementation. When we use Spring, we can write a bean of type **`DriverManagerDataSource`** in XML or Java code. Here, the container will create an object according to the configurations provided by the developer.

Note: **Here, the interviewer is keen to check the theoretical as well as practical knowledge of the participants. So, it is better to go with a bit of theory about what is DI, types of DIs, and then explain the practical implementation. We have already discussed the theoretical answer about Dependency Injection in the earlier question.**

Is DriverManagerDataSource the only implementation provided by the framework?

No, **BasicDataSource**, **ComboPooledDataSource**, and **SingleConnectionDataSource** are also provided by the framework. Each of these implementations serves different purposes. For example, **BasicDataSource** (from Apache DBCP) and **ComboPooledDataSource** (from C3P0) provide connection pooling support, which is recommended for production environments. In contrast, **DriverManagerDataSource** and **SingleConnectionDataSource** are typically used for testing or simple standalone applications, as they do not offer robust connection pooling capabilities.

Consider a scenario in which multiple requests for obtaining connections are fired. Will it be feasible to use DriverManagerDataSource?

In practical scenarios, the application may need to obtain multiple database connections. However, **DriverManagerDataSource** does not provide a facility for connection pooling and may affect the application performance. Thus, alternatives such as **BasicDataSource** and **ComboPooledDataSource** can be used.

What is inversion-of-control?

A very simple meaning of IoC is inverting the responsibility.

The major task of a Java developer is to create an object by setting the values of the data members. Now, instead of developers creating objects themselves, the developers get objects from the containers. Thus, the developers are inverting their responsibilities and letting the container create and manage an object.

Could you explain the working of the Spring IoC container?

The IoC container is responsible for instantiating a bean, managing the life cycle of a bean, and injecting its dependencies. Spring has **BeanFactory** and **ApplicationContext** as containers. **BeanFactory** provides the basic functionalities and configuration. **ApplicationContextInterface** is an extension of the **BeanFactory** interface.

ApplicationContext makes it easy to handle message resources for internationalization support, integration of AOP features, and publishing of events.

What is a bean, according to you?

This could also be asked as: *Could you explain what bean is, with reference to the Spring Framework?*

Bean is an object that is instantiated or managed by the container depending upon the configuration provided.

In the Spring Framework, a bean is created by the IoC container, and its entire lifecycle, such as initialization, Dependency Injection, and destruction, is handled by the container. Beans are typically defined using annotations (like `@Component`, `@Service`, `@Repository`, `@Controller`) or through XML/Java-based configuration.

You just mentioned the ApplicationContext interface. If it is an interface, do we need to provide its implementation?

Though there are different flavors of a question, the answer will remain the same.

The `ApplicationContext` interface is implemented by:

- **ClassPathXmlApplicationContext**: This class is used to load the bean configuration file from the class path.
- **FileSystemXmlApplicationContext**: This class is used to load the bean configuration file from the file system.
- **AnnotationConfigApplicationContext**: The class is used to create the Spring IoC container and the instantiation of beans from annotation-based configuration.

Ideally, the preceding answer is sufficient, but sometimes, if the interviewer finds you confident and having sound knowledge, they can go into further depth. In such a case, they might be interested in knowing the differentiation between console and web-based implementations, particularly in terms of configuration, deployment, request handling, and lifecycle management.

Note: **The preceding implemented classes discussed in the previous question play an important role in console-based applications. We also have Web implementations for Web applications. So, you might expect some questions on Web-based containers as well.**

Did you work with web-based containers? Can you explain web containers as well?

The following are some of the web-based containers provided by the Spring Framework:

- **XmlWebApplicationContext**: This class is used for containers used in web-based applications. It loads the XML file containing the bean definition from **`WEB-INF/applicationContext.xml`**.
- **AnnotationConfigWebApplicationContext**: The class facilitates an application context for the web-based application with annotation-based configuration for bean definitions.

Can you tell us an overall process to use ClassPathXmlApplicationContext?

We can define a bean configuration file in **`classpath`**. For example, the **`beans.xml`** file uses the **`<bean>`** tag.

Now, we can load this file using **`ClassPathXmlApplicationContext`** as follows:

```
ApplicationContext context = new ClassPathXmlApplicationContext(" beans.xml")
```

Further, using this context, we can get the beans from the containers as follows:

```
context.getBean("mybean")
```

Where **`mybean`** is an ID of one of the beans defined in the **`beans.xml`** file.

The following code snippet shows the contents of **`beans.xml`**:

```
<?xml version="1.0" encoding="UTF-8"?>
<beans xmlns="http://www.springframework.org/schema/beans"
    xmlns:xsi="http://www.w3.org/2001/XMLSchema-
    instance" xmlns:context="http://www.springframework.org/schema/context"
    xsi:schemaLocation="http://www.springframework.org/schema/beans
    http://www.springframework.org/schema/beans/spring-beans.xsd
    http://www.springframework.org/schema/context/
    http://www.springframework.org/schema/context/spring-context.xsd">
        <bean id="mybean"    class="com.beans.Employee"></bean>
</beans>
```

In this configuration file, a bean with the id **`"mybean"`** is defined for the class **`com.beans.Employee`**. The Spring IoC container will create an instance of this class and manage its lifecycle.

This XML-based configuration is one of the traditional ways of defining beans in the Spring Framework, although modern applications commonly use annotation-based or Java-based configuration.

Can we use a different file name for the bean configuration, or is it mandatory to use beans.xml as the file name?

We can use any valid name for the bean confirmation file. The only thing we need to do is to use the changed name while creating the container instance.

In the Spring Framework, the container (such as **`ClassPathXmlApplicationContext`**) loads the configuration file based on the name we provide. Therefore, the file name is not mandatory; it is simply a convention. What matters is that the correct file name and path are specified while initializing the container.

Is the location of the beans.xml file fixed? Can we change the location of the file?

The location of the file is the choice of the developer. While instantiating the container, we need to load the configuration file from the relevant location. If the file is in classpath or relative to classpath, we can use **`ClassPathXmlApplicationContext`**; if the file is not relevant to classpath, we can use **`FileSystemXmlApplicationContext`**.

Can we use more than one configuration file? Is it possible to distribute the beans in more than one configuration file in a single application?

Yes, we can use more than one configuration file to configure the beans. The files can then be loaded at the time of Spring container initialization.

In the Spring Framework, multiple XML configuration files can be passed while creating the container, and all bean definitions will be combined into a single **`ApplicationContext`**. This approach is useful in large applications where configuration can be modularized; for example, separating DAO, service, and controller bean definitions into different files for better maintainability and clarity.

What are the ways to get the container instantiation for more than one bean configuration file? How to load more than one bean configuration file while creating the container?

The following are the different ways to load beans from multiple configuration files in the Spring Framework:

- We can use the constructor of **ClassPathXmlApplicationContext** to load the XML files containing the configuration as follows:

  ```
  ApplicationContext context = new
   ClassPathXmlApplicationContext("beans.xml","beans1.xml","beans2.xml");
  ```

- We can write more than one file containing bean configuration, and then use the **<import>** tag to load the bean definitions from other files.

Note: **You might also face some questions on how to get the configured beans from XML. Be ready for such questions as well.**

Could you write a standard way of configuring bean in an XML file?

We can configure the bean either using the setter injection or the constructor injection, shown as follows:

- **For setter-based injection**:

  ```
  <bean id="valid_bean_id" class="fully_qualified_class_name">
          <property name="name_of_data_member"
                       value="value_of_the_data_member"/>
  </bean>
  ```

  In setter-based injection, the Spring container first creates the bean using the default constructor and then injects the dependencies using the corresponding setter methods. This approach provides flexibility, as dependencies can be modified or reconfigured easily and are not mandatory at the time of object creation.

- **For constructor-based configuration**:

```
<bean id="valid_bean_id" class="fully_qualified_class_name">
      <constructor-arg value="value_of_the_data_member"/>
</bean>
```

In constructor-based injection, the Spring container invokes the parameterized constructor instead of the default constructor of the bean and injects the required dependencies mentioned in the arguments of the constructor at the time of object creation. This ensures that all mandatory dependencies are provided and the bean is fully initialized before it is used. This approach is generally preferred when dependencies are required and should not be changed after the object is created. Though we can change such dependencies explicitly through programming, it is required.

What is the way to configure a bean having has-a-kind relation?

An interviewer might give a class definition as shown in the following code and ask you to configure it:

```
package com.pojo;
class Address{
      long pincode;
      String cityName;
     //getters and setters
}

class Publication{
     Address add;
     String publicationName;
     //default and parameterized constructor
}
```

Here, we need to define two beans as follows:

```
<bean id="add" class="com.pojo.Address">
  <property name="pincode" value="12345"/>
  <property name="cityName" value="city1"/>
<bean>

<bean id="obj" class="com.pojo.Publication">
  <constructor-arg ref="add"/>
<bean>
```

When we are using a *has-a-kind* of relationship, we need to use the *ref* attribute in the configuration file. In the preceding snippet, we have used `<constructor-arg ref=" ">` instead of `<constructor-arg value=" ">`.

You just mentioned a couple of bean configurations; how many instances will the container create for such a bean configuration?

The same question can be reframed as: *When you define a bean configuration, how many instances does a container create?*

Spring by default supports singleton scope of beans, which means bean will be instantiated only once by Spring. The Spring container merely returns the same instance again and again for multiple requests for that bean.

Simply put, only one object is created for one bean configured in XML.

Does that mean the developer gets only one instance to work with from the container?

This question can be reframed in different ways as:

- *Is there a possibility of getting more than one instance from the same bean configuration?*
- *What is the scope of a bean?*
- *What are the scopes available in Spring?*

The scope of a bean defines how many instances of a bean configuration to create or how long a bean instance will live.

The following five scopes are provided by the Spring Framework:

- **singleton**: The Spring IoC container creates only one instance for the configured bean. This is the default scope of a bean.
- **prototype**: The Spring IoC container creates a new instance for every new request made.
- **request**: The Spring IoC container creates a new instance for every new HTTP request made. The request scope is valid only when the context is web-aware.
- **session**: The Spring IoC container creates a new instance for a new creation of *HttpSession*. The session scope is valid only when the context is web-aware.
- **application**: The application scopes a single bean definition to the life cycle of a *ServletContext*. The scope is valid only when the context is web-aware.

- **websocket**: The application scopes a single bean definition to the life cycle of a *WebSocket*. This scope is also valid only when the context is web-aware.

What is the default scope of a bean?

The default scope of bean is *singleton*. In the Spring Framework, a *singleton* bean means that only one instance of the bean is created per IoC container, and the same instance is shared wherever it is injected or requested. This helps in managing shared resources efficiently.

You just said beans are by default singleton. Can we change the default singleton scope?

This question can be reframed with two types of questions by the interviewer in the following ways as well:

- *How to change the scope of a bean?*
- *How to configure the scope of a bean?*

Yes, we can change the scope by modifying the configuration, as shown in the following code:

```
<bean id="add" class="com.pojo.Address" scope="prototype">
      <property name="pincode" value="12345"/>
      <property name="city_name" value="city1"/>
<bean>
```

Instead of *prototype,* we can specify *singleton, request, session,* or *global-session.*

Is it possible to define the bean scopes using annotations?

Yes, it is. We can define the request scope using annotation-driven components by using **`@RequestScope`**, session scope with **`@SessionScope`,** and application scope by **`@ApplicationScope`**.

Is it possible to create user-defined scopes?

Yes, a developer can develop a new scope, which is termed as *custom* scope.

Note: If you are aware of how to create it, you can explain how to create custom scope. Go for it only when you know the process and you are not explaining just to impress the panel. They are only making sure you are aware of the framework features. Being smart is perfectly fine, but do not try to be extra-smart, that too when you have limited knowledge.

To define a *custom* scope, we need to implement the **`org.springframework.beans.factory.config.Scope`** interface and override the following methods:

- **`Object get(String name, ObjectFactoryobjectFactory)`**
- **`Object remove(String name)`**
- **`void registerDestructionCallback(String name, Runnable destructionCallback)`**
- **`String getConversationId()`**

When does the instantiation process take place by the container? Is the bean initialized eagerly or lazily?

By default, the Spring container (**`ApplicationContext`** implementation) eagerly creates the instance for each one of the configured beans.

This means that all singleton beans are instantiated at the time the container is initialized, not when they are first requested. The purpose of eager initialization is to detect configuration or dependency errors at startup itself.

However, lazy initialization can be enabled using the *lazy-init* attribute in XML configuration or the **`@Lazy`** annotation in the Spring Framework, so that the bean is created only when it is actually needed.

Is it possible to change the default mechanism of bean instantiation?

This question can be reframed differently as follows:

- *Can we instruct the container for lazy initialization?*
- *How is the lazy initialization configured?*

The default mechanism of eager initialization can be changed by configuring the **`lazy-init`** attribute in XML configuration. The configuration can be written as follows:

```
<bean id="valid_bean_id" class="fully_qualified_class_name"
        lazy-init="true">
<property name="name_of_data_member" value="value_of_the_data_member"/>
<bean>
```

When **lazy-init="true"** is specified, the bean will not be instantiated during container startup. Instead, it will be created only when it is requested for the first time.

This approach can improve startup performance, especially in large applications where certain beans are rarely used. In the Spring Framework, lazy initialization can also be applied globally at the container level or locally at the individual bean level.

Can a bean be initialized lazily? Is it possible to control lazy initialization at the controller layer?

Yes, it is possible to initialize beans lazily at the container level. The code shown in the previous question shows how to configure the bean so that it can be initialized lazily.

In your opinion, which initialization is desired, eager or lazy, and why?

The errors in the configuration or problems in environment can be discovered immediately at the time of XML configuration instead of discovering the issues in the later phase. Under the situation when it is not desired to create an instance eagerly, we can configure the attribute **lazy-init=true** to create the instance when asked.

What is auto-wiring? Can we use auto-wiring for primary dependencies?

Usually, while defining the bean configuration, we need to mention all the dependencies of the bean explicitly. **Auto-wiring** facilitates us to inject the object dependencies explicitly automatically.

Auto-wiring is used for a *has-a-kind* relation where one object needs to be injected in another. It is not applicable to primary dependencies of an object of type **int**, **float**, **long,** and so on as well as dependencies of type String.

What are the types of auto-wiring, and how to configure them?

Different types of auto-wiring are:

- **no**: The default mode of auto-wiring is **`no`**. It means the developer needs to mention a way to inject the required object dependencies implicitly.
- **byName**: The **`byName`** auto-wiring mode facilitates the injection of the missing object depending upon the name of data member.
- **byType**: The **`byType`** auto-wiring mode facilitates the injection of the missing object depending upon the type of data member.
- **constructor**: The **`constructor`** auto-wiring mode injects the dependency by invoking the parameterized constructor of that class.

Could you explain the bean life cycle?

The interviewer might ask the following questions on the similar concepts:

- *What are the callback methods in bean life cycle?*
- *Is it possible to customize the nature of bean?*

Yes, certain callbacks can be used to customize the bean nature. The following figure shows the life cycle of bean:

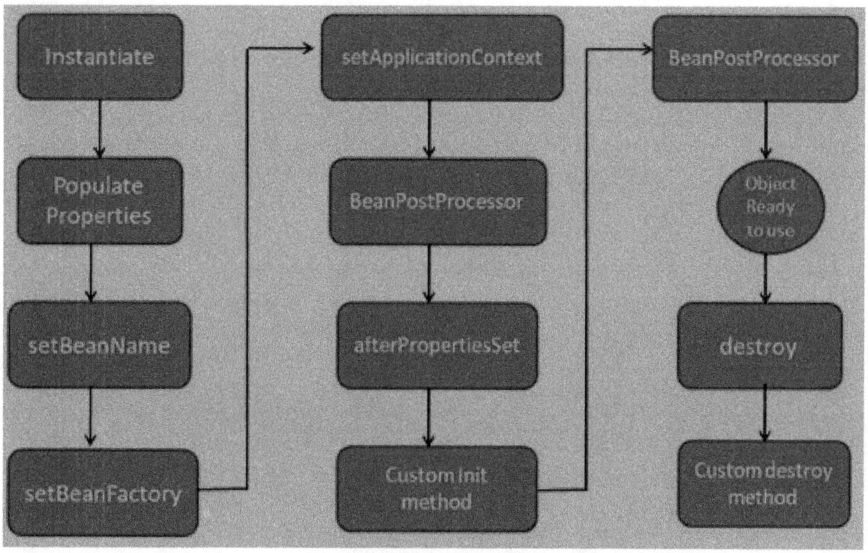

***Figure 12.2**: Spring life cycle*

Is it possible to set a mechanism to modify the bean properties after its instantiation?

This question can take multiple forms as follows:

- *What is the use of init-method attribute?*

- *When can we use the InitializingBean interface?*
- *What is the use of InitializingBean?*

After instantiation, if we need to modify the properties of the bean, we can use the **`init`** method.

There are different ways to achieve this:

- Declare a **`public void`** method with **`no`** arguments in the class and use the attribute **`init-method=method_name`**.
- We can implement the **`InitializingBean`** interface in the class and override the **`afterPropertiesSet`** method to modify the properties of the bean.
- Alternatively, we can write a generic method and annotate it with **`@PostConstruct`**.

Using init-method as an attribute and implementing InitializingBean interface are two ways for modifying the bean properties after instantiation. Which one is preferable?

We should not categorize these approaches as good or bad; instead, it is better to consider certain scenarios that help in deciding which one to choose. A key advantage of implementing the interface is that there is no need to explicitly specify the method to be invoked by the container after the bean's instantiation.

At the same time, if we are configuring the bean using XML, then we can use **`init-method`**. The configuration file can be changed at any moment. So, it is a good choice if we do not wish to prefer tightly coupled classes.

Can we have custom cleanup methods?

This question can be reframed in different ways as:

- *Is it possible to write a method that will release resources before destroying the bean?*
- *What is the use of destroy-method attribute? Why use the DisposableBean interface?*
- *Can you suggest an elegant way to provide a cleanup mechanism?*

Yes, we can have a custom cleanup mechanism.

This cleanup method allows a developer to provide a way to close all the open resources or to perform some back steps before the container containing the bean is destroyed.

There are three ways by which the cleanup mechanism can be provided:

- In a class, provide a void no-argument cleanup method and configure **destroy-method=method_name** for the bean configuration in XML.
- The second way to achieve this is by implementing the **DisposableBean** interface by a class and overriding the destroy method to provide the cleanup mechanism.
- Alternatively, we can also write a general method and annotate it by **@PreDestroy**

Providing each time init-method or destroy-method in every individual bean configuration is repetitive as well as time-consuming. Can we have an alternative way to provide a default initialization or a destroy method?

Yes, configuring each bean for initializing and destroy method is repetitive. To avoid this, we can add the same methods in every class, which will represent the **init()** and **destroy()** methods. Instead of specifying these methods for every bean, the **default-init-method** and **default-destroy-method** attributes can be configured at the **<beans>** level. By providing the method names in these attributes, the container automatically applies them to all eligible beans, resulting in cleaner configuration and improved maintainability.

What is the purpose of ApplicationContextAware, BeanFactoryAware, or BeanNameAware interfaces in the Spring Framework?

Sometimes, beans need to access the **ApplicationContext** to look up some other beans. **ApplicationContextAware**, **BeanFactoryAware** enables the bean to obtain the reference to the container and access its managed resources.

Sometimes, the beans expect that the **BeanFactory** should be aware of their assigned name in the container. In such a case, the class can implement **BeanNameAware**.

What is the parent attribute in the bean configuration used for?

This question can be reframed as:

- *Why use the parent attribute?*
- *Explain the use of the parent attribute.*

Spring always supports a reduction in boilerplate code. And, it is applicable even to an XML configuration. Suppose we have two bean definitions whose properties are the same, along with their values. Instead of repeating the same configuration, we can reuse it in another by providing the **parent** attribute. We can either use all the property values from the parent or, at the same time, override values for a couple of properties.

The best part is that the child bean definition inherits scope, method overrides from the parent, constructor argument values, along with property values, and the option to add new values is still open.

XML and annotation-based are two different ways of configuration; which one do you prefer?

Both of these approaches have their pros and cons. It depends on the situation/scenario to decide which one is better and which is not.

An XML-based configuration is decoupled from the source code. So, we can modify the configuration without modifying the source code.

When we use annotation-based configuration, it provides a context in the declaration. No extra configuration file needs to be maintained. Annotation-based configuration is more concise.

One more aspect to consider is that XML enables placing the configuration at a centralized location. It means controlling the changes becomes easier. However, when we use annotations for the configuration, they are distributed all over the code, and then to control such a decentralized configuration.

Are the annotations by default enabled?

Or the interviewer might ask: *How to enable annotation-based configurations?*

When we consider an XML-based configuration, annotations are disabled by default. When we intend to enable annotations, we need to configure **<context:annotation-config>** or **<context:component-scan>** on top of our XML file.

Both <context:annotation-config> and <context:component-scan>, which are written on the top of our XML file, activate annotation-based configurations. Are they the same or different?

The **<context:annotation-config>** annotation is mainly used to enable the annotations for Dependency Injections. The configuration activates the annotations for the beans that are already registered in the application context.

The configuration **`<context:component-scan>`** scans the packages to automatically detect the annotations from the classes. This eliminates the need for explicit bean declaration in the configuration.

Which annotation activates package scanning for annotation?

This can also be asked as: *What is achieved by applying the @ComponantScan annotation?*

`@ComponantScan` allows scanning of packages for the classes and interfaces for the annotations applied for stereotype and auto-wiring. It automatically registers detected classes such as **`@Component`**, **`@Service`**, **`@Repository`**, and **`@Controller`** as Spring beans in the application context. This reduces manual configuration and promotes a convention-over-configuration approach.

What is stereotype annotation?

Stereotype annotations, when applied to a class, mark the class as Spring-managed component. Additionally, because of this, the class registers the application context as a bean during the component scan. As the class is registered in the context, it is now available for Dependency Injection in the other classes.

What are the stereotype annotations?

The following are the different stereotype annotations present in the Spring Framework:

- **@Component**: This is a generic annotation that can be applied to any Spring-managed component.
- **@Service**: This annotation is applied to the classes that perform some business logic or API invocations to perform some functionalities.
- **@Controller**: This annotation is applied to the classes that are responsible for handling HTTP requests and responses.
- **@Repository**: The **`@Repository`** annotation is applied to the classes that are involved in database communication.

Could you explain @Configuration annotation?

The **`@Configuration`** is a class-level annotation. When a class is applied with **`@Configuration`**, it indicates that a class is used by the Spring container as the source for bean definitions.

What is the @Bean annotation?

The **@Bean** annotation is applied to the methods. The annotation indicates that the bean returned from this method is registered with the Spring context.

It is typically used within **@Configuration** classes to explicitly define and configure beans. Unlike stereotype annotations, which rely on component scanning, **@Bean** provides fine-grained control over the instantiation, configuration, and lifecycle of the bean.

Why use @Autowired annotation?

This annotation is used for auto-wiring of the dependencies. **@Autowired** can be used on data member, constructor, or setter functionality. It allows the Spring container to resolve and inject collaborating objects automatically, reducing the need for explicit configuration in XML or manual object creation.

When should you use the @Qualifier annotation?

The **@Autowired** annotation, when applied to the dependency, usually indicates auto-wiring by type. **@Qualifier** is applied when the property name needs to be used for discovering the missing property for injection (This is similar to **autowire=byName**).

What does the @Required annotation signify?

@Required is a method-level annotation. When it is applied to a setter method, it indicates that the property must be injected into the bean at the time of configuration.

However, it is important to note that **@Required** has been deprecated since Spring 5.1 and is no longer recommended for use. In modern Spring applications, constructor-based Dependency Injection is preferred to enforce mandatory dependencies at the time of object creation.

Are @Autowired and @Required the same? Which one is recommended to use?

@Autowired and **@Required** annotations play different roles in a Spring-based application:

- **@Autowired** is used to denote the auto-wiring of the dependencies. However, **@ Required** is useful to check whether the property has been set or not.
- **@Autowired** can be applied to data members, constructors, or setter functionality, but **@Required** is applied to setter methods.
- When **@Autowired** is applied to a dependency, it indicates the injection of the property. If the dependency is not discovered or available, then exception will be thrown.

Under the uncertain situation when it is not must to inject the bean, we can configure `@Autowired(required=false)` to overlook the default behavior of injection.

When should you use the @Scope annotation?

By default, beans configured in spring are singleton by scope. When the developers intend to change the default scope, the class is applied with the annotation as `@Scope("prototype")`.

Spring MVC framework

The Spring MVC framework can be explained with the help of *Figure 12.3*:

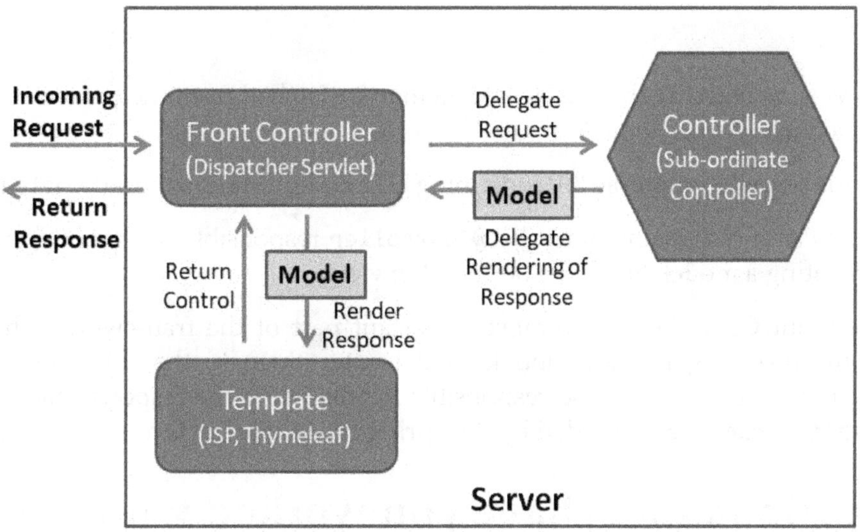

***Figure 12.3**: Spring MVC framework*

Spring MVC is designed around the Front Controller MVC design pattern. Each time a request is made, it is attended to by the Front Controller. Depending upon the request pattern, the request is delegated to the respective controllers. The controller is responsible for reading the data from the incoming request and then performing logic on it. Once the logical part is done, it is time to communicate the response to the user. The data that the controller sends to the user is bound to a *Model* object. This *Model* object will now be bound in the view template by the Front Controller. This response, containing a template with data, is returned to the user.

Can you explain some features of the Spring MVC framework?

The following are some of the key features of the Spring MVC framework:

- It is designed around the Front Controller MVC design pattern.

- It supports clear separation of the roles with Controllers, Validators, Model and View objects.
- Easy binding and validation of the data.
- Provides JSTL tags for easy binding of the data

Could you explain the components of the Spring MVC design pattern?

Spring MVC is designed around the Front Controller MVC design pattern. MVC stands for *Model, View, and Controller*.

Here:

- *Model* is an object with data. This data may be fetched from the database or an object created using some logic.
- *View* is played by a simple JSP containing JSTL code; it can also be a `Thymeleaf` template.
- *Controller* is a class annotated by **`@Controller`** responsible for handling request and generating a model which the bounded in view.

  The Front Controller is the most important part of the framework, which attends all the incoming requests and then delegates them to the subsequent controller. The Front Controller is also responsible for returning the response back to the user. `DispatcherServlet` provided by the Spring Framework acts as the Front Controller.

Which annotations have you worked with while dealing with the Spring MVC framework?

Different annotations that are present in the Spring MVC framework are as follows:

- **@Controller**: The class that handles an Http request and response is annotated with `@Controller`.
- **@RequestMapping:** This annotation is used to map web requests onto specific handler classes and / or handler methods where some logic is performed so as to generate some data that can be returned as a response.
- **@Valid**: This annotation is applied to an input parameter whose validation needs to be performed.
- **@ModelAttribute**: This annotation is applied to a method parameter or the returned value from a method. The annotated parameter is then exposed to the web view.

How does the Front Controller delegate the request to the controller?

The Front Controller is mapped in **web.xml** or **Deployment Descriptor** (**DD**) with the **<servlet>** tag. The mapping to discover the controllers to dispatch the request is available in the **WEB-INF/servlet_name-servlet.xml** file.

Note: **Try to hold yourself from giving more information on mapping. Do not go ahead with mapping.**

You just said that request mapping is available in WEB-INF/servlet_name-servlet.xml file. Is this location mandatory, or can the file name and its location be customized?

By default, the **WEB-INF/servlet_name-servlet.xml** file is the location. However, it is possible to change the location or even the name of the file. We can configure the **init** parameter to the **<servlet>** tag in DD to change the location as:

```
<init-param>
    <param-name>contextConfigLocation</param-name>
    <param-value>
        /WEB-INF/sub_folder_name/file_name_with_extension
    </param-value>
</init-param>
```

By specifying this parameter, the Spring container loads the configuration file from the provided path instead of the default location, offering greater flexibility in organizing application configuration files.

What is the purpose of the <load-on-startup> element in web.xml file and what does specifying <load-on-startup>1</load-on-startup> indicate?

The tag **<load-on-startup>** in DD specifies whether the servlet will be loaded at the project deployment time or server start. The container loads the servlets in ascending order of the integer values, which are declared within the **<load-on-startup>** tag. If we do not specify this tag, then the servlets will be loaded on demand.

Specifying **<load-on-startup>1</load-on-startup>** indicates that the servlet will be loaded and initialized when the server starts or the application is deployed, rather than waiting for the first client request.

The value 1 represents the loading priority. Since servlets are loaded in ascending order of the integer value, a value of 1 means the servlet has a high priority and will be loaded before servlets with higher values, like 2, 3, and so on.

What types of beans are typically defined and managed within WebApplicationContext in Spring-based web application?

The following beans are present in **WebApplicationContext**:

- **HandlerMapping**: This bean is responsible for mapping the incoming request to the respective handlers.
- **ViewResolver**: This bean helps in resolving the local name to the actual view file name. **ViewResolver** defines the prefix and postfix attributes, which can be applied to the local file name, based on which the actual view file is located by the framework.

What is the use of a message resource bundle?

ResourceBundleMessageSource helps in resolving the messages from the properties file. This implements **MessageSource** and uses **ResourceBundle**. One of the main uses of **ResourceBundleMessage** is to store the messages that can be used in the process of internationalization.

What are the ways of providing validation, and why do we need it?

Interaction with a user is what software is meant for. The user interacts with software by providing some inputs, based on which the software generates some output. Yet whenever a user inputs some data, there is a potential chance of irrelevant or incorrect data being entered by the user. For example, let us say the application expects to enter the email address from a user, and the user does not provide an email address in a proper format, or imagine you ask a user to enter age and the user enters a value less than 0 or greater than 100. In these cases, the business logic that is written (assuming the user is smart) will fail. So, there has to be a way to ensure the correctness of the user's data. The process to ensure this correctness is validation.

Validation can be done at the client or server side. Client-side validation can be done using JavaScript. Spring provides **Validators** to perform server-side validations.

To work with custom validators, we need to write a class implementing **Validator** and override the **support** and **validate** methods. The **support** method checks if the object that is to be validated is of the expected type or not. The **validate** method has the logic to apply validation rules. To perform such validation, **validator** has to be registered to the container as a bean.

Writing a custom validator is one of the ways to perform validation. Another way to perform validation is to use Hibernate validators. We can apply **@NotNull, @Min, @Max, @Size** annotations to the POJO data members. Now, we can use **@Valid** annotation on the argument of the request handler method of the controller that we intend to validate.

Aspect-oriented programming

Aspect-oriented programming (AOP) to write cross-cutting concerns and facilitates getting rid of code duplication. Cross-cutting concerns, such as logging, transaction management, security, and exception handling, typically span multiple modules and can lead to code duplication if implemented directly within each component.

By using AOP, these concerns are modularized into separate units termed *aspects*, promoting better code organization, improved maintainability, and reduced duplication.

Under which circumstances will you prefer AOP?

The most important responsibility of the developer is to provide a confined solution to the client, which should solve a certain issue or problem. Along with developing the solution, the developer also needs to think about and implement the exception handling, transaction management, and logging. These concerns are distributed through all the layers of the application and lead to duplication of the code. AOP allows us to write the code in one place for such concerns, and according to the pointcut, it can be applied to the JoinPoint.

Could you explain the terminologies used in AOP?

AOP consists of different terminologies, such as:

- **Aspects**: Aspect is a component containing cross-cutting concerns such as transaction management or logging.
- **JoinPoint**: A point in the application where the aspect can be applied.
- **Advice**: Advice is the action to be taken on a particular JoinPoint.
- **Pointcut**: An expression that allows selection of the JoinPoint where the advice is to be applied.

- **Target object**: The object on which the advice is going to be applied is a target object.
- **Weaving**: It is the process of linking aspects with other application objects to create an advised object.

What is an advice, and what types of advice are available?

Advice is the action to be taken on a particular *JoinPoint*.

Types of advice are:

- **Before advice**: Advice that executes before the join point.
- **After advice**: Advice that executes after the join point.
- **After returning advice**: Advice that executes after the join point completes normally.
- **After throwing advice**: Advice that executes after the method throws an exception.
- **Around advice**: The advice executes before and after the join point.

Which types of weaving are supported by Spring AOP?

Weaving can be done at Compile-time, Load-time, or Runtime. Spring AOP supports only runtime weaving.

Could you explain how to write the pointcut expression using a couple of examples?

The following expressions can be written to weave **PointCuts**:

- **Any public method: `execution(public * *(..))`**
- **Any method with a name beginning with "set": `execution(* set*(..))`**
- **Any method with a name beginning with "get": `execution(* get*(..))`**
- **Any method defined by the MyService interface:**
  `execution(* com.service.MyService.*(..))`
- **Any method defined in the dao package or a sub-package:**
  `execution(* com.dao..*.*(..))`
- **Any JoinPoint within the dao package: `within(com.dao.*)`**
- **Any JoinPoint within the dao package or a sub-package: `within(com.dao..*)`**

- **Any JoinPoint where the proxy implements the MyService interface**:
  `this(com.xyz.service.AccountService)`

Can you write Pointcut expression to track all the methods from the package com.dao?

We can write the Pointcut expressions such as:

- `@Pointcut("execution(public * *(..))")` is used for tracking all the join points from all the methods from all the packages.
- `@Pointcut("within(com.dao.MyClass.*(..)")` is used for tracking join points for all the methods from the `class com.dao.MyClass`.
- `@Pointcut("within(com.dao.*.*(..)")` expression to track all the methods from the `package com.dao`.

Could you explain the Pointcut designators you have used, or explain the Pointcut designators you know?

The different pointcut designators are as follows:

- **execution**: The execution designator is used for matching method execution Join Points.
- **within**: To limit matching to `JoinPoints` within certain types such as packages, the within designator is used.
- **this**: It is used to limit matching to `JoinPoints` where the bean reference is an instance of the given type.
- **target**: The target designator is used to limit matching to `JoinPoints` where the target object is an instance of the given type.
- **@target**: The `@target` annotation limits matching to `JoinPoints` where the class of the executing object has an annotation of the given type.
- **@args**: The annotation limits matching to `JoinPoints` where the runtime type of the actual arguments passed has annotations of the given type.
- **@within**: The designator limits matching to `JoinPoints` within types that have the `@within` annotation.
- **@annotation**: This annotation is used to limit matching to `JoinPoints` where the subject of the `JoinPoint` has the given annotation.

Can you explain Around advice?

This question can also be re-framed as:

- *In what ways does Around advice differ from other advices?*
- *When can we use Around advice?*

Around advice runs at the matched Pointcut. It enables performing the work both before and after the method execution. It also allows us to determine when and how the method actually gets executed. It is said to be powerful whenever we need to share the state. The Around advice is often used whenever we need to share the state before the method execution and then after the method execution. For example, it can be used to calculate the time taken to complete the method execution.

Spring Boot Framework

Spring Boot is an extension of the Spring Framework that simplifies the development of production-ready applications. It provides auto-configuration, starter dependencies, and embedded servers to reduce manual setup and configuration. Spring Boot follows the convention-over-configuration approach, enabling developers to quickly build stand-alone, microservices-based applications. It also offers features such as Actuator for monitoring and easy integration with external systems and cloud platforms.

Did you work with Spring Boot projects? Which starters have you worked with?

The following are the available Spring Boot starters:

- `spring-boot-starter`
- `spring-boot-starter-web`
- `spring-boot-starter-jdbc`
- `spring-boot-starter-data-jpa`
- `spring-boot-starter-hateoas`
- `spring-boot-starter-security`
- `spring-boot-starter-data-rest`

Note: If you did not work with all of them, then do not worry. You can list all the starters and then let the interviewer know that, though you know the list, you have worked with only a couple of them.

There are many ways to create Spring Boot applications. Can you tell us the ways of creating a Spring Boot project?

The Spring Boot application can be created using the following approaches:

- **Spring Initializer**: A web-based tool that generates a ready-to-use Spring Boot project with the required dependencies and build configuration.
- **Spring Boot CLI**: A command-line interface that allows developers to quickly create and run Spring Boot applications using Groovy scripts or Java code.
- **Spring Tool Suites**: An IDE based on Eclipse that provides built-in support for creating, developing, and running Spring Boot applications.

How does Spring Boot's auto-configuration mechanism work internally?

When we execute any Spring Boot application, the following steps are followed internally by the framework:

- The class with **`@SpringBootApplication`** executes. This annotation internally includes **`@Configuraton`**, **`@EnableAutoConfiguration`**, and **`@ComponentScan`**.
- **`@EnableAutoConfiguration`** loads the auto-configuration classes.
- **`@ComponentScans`** the packages and loads the beans which are annotated with **`@ Component`**, **`@Service`**, and **`@RestController`**, etc. These beans get registered with the container.
- The methods from the controller are executed only when the client sends the HTTP Request.

Which annotations have you worked on for creating REST applications?

This question can be reframed as:

- *Can you explain the couple of annotations used in REST applications?*
- *Explain annotations used for REST application development?*

Different annotations that are used in REST applications are:

- **@RestController**: It provides a convenient way to declare a class responsible for creating REST web services. The annotation is introduced in 4.0, which combines **`@Controller`** and **`@ResponseBody`**.
- **@RequestMapping**: **`@RequestMapping`** is a very commonly used annotation. It allows mapping HTTP requests to handler methods of REST controllers.
- **@GetMapping**: The annotation enables mapping HTTP GET requests to specific handler methods. It is a shortcut for **`@RequestMapping(method = RequestMethod.GET)`**.
- **`@PostMapping`**, **`@PutMapping`**, **`@DeleteMapping`**, and **`@PatchMapping`** are the annotations introduced for mapping method handlers for POST, PUT, DELETE, and PATCH methods.
- **@ResponseBody**: The **`@ResponseBody`** annotation tells a controller that the object returned is automatically serialized into JSON and passed back into the response object.

What is the use of @PathVariable annotation in Spring Boot application?

This annotation is used to extract the values from the URI path and pass them as method parameters in the controller method.

The following code snippet shows the usage of the **`@PathVariable`** annotation:

```
@GetMapping("/users/{id}")
 public User getUserById(@PathVariable("id") Long userId) {
    // userId will be populated from the URL
    return userService.findById(userId);
}
```

This code defines a REST endpoint **`/users/{id}`** that handles **`HTTP GET`** requests. The **`@PathVariable("id")`** annotation extracts the **`{id}`** value from the URL and passes it to the method as **userId**, which is then used to fetch and return the corresponding User from **userService**.

Can you explain the @PutMapping and @PatchMapping annotations?

This can also be reframed as: *Can you explain when to use the PUT and PATCH methods?*

We can create different methods that will represent the **PUT** and **PATCH** methods. Furthermore, we can apply **@PutMapping** and **@PatchMapping** on those methods, respectively. The scenarios in which we can apply **@PutMapping** and **@PatchMapping** are as follows:

- Whenever we have a resource and a client needs to replace the existing resource entirely, it is feasible to use the **PUT** method.
- Whenever we have a resource and a client needs to replace the existing resource partially, it is feasible to use the **PATCH** method.

Which annotations are used to map handler methods?

Different annotations that can be used to map handler methods are as follows:

- The **@GetMapping** annotation enables mapping **HTTP GET** requests to specific handler methods. It is a shortcut for **@RequestMapping(method = RequestMethod.GET)**.
- **@PostMapping**, **@PutMapping**, **@DeleteMapping**, and **@PatchMapping** are the annotations introduced for mapping method handlers for **POST**, **PUT**, **DELETE**, and **PATCH** methods.

What are runners in Spring Boot?

Runner is an interface that facilitates the execution of the code after the application starts. Spring Boot provides **ApplicationRunner** and **CommandLineRunner**.

CommandLineRunner is an interface. It is used to indicate that a bean should run when it is contained within a **SpringApplication**. It allows the creation of standalone applications. **ApplicationRunner** is similar to **CommandLineRunner** but provides arguments as an **ApplicationArguments** object instead of a simple string array, making it easier to work with structured and option-based arguments.

How can you read the input from a request in Spring Boot application?

We can read the input from the request by using annotations like:

- **@RequestParam:** This annotation is used to read the data from the request, such as form data, and then bind it automatically to the method argument.
- **@RequestBody:** This annotation maps the request body to *Transfer Domain Object* to the method argument of a type.

What is the difference between @RequestParam and @QueryParam annotations?

Both of these annotations are used to read request parameters.

`@QueryParam` is an annotation provided by the JAX-RS framework used to bind query parameters from URL to method parameters in RESTful web services. On the other hand, `@RequestParam` is an annotation from the Spring Framework and is commonly used in Spring MVC and Spring Boot applications to bind the query parameters, form data, or request parameters to method arguments in controller classes.

Did you work with Spring Boot's internal database?

The answer to this question will be followed by different questions like:

- *How to configure H2 database?*
- *Is it good to use H2 database?*
- *When and how to use H2 database?*

H2 is an in-memory database written in Java. It can be embedded in Java applications. Spring Boot supports integration of H2 in the Spring Boot application.

To configure H2 in Spring Boot, we need to add the H2 dependency in the **`pom.xml`** file and then configure database properties in the **`application.properties`** file. Now, configure, **`spring.h2.console.enabled=true`** and **`spring.h2.console.path=/h2`** in the properties file. Sometimes, installing a database on a system is not possible or not feasible. Then, we can use an internal database for testing the code without having to worry about installing and managing a dedicated database server upfront.

When H2 is going to be used for production as well, using H2 is a better choice. However, when we are using a different database in production, testing code against H2 is a bad choice.

How do you configure Spring Boot application?

Configuring a Spring Boot application means defining how the application behaves, such as database settings, server port, logging level, profiles, security, etc. The following are the different ways to configure the Spring Boot application:

- Using **`application.properties`** or **`application.yml`**
- Using environment variables
- Using command-line arguments
- Using **`@ConfigurationProperties`**
- Using **`@Value annotation`**

What are the different Spring Boot profiles?

The most common Spring Boot profiles are as follows:

- **`dev`**
- **`test`**
- **`prod`**

We can define profile-specific files as:

- **`application-dev.properties`**
- **`application-test.properties`**
- **`application-prod.properties`**

We can activate the desired profile by setting the property in the **`application.properties`** file as **`"spring.profiles.active=dev"`**.

We can replace dev with test or prod to activate the **test** profile or the **prod** profile, respectively.

How to execute database schemas to create a table or insert records into a table?

Spring Boot allows an easy way to create a table and manipulate data in it. To do this, you can create **`.sql`** files containing DML or DDL statements to execute. You have to create this file in the directory **`/src/main/resources/`**.

The file will be loaded at startup and executed to create a table or insert records in it according to SQL statements written within it.

What is the use of RestTemplate? How to use RestTemplate?

`RestTemplate` is used for consuming REST applications. **`RestTemplate`** provides different methods for web communication, which are as follows:

- **exchange()**: This method executes a specified **`HTTP`** method as **`GET`** or **`POST`**, and it returns **`ResponseEntity`**. **`ResponseEntity`** can contain the **`HTTP`** status code, the resource as an object, or both.

- **execute()**: This method expects **RequestCallback** and a **ResultSetExtractor** as parameters. It facilitates the creation of complex requests or may process complex responses.
- **getForEntity()**: This method executes a **GET** request and returns **ResponseEntity** containing the status code and the resource as an object. It provides access to additional response details such as **HTTP** headers, status code, and the response body, offering more control compared to **getForObject()**.
- **getForObject()**: This method executes a **GET** request and returns the resource directly. It automatically converts the HTTP response body into the specified Java type using configured message converters.

Note: **Though this answer is enough, you can add an extra spoon of sugar by adding that same as getForEntity() and getForObject() for GET, we have counterpart methods for POST and PUT.**

What is HATEAOS?

HATEAOS is an acronym for *Hypertext As the Engine of Application State.*

Usually, in HTML pages, we can place a hyperlink to browse or link between two resources. In a web service, response linking to two resources is provided by **HATEAOS**. It facilitates creating links between two resources to retrieve relevant information. It enables creating links for model classes for link and resource representation models. It supports the APIs for link builders to create links that point to the methods declared in Spring MVC controllers.

How to provide HATEAOS support in an application?

To enable **HATEAOS**, we have to follow different steps:

- Add a dependency for **HATEAOS** in the **pom.xml** file.
- Create a POJO class extended by **RepresentationModel**.
- In the controller, create the links between resources by using the **linkTo()** method of **WebMvcLinkBuilder**.

What are the default security configurations in Spring Boot?

The following are the default security configurations of Spring Boot:

- Basic authentication is enabled (requires username and password).
- A default username is **`user`**, and a random password is generated (this can be modified in the **`application.properties`**).
- All endpoints are secured by default.
- Form Login is disabled.
- HttpSession is created when required.

How does Spring Boot manage transactions using @ Transactional?

In Spring Boot, transactions are managed declaratively using the **`@Transactional`** annotation, which works through Spring's AOP proxy mechanism. When a method annotated with **`@Transactional`** is invoked, Spring creates a proxy around the target bean that intercepts the method invocation, starts a transaction using a **`PlatformTransactionManager`** (such as **`JpaTransactionManager`**), executes the method, and then commits the transaction if it completes successfully or rolls it back if a **`RuntimeException`** or **`Error`** occurs.

What is Swagger, and why use it?

In REST applications, there are many handler methods mapped for different request parameters and response types. It is important to properly communicate the REST API documentation to the client. **Swagger2** is an open-source project that is used to generate the REST API documentation. It also provides a user interface to access our RESTful Web services via a web browser.

Finally, this interesting journey had reached its destination. The Spring Framework is huge in size, and covering the features in a single chapter is difficult. Despite that, we have covered almost every concept that may be required to answer the questions based on Spring and Spring Boot.

Conclusion

In this chapter, we explored the entire Spring Framework. We discussed the different components of the Spring Framework and what interview questions could be asked about those components. We also discussed the different questions on how Spring is useful in application development and how we can customize the behavior of an application using XML files and annotations.

We also talked about how Spring Boot helps to create a REST-based web application, which is becoming the need of the current era of software development.

In the next chapter, we will be expanding our knowledge to understand another interesting framework, Hibernate. We will also discuss how interviewers typically evaluate a candidate's understanding and practical skills related to Hibernate.

CHAPTER 13
Hibernate

Introduction

Storing data in a database is one of the most important aspects of application development. Whatever the type of application, we need to store the data permanently. In our earlier chapter on *JDBC*, we saw how to store the data in the database using the *JDBC API*. You are also well aware that writing the *JDBC* code is not easy. Often, the developers get frustrated by writing boilerplate code to implement different interfaces that are part of *JDBC API*. The *Hibernate* framework is for rescue. It provides a simplified way to persist the data in the database. *Hibernate* uses a Java object to represent data, which is mapped to a table where it can be persisted. This approach of storing objects in a database is termed **Object-Relational Mapping** (**ORM**), and *Hibernate* is one of the implementations of it. *Hibernate* makes the job of a developer way simpler by providing configuration to achieve object persistency. We can configure *Hibernate* by using configuration files, and we can also make use of different annotations provided by the *Hibernate API*.

Structure

We will be covering interview questions based on the following topics in this chapter:

- Object-Relational Mapping
- Architecture of Hibernate
- Hibernate Query Language

Objectives

At the end of this chapter, you will be able to understand the automotive approach of persistency, *Hibernate*. You will be able to work with different configuration settings of *Hibernate* and also annotations that are used in this framework. Along with this, we will also discuss different interview questions based on the *Hibernate* framework.

Object-Relational Mapping

Object–Relational Mapping (**ORM**) was introduced to bridge the gap between object-oriented programming languages and relational databases. It eliminates the need to write large amounts of SQL by automatically mapping Java objects to database tables. ORM frameworks simplify data access, reduce boilerplate code, and improve developer productivity. It is because of these advantages that ORM tools like *Hibernate* have become widely adopted in enterprise applications for efficient and maintainable data persistence.

Could you list the different frameworks that support ORM?

Several frameworks support ORM and help developers map objects in programming languages to relational database tables. Some of the commonly used ORM frameworks are:

- Hibernate ORM
- **Java Persistence API** (**JPA**) implementations such as EclipseLink
- Apache OpenJPA
- MyBatis (SQL mapping framework with ORM-like capabilities)
- Spring Data JPA

These frameworks simplify database interactions by automatically mapping objects to database tables and managing persistence operations in enterprise applications.

What are the features of ORM? How does ORM help developers?

The following are the different features of ORM:

- ORM helps in fast application development.
- ORM takes away all the crude-level details.
- Makes it easy to map inheritance and collection management.
- It manages the transaction.

Are there any drawbacks to ORM or Hibernate?

Though ORM provides many features for an application developer, it has some drawbacks:

- Development is faster, but the application performance is slower than traditional *JDBC*.
- Debugging of the application becomes difficult.
- *Hibernate* does not allow multiple inserts.
- It is advisable to use pure *JDBC* for batch processing instead of *Hibernate* because its performance is not good in batch processing.
- The learning curve of *Hibernate* is a bit time-consuming.

In what scenarios can ORM be a bad choice? Why?

ORM frameworks such as *Hibernate* ORM may not be suitable in certain scenarios. They can generate inefficient queries for complex or highly optimized SQL operations, making direct SQL a better option. ORM can also introduce unnecessary overhead in very simple applications that perform only basic database operations. Additionally, during large batch processing, ORM may consume more memory due to object state tracking. In such cases, using direct database access can provide better performance and control.

Architecture of Hibernate

The architecture of *Hibernate* ORM describes the internal structure and interaction of its core components that enable Object-Relational Mapping. It includes components such as Configuration, SessionFactory, Session, Transaction, and Query, which work together to manage the persistence of Java objects and handle communication with the relational database efficiently.

The following figure shows the different components of the *Hibernate* framework:

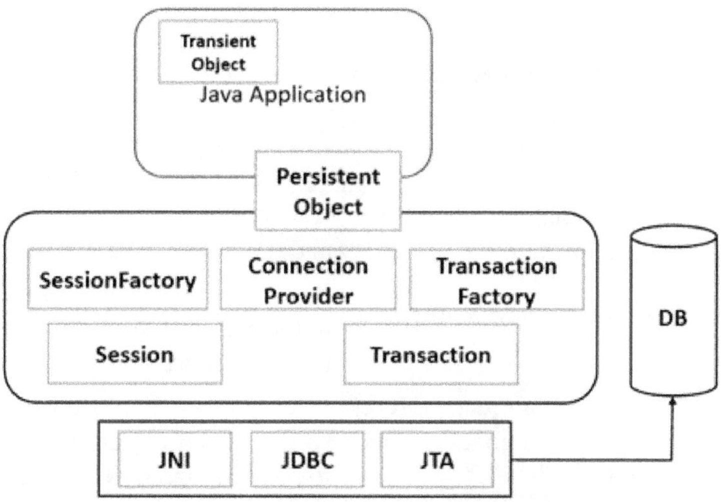

***Figure 13.1**: Architecture of Hibernate*

As shown in *Figure 13.1*, the *Hibernate* framework consists of different components, shown as follows:

- SessionFactory
- Connection Provider
- Transaction Factory
- Session
- Transaction

How do the SessionFactory, Session, Transaction, and Query communicate with each other?

In *Hibernate* ORM, the **`SessionFactory`** is responsible for creating Session objects. A Session represents a connection with the database and is used to perform persistence operations. Within a session, a Transaction is started to ensure that database operations are executed atomically. The Query object is created using the session to retrieve or manipulate data, and its execution occurs within the scope of the active transaction.

What is Hibernate? Are JPA and Hibernate the same?

JPA is a specification that facilitates accessing, managing, and persisting objects to the database. JPA provides an API and does not provide any implementation, so it requires an implementation.

ORM tools like *Hibernate, TopLink*, and *iBatis* provide an implementation of *JPA* specifications for data persistency.

Hibernate and JPA are related to each other, but they have some fundamental differences as follows:

Hibernate	JPA
Hibernate is an ORM tool that is used to save the state of an object into the database.	JPA defines the API for managing the relational data in the Java applications.
It uses a **`SessionFactory`** interface to create **`Session`** instances.	It uses the **`EntityManagerFactory`** interface to interact with the entity manager factory for the persistence unit.
It uses the **Hibernate Query Language** (**HQL**) as an object-oriented query language to perform database operations.	It uses **Java Persistence Query Language** (**JPQL**) as an object-oriented query language to perform database operations.

***Table 13.1**: Differences between Hibernate and JPA*

What are the interfaces or core components you worked with in Hibernate?

The core interfaces of the *Hibernate* framework are:

- **Configuration**: An instance of **Configuration** facilitates the application to specify properties and mapping documents, which can be used to create **SessionFactory**. Usually, in an application, we create a single **Configuration** to build a single instance of **SessionFactory**. By default, a new **Configuration** will be created from the properties, which are specified in the **hibernate.properties** file.
- **SessionFactory**: Usually, an application has a single **SessionFactory** instance, and the threads that are servicing client requests obtain **Session** instances from this factory.

  The internal state of a **SessionFactory** is always immutable. Once an instance is created, this internal state is set, which includes the metadata about Object-Relational Mapping.
- **Session**: The main purpose of the **Session** is to offer means for creating, reading, and deleting operations for instances of mapped entity classes.
- **Query**: The session interface facilitates performing CRUD operations, which are performed on the database using the primary key. The **Query** interface, on the other hand, provides a way to retrieve the rows without using the primary key. The **Query** interface provides methods such as **executeUpdate()**, **list()**, **setMaxResult()**, and **setFirstResult()** to perform operations on the database for processing the data.

  The following code snippet describes how to create and use the **Query** object:

  ```
  1. Query query=session.createQuery("from Employee", Employee.class);
  2. Query q=session.createQuery("select sum(salary) from Employee",
             Employee.class);
  ```
- **Transaction**: Transaction allows the application to define units of work by maintaining abstraction from the underlying transaction implementation, such as *JTA, JDBC*. An instance of transaction is associated with a **Session** and is usually instantiated by invoking **Session.beginTransaction()**.

In how many ways can a class be mapped to table(s)? How does Hibernate map objects to the table?

Hibernate maps a class to the table. We can use two different approaches to do this mapping. Firstly, by configuring it in the **XXX.hbm.xml** file and by using predefined annotations on the

POJO class. The XML-based approach provides external configuration and greater flexibility, while the annotation-based approach keeps the mapping information directly within the source code, making the configuration simpler and easier to maintain. In modern applications, the annotation-based approach is more commonly used.

Which files are needed to maintain the configuration in Hibernate?

Hibernate needs information about how to communicate with the database and how a class is to be mapped to a table in the database. To achieve this, *Hibernate* uses the **hibernate.cfg.xml** file to configure the properties used to communicate with the database. And, the **XXX.hbm.xml** (*Hibernate Bean Mapping*) file helps in mapping a class to the table.

Can we change the name of the hibernate.cfg.xml file?

By default, **hibernate.cfg.xml** from the class path is used to obtain the instance of **Configuration**. However, it is possible to change the location as well as the name of the file.

We can use the following syntax to use another file name:

```
Configuration configuration = new Configuration();
configuration.configure("New_File_Name.cfg.xml");
```

This allows us to explicitly specify a custom *Hibernate* configuration file instead of relying on the default **hibernate.cfg.xml**, giving more flexibility in managing multiple configurations.

How to obtain SessionFactory?

We can obtain **SessionFactory**, as shown in the following code snippet:

```
Configuration configuration = new Configuration();
SessionFactory factory=configuration.configure().buildSessionFactory();
```

The **Configuration** object reads the Hibernate configuration file and loads the necessary settings required to establish the database connection. After processing the configuration details and mapping information, it builds the **SessionFactory** object, which is responsible for creating **Session** instances used to perform database operations.

How many SessionFactory objects are usually created and can be used by a developer in an application?

This question can be reframed as:

- *How many times have you created an instance of SessionFactory?*
- *It is a usual process to create and use a single instance of SessionFactory per database in Hibernate. Can you tell us the reason?*

Usually, in an application, a single database is more than sufficient for persistency. However, in some situations, more than one database is used in the application. **SessionFactory** is a heavyweight object, and creating more than one instance in an application may affect the application's performance, so it is recommended to use one instance per application.

However, *Hibernate* supports configuring more than one database to work with within the same application.

If we intend to configure more than one database within the application, you need to simply add more configuration files, as one configuration file is used to obtain a single instance of **SessionFactory**.

The following code can be used to work with two databases.

The default **hibernate.cfg.xml** for the first database can be used for obtaining an instance of **SessionFactory** as:

```
Configuration configuration = new Configuration();
SessionFactory factory=configuration.configure().buildSessionFactory();
```

The second database can be configured to obtain another **SessionFactory** instance in the same application as:

```
Configuration configuration1 = new Configuration();
SessionFactory factory1=configuration1.configure().
                                        buildSessionFactory();
```

This allows the application to connect to multiple databases by creating separate **SessionFactory** instances for each database configuration. Each **SessionFactory** maintains its own configuration settings, mappings, and database connection details, ensuring that operations performed through one factory do not interfere with the other.

Is SessionFactory a thread-safe object?

Yes, **SessionFactory** is a thread-safe object; many threads cannot access it simultaneously. t is designed to be created **once during application startup** and shared across multiple threads throughout the application. Since creating a **SessionFactory** is an **expensive operation**, it is recommended to reuse the same instance rather than creating it repeatedly.

Is Session a thread-tsafe object?

No, `Session` is not a thread-safe object; many threads can access it simultaneously. In other words, you can share it between threads.

Could you explain the phases of an entity?

The following figure shows the different phases of an entity:

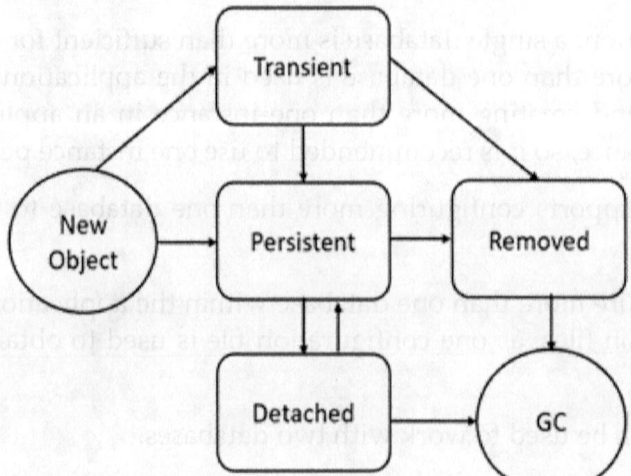

Figure 13.2: Phases of entity

- **New object**: The new object state is achieved by methods like `get()`, `load()`, `uniqueResult`, `iterate()`, and `scroll()`. This newly created object is ready for persistency.
- **Transient state**: The object is in a transient state if it is just created but has no identifier or primary key in a table. It does not associate with a session.
- **Persistent state**: The `Session` object invokes methods like `save()`, `saveOrUpdate()` on a transient object to convert the transient object to persistent object. In the persistent state, an object in the application represents a row in the database within a live session. In this state, it is associated with a unique `Session`. Or, the object is in a persistent state if a session is open, and you just saved the instance in the database or retrieved the instance from the database.
- **Detached state**: In the detached phase, an object in an application is not in live communication with the database. We can achieve this state by invoking the `evict()`, `clear()`, or `close()` method on the persisted object. The object is in a detached state if a session is closed. It is not possible to work with an object in the detached phase. The object comes to the persistent state if we invoke the `lock()` or `update()` method.
- **Removed state**: The entity is pushed into removed state when the `delete()` method is invoked on it. The objects in this state are pushed to the garbage collector.

How to map a class to a table? Could you explain the annotations to map an entity to a row in a table?

Hibernate supports both XML- and annotation-based confirmation to map an entity to the table.

XML-based configuration:

```
<hibernate-mapping>
  <class name = "Employee" table = "EMPLOYEE">
   <id name = "name_of_data_memember_to_consider_as_primary key"
       type = "data_type"  column = "column_name">
    <generator class="generator_class_name"/>
   </id>
   <property name = "property_name" column = "column_name"
             type = "data_type"/>
 </class>
</hibernate-mapping>
```

This XML file defines the mapping between the Java class and the corresponding database table. The **`<class>`** tag specifies the name of the POJO class and the table to which it is mapped. The **`<id>`** tag is used to define the primary key of the table along with the key generation strategy, while the **`<property>`** tag maps the remaining class attributes to the respective table columns.

Annotation-based configuration:

- Annotate the POJO class with **`@Entity.`**
- Annotate the data member with **`@Id`**, which needs to be considered as the primary key in the table.
- Other data members by default become the columns of the table. By default, the name of the data member is considered the name of the column. However, the column name can be changed by annotating the data member with **`@Column`**. The annotation allows customizing properties such as **`length`** and **`constraint`**.

What does the @Id annotation do?

When we annotate the data member with **`@Id`**, that data member value is considered a primary key in the table. It uniquely identifies each record in the database table. The **`@Id`** annotation is usually used along with **`@GeneratedValue`** to automatically generate the primary key value using strategies such as auto-increment or sequence generation.

What does @NaturalId do?

The **`@Id`** annotation is used to denote a data member as a primary key. We can use **`@ID`** along with **`@GeneratedValue`** to create primary keys for records in the database. Sometimes, however, instead of using the primary key as identification, an entity may use another property of itself, which can be treated as a natural ID. If you intend to assign any other property of the entity as a natural ID, then you can annotate it with **`@NaturalId`**.

Can you give any real-time examples of @Id and @ NaturalId?

If you consider the **`Employee`** entity, then **`empId`** will always be treated as a property, which is a primary key, which can be annotated by **`@Id`**. However, **`emailAddress`** connected with **`Employee`** will also be unique, and in some scenarios, the employee can be identified by their email address. Thus, the **`emailAddress`** property can be annotated by **`@NaturalId`**.

Is it possible to stop a data member from being persisted or ignore fields to save in the database?

Yes, it is possible to ignore one or more data members from being persisted in the database. To achieve this, we need to simply add **`@Transient`** to annotate a property or field of an entity class, mapped super class, or embeddable class. **`@Transient`** helps in ignoring field from the process of adding in the database.

What methods are provided by Session object?

The Session interface provides the following methods:

- **save(Object object)**: The method saves the given transient instance.
- **saveOrUpdate(Object object)**: The method enables either save the new instance or update the given instance in the table.
- **update(Object object)**: The method enables updating the persistent instance with the identifier of the given detached instance.
- **delete(Object object)**: This method enables removing a persistent instance from the datastore.
- **get(String entity_name, Serializable id)**: This method returns the persistent instance of the given named entity with the given identifier. It may return **`null`** if there is no such persistent instance.
- **getTransaction()**: This method gets the **`Transaction`** instance associated with the current **`session`**.

- **beginTransaction()**: The method begins a unit of work and returns the associated **`Transaction`** object.
- **createCriteria(String entity_name)**: The method creates a new **`Criteria`** instance for the given entity name.
- **createQuery(String query_to_execute)**: The method creates a new instance of **`Query`** for the specified HQL query string.
- **clear()**: This method clears the session.
- **close()**: This method allows ending the session by releasing the JDBC connection and cleaning up.

How do the persist() and save() methods of the Session interface differ?

The following are the differences between **`persist()`** and **`save()`** methods:

- Both methods enable inserting records into the database. However, the **`return`** type of the **`persist()`** method is **`void`**, while that of the **`save()`** method is a serializable object.
- Both methods convert a transient instance to a persistent instance. However, the **`persist()`** method does not guarantee that the identifier value will be assigned to the persistent instance immediately. It might be performing the assignment of it at the **`flush()`** time.
- Both methods behave differently on the outside of transaction boundaries. The **`persist()`** method guarantees that it will not execute an insert statement if it is invoked outside of transaction boundaries. However, the **`save()`** method does not guarantee the same; it returns an identifier after the insertion. If an insertion has to be executed to get the identifier, the insertion has to happen immediately, no matter whether it is executed inside the transaction or outside the transaction.
- The **`persist()`** method used outside the transaction boundary is useful in long-running conversations with an extended **`Session`** context. In contrast, the **`save()`** method is not good in a long-running conversation with an extended **`Session`** context.

Explain the differences between the save(), saveOrUpdate(), and persist() methods of Hibernate. Which one should we use?

Understanding the behavior and lifecycle implications of these methods is important for choosing the right one in different persistence scenarios:

- The **persist()** method is useful for adding a new entity instance to the persistence context. We usually invoke it when we wish to add a record to the database, that is, when we wish to persist an entity instance. The following code snippet shows how to use this method:

```
Employee emp=new Employee(12,"ABC","Java");
session.persist(emp);
```

  When the **persist()** method is invoked on an already persistent instance, nothing happens. When we try to persist a detached instance, the implementation is bound to throw an exception.

- The basic purpose of **save()** is the same as that of **persist()**. However, this method is guaranteed to return the serializable value of this identifier. The following code snippet shows how to use the **save()** method:

```
Employee emp=new Employee(12,"ABC","Java");
Long id= session.save(emp); //Long is the data type of primary key
```

  When we invoke **save()** on a detached instance, it creates a new persistent instance and assigns it a new identifier. It results in a duplicate record in a database upon committing or flushing.

- The **merge()** method is used to update a persistent entity instance with new field values from a detached entity instance. The **merge()** method finds an entity instance by ID taken from the already passed object and then copies its fields to this new instance. Finally, it returns a newly updated instance. The following code snippet shows how to use the **merge()** method:

```
Employee emp=new Employee(12,"ABC","Java");
session.save(emp);
session.evict(emp);

emp.setName("new name");
Employee emp_new=(Employee)session.merge(emp);
```

- The **update()** method is used to update the data. The method acts on the object passed as an argument. The **update()** method transits the already passed object from the detached to the persistent state. The method throws an exception if you pass a transient entity to it. The following code snippet shows how to use the **update()** method:

```
Employee emp=new Employee(12,"ABC","Java");
session.save(emp);
session.evict(emp);

emp.setName("new name");
session.update(emp);
```

An **Employee** object is first saved to the database using **`save()`**, which makes the object persistent within the session. The **`evict()`** method then removes the object from the session cache, making it detached. After modifying the object's state, the **`update()`** method is used to reattach the detached object to the session so that the changes can be synchronized with the database.

Note: **We did not put the result of the update operation in a separate variable because the update takes place on the Employee object itself. It means that we are reattaching the existing entity instance to the persistence context.**

- The **`saveOrUpdate()`** method is a safer method. This method does not throw an exception when applied to a transient instance. In case we are not sure whether an identifier exists in the table, we can use the **`saveOrUpdate()`** method. It will add a new row to the table if it does not exist.

What will be the output of a given code?

Considering the given code snippet:

```
Employee emp=new Employee(12,"ABC","Java");
emp.setName("new name");
session.update(emp);
```

The **`update()`** method invoked on a transient instance will result in an exception. Thus, when we run the given code, it will not work. This is because the **`update()`** method expects a detached instance that already exists in the database. Since the object is still in the transient state and has never been persisted before, *Hibernate* cannot associate it with any existing record in the database, which leads to an exception in *Hibernate* ORM.

What is the difference between the get() and load() methods?

Both methods are actually used to pull the object. However, they have some differences as well. These differences are discussed in the following table:

load() method	get() method
If an object is not found, it throws `ObjectNotFoundException`.	If an object is not found, the method returns null.
The `load()` method does not hit the database.	The `get()` method always hit the database.
It returns the proxy object.	It returns the real object, not the proxy.
It should be used if you are sure that an instance exists.	It should be used if you are not sure about the existence of an instance.

Table 13.2: Difference between get() and load()

Do you know generator classes? How many generator classes have you worked with? Could you explain the different generator classes in Hibernate?

Every table in a database will have a primary key. Either the key is assigned by the application for that row, or it can be generated by the underlying database. It is used to generate the unique identifier for the objects of the persistent class. The **`<generator>`** element or **`@GeneratedValue`** can be used to generate the primary key.

Which generator class has to be used is dependent on the underlying database. *Hibernate* supports **`assigned`**, **`increment`**, **`sequence`**, **`hilo`**, **`native`**, **`identity`**, **`seqhilo`**, **`uuid`**, **`select`**, **`foreign`**, **`sequence-identity`**.

We can use **`@GeneratedValue(strategy = )`** to generate a primary key according to a strategy.

We can specify strategies as:

- `GenerationType.AUTO`
- `GenerationType.IDENTITY`
- `GenerationType.SEQUENCE`
- `GenerationType.TABLE`

What is the purpose of hibernate.hbm2ddl.auto property?

The property **`hbm2ddl.auto`** property is used to validate and export the schema of DDL to the database when **`SessionFactory`** is created. The possible values of this property are:

- **Create**: Creates a schema
- **Update**: Updates an existing schema

- **Validate**: Validates existing schema
- **Create-drop**: Creates and drops the schema automatically when a session starts and ends

What is the purpose of hibernate.dialect property?

Hibernate takes away the responsibility of writing SQL queries from the developer. Instead of the developer, *Hibernate* generates these queries. However, we cannot overlook different data types and the way queries and procedures are written in SQL. The dialect specifies the type of database used in *Hibernate* to ensure the appropriate generation of the type of SQL statements. When we connect *Hibernate* to an application, it is essential to configure the dialect.

Could you list the different mapping strategies to implement inheritance in Hibernate?

We can map the hierarchical classified classes with the table of the database using one of the three inheritance mapping strategies:

- Table-Per-Class Hierarchy
- Table-Per-Concrete Class
- Table-Per-Subclass

How to map the Table-Per-Class Hierarchy, Table-Per-Concrete Class, and Table-Per-Subclass inheritance strategies in Hibernate ORM?

Let us understand these:

- **Table-Per-Class Hierarchy**: In the *Table-Per-Class* Hierarchy mapping, a single table is required to map the whole hierarchy. We specify an extra column in the configuration (discriminator column), which is added to identify the class. We can specify the discriminator column through XML, or we can also provide an annotation for it, as shown:

    - **By using XML file configuration**:

      ```
      <discriminator column="type" type="string"></discriminator>
      ```

      The `<discriminator>` element specifies the column used to identify different subclasses in an inheritance hierarchy. Based on the value stored in this column, *Hibernate* ORM determines which subclass object should be instantiated.

- **By using annotations**:

```
@DiscriminatorColumn(name="type",
                          discriminatorType=DiscriminatorType.STRING)
@DiscriminatorValue(value="employee")
```

The **`@DiscriminatorColumn`** annotation specifies the column used to identify different subclasses in an inheritance hierarchy, while **`@DiscriminatorValue`** defines the value stored in that column for a particular subclass in *Hibernate* ORM.

- **Table-Per-Concrete Class**: In the case of *Table-Per-Concrete* Class, tables are created as per the class. Though the data is stored as per class definitions, duplicate columns are always added in subclass tables.

  The strategy can be mapped in two ways, shown as follows:

  - **By using the union-subclass element**:

```
<class name="com.Employee" >
    <id name="id">
        <generator class="increment"></generator>
    </id>

    <property name="name"></property>

    <union-subclass name="com.Child_Employee1">
        <property name="salary"></property>
        <property name="projects"></property>
    </union-subclass>

    <union-subclass name="com.Child_Employee2" >
        <property name="wages_per_hour"></property>
        <property name="contract_duration"></property>
    </union-subclass>
</class>
```

This approach maps each subclass to its own table while allowing *Hibernate* to combine the results using SQL UNION queries when fetching the parent class data.

  - **By using the self-created table for each class**:

```
<class name="com.Employee" >
        <id name="id">
```

```
            <generator class="increment"></generator>
        </id>

        <property name="name"></property>
</class>
<class name="com.Child_Employee1">
        <id name="id">
            <generator class="increment"></generator>
        </id>
        <property name="name"></property>
        <property name="salary"></property>
        <property name="projects"></property>
</class>
<class name="com.Child_Employee2" >
        <id name="id">
            <generator class="increment"></generator>
        </id>
        <property name="name"></property>
        <property name="wages_per_hour"></property>
        <property name="contract_duration"></property>
</class>
```

We can also make use of annotations to set up this relationship. To use the annotation-based configuration, specify **`@Inheritance(strategy = InheritanceType.TABLE_PER_CLASS)`**. The annotation denotes the table per concrete class strategy. It should be specified in the parent class only. The **`@AttributeOverrides`** annotation defines that parent class attributes are overridden in this child class. In the table structure, the parent class table columns will be added to the subclass table.

- **Table-Per-Subclass**: In this strategy, tables are created as per the class but are related by a foreign key. In *Table-Per-Subclass,* the subclass-mapped tables related to the parent class mapped table are joined by the primary key–foreign key relationship. This is achieved by using XML-based configuration and by using annotations shown as follows:

    - **By using XML-based configuration**: We need to use the **`<joined-subclass>`** element of the class to map the child class with the parent using the primary key and foreign key relation:

```
<class name="com.Employee" >
        <id name="id">
```

```
            <generator class="increment"></generator>
        </id>

        <property name="name"></property>

    <joined-subclass name="com.Child_Employee1" >
            <key column="empid"></key>
            <property name="salary"></property>
            <property name="projects"></property>
    </joined-subclass>

    <joined-subclass name="com.Child_Employee2">
            <key column="empid"></key>
            <property name="wages_per_hour"></property>
            <property name="contract_duration"></property>
    </joined-subclass>
</class>
```

- **By using annotation-based configuration**: To use the annotation-based configuration, we need to specify **`@Inheritance(strategy=InheritanceType.JOINED)`** in the parent class and the **`@PrimaryKeyJoinColumn`** annotation in the subclasses.

Can you explain the advantages and disadvantages of different inheritance mapping strategies?

The following are the advantages and disadvantages of each of the strategies:

- **Table-Per-Class strategy**:
  - **Advantage**: This strategy offers the best performance even in the deep hierarchy because single selection is sufficient.
  - **Disadvantage**: Whenever there are changes to the members of the hierarchy, it requires the column to be altered, added, or removed from the table.
- **Table-Per-Subclass strategy**:
  - **Advantages**:
    - This strategy does not require complex changes to the database schema when a parent class is modified.
    - It works well with shallow hierarchy.

- **Disadvantages**:
  - With a growing hierarchy, it may result in poor performance.
  - The number of joins required to construct a subclass also grows.

- **Table-Per-Concrete Class strategy**:
  - **Advantage**: It is the easiest method of inheritance mapping to implement.
  - **Disadvantages**:
    - The data belonging to a parent class is scattered and duplicated across a number of subclass tables, which represent the concrete classes.
    - Whenever there are changes to a parent class, they are reflected to large number of tables.
    - It causes a large number of select operations.

What are the different association models available in Hibernate?

The following are the different association models present in *Hibernate*:

- One-to-one
- Many-to-one
- One-to-many
- Many-to-many

Can you explain how to configure the many-to-one association with a relevant example?

The **many-to-one association** represents two-way relationships between entities where one object refers to multiple references of another object, and the other object in turn can contain a single reference to the first object. The typical example of this pattern can be represented by **`Movie`** and **`Review`** entities. **`Movie`** can have multiple **`Reviews`**, whereas each **`Review`** entity can refer to a single **`Movie`**.

The following code snippet shows how to configure the **`Movie`** and **`Review`** classes to represent this association:

`Movie.java`

```
@Entity
public class Movie{
   @Id
```

```java
    @GeneratedValue(strategy = GenerationType.AUTO)
    @Column(name = "id", updatable = false, nullable = false)
    private Long id;

    @OneToMany(mappedBy = "movie")
    private List<Review> reviews = new ArrayList<Review>();
...
}
```

In this class, the **@OneToMany** annotation defines the one-to-many relationship between **Movie** and **Review**. The **mappedBy** attribute indicates that the relationship is managed by the movie field in the **Review** entity, making **Movie** the inverse side of the association.

Review.java:

```java
@Entity
public class Review {
    @Id
    @GeneratedValue(strategy = GenerationType.AUTO)
    @Column(name = "id")
    private Long id;

    @ManyToOne
    @JoinColumn(name = "fk_movie")
    private Movie movie;
...
}
```

In this class, the **@ManyToOne** annotation establishes the many-to-one relationship with the **Movie** entity. The **@JoinColumn** annotation specifies the foreign key column (**fk_movie**) that links each review to its corresponding movie in *Hibernate* ORM.

Note: This question can also be an answer to the question, how do you map collections in Hibernate?

Can you explain many-to-many association, and how to configure that with some real-time examples?

When one entity can refer multiple entities, and in turn the other entity can also refer multiple references of the first entity, such an association is termed a many-to-many association. A real-time example could be **Movie** and **Writer**. **Movie** can have multiple writers, and multiple writers can write multiple movies.

The following code snippet shows how to write configurations for the same:

Movie.java:

```
@Entity
   public class Movie{
    @Id
    @GeneratedValue(strategy = GenerationType.AUTO)
    @Column(name = "id", updatable = false, nullable = false)
    private Long id;
    @ManyToMany
    @JoinTable(
    name = "movie_writer",
    joinColumns = { @JoinColumn(name = "fk_movie") },
    private List<Writer> authors = new ArrayList<Writer>();
...
}
```

In this class, the **@ManyToMany** annotation defines a many-to-many relationship between **Movie** and **Writer**. The **@JoinTable** annotation specifies the intermediate table (**movie_writer**) that stores the foreign keys (**fk_movie** and **fk_writer**) used to associate movies with their writers.

Writer.java:

```
@Entity
public class Writer {
   @Id
   @GeneratedValue(strategy = GenerationType.AUTO)
   @Column(name = "id")
   private Long id;
   @ManyToMany(mappedBy="movie_writer")
   private List<Movie> books = new ArrayList<Movie>();
...
}
```

In this class, the **`@ManyToMany`** annotation with the **`mappedBy`** attribute indicates that the relationship is managed by the authors field in the **`Movie`** entity. This makes the **`Writer`** class the inverse side of the many-to-many association in *Hibernate* ORM.

What is uni-directional and bi-directional mapping?

In *Hibernate* ORM, associations between entities can be defined either as unidirectional or bidirectional, depending on whether the relationship is navigable from one side or from both sides of the entities involved. These mapping can be described as:

- **Uni-directional mapping**: As the name suggests, it is mapping in one direction. When only one of the entities contains a reference to the other, the association is unidirectional. When only one of the entities supports a *has-a* kind of relation, it is a unidirectional mapping. It suggests we can fetch one instance from another, while another instance has no reference to the earlier. Let us consider that **`User`** has an **`Address`**. The **`User`** instance can access **`address`** and update **`address`**. However, the Address object is not aware that it is associated with the **`User`** object, as the **`Address`** model does not maintain any reference to the User model.
- **Bi-directional mapping**: When the association between both entities is mutual, it is known as bi-directional mapping. In other words, when both entities have references to each other, it is termed bi-directional mapping. It means one instance can fetch and update another instance easily. The bi-directional mapping provides navigational access in both directions. Let us consider the same example. **`User`** has an **`Address`**, and now, as we are using the bi-directional mapping, **`Address`** also has **`User`**. Both the **`User`** instance and **`Address`** can access and update each other.

One of the attributes of entity needs to be calculated by some expression. How can you map such an attribute using Hibernate?

To achieve this, we can apply the **`@Formula`** annotation on that attribute. We can use either SQL expression or a normal expression to generate a value, which can be used by *Hibernate* for persistency.

What are lazy and eager fetching strategies in Hibernate ORM?

Lazy and Eager are two types of data loading strategies supported by *Hibernate* in case of associations such as one-to-one, one-to-many, etc.:

- **Eager loading/fetching**: In eager fetching, the data loading happens at the time their parent is fetched. Associations like many-to-one and one-to-one use the eager loading strategy by default. Initial loading of data may take more time, as children also need to be loaded when the parent is loaded. The use of the **`fetch = FetchType.EAGER`** attribute enables eager fetching.

- **Lazy loading/fetching**: In lazy fetching, the data loading happens only when developers explicitly invoke the **`get()`** or **`size()`** method. By default, many-to-many and one-to-many associations use the lazy loading strategy. In this case, the initial loading time is much smaller than eager loading, as children will be loaded only when explicitly asked. To enable lazy fetching, we can use the **`fetch = FetchType.LAZY`** attribute.

What is cascading? What does CASCADE.ALL mean? What are the commonly used cascading options available?

The simplest dictionary meaning of **cascading** is *a process whereby something, typically information or knowledge, is successively passed on.*

In *Hibernate*, an entity has an association with another entity. Thus, when we perform some action on the target entity, that action must be propagated to the other entity that has an association with it. This can be achieved by cascading. Let us consider **`User`** has an address. When one performs an update on **`User`**, whether to update the address or not is decided by the value provided to the cascading attribute.

We have cascading options as follows:

- **ALL**: This means that *all* the operations performed on the container will also be applied to the contained entity.
- **PERSIST**: In this case, when the parent entity is persisted, all its related entities will also be persisted. It means that **`save()`** or **`persist()`** operations are cascaded to related entities.
- **REMOVE**: In this case, if the parent entity is removed, then all its related entities will also be removed.
- **MERGE**: When the parent entity is merged, all its related entities will also be merged.
- **DETACH**: When the parent entity is detached, all its related entities will also be detached.
- **REFRESH**: When the parent entity is refreshed, all its related entities will also be refreshed.

There is no default cascade type in JPA; it means that by default, no operations are cascaded to any particular cascading strategy.

How to map java.util.Date in Hibernate?

When we map **`java.util.Date`**, which is part of our entity in the database, *Hibernate*, by default, stores the same in the nanoseconds format. However, you can change this format to different types, such as:

- **TIMESTAMP**: Persists the data of date and time in nanoseconds.
- **TIME**: Persists data of time in nanoseconds.
- **DATE**: Persists data of only date in years, months, and days.

To use these types, you can use the **`@Temporal`** annotation as **`@Temporal(TemporalType.DATE)`**.

How can you map enum to a database using the Hibernate framework?

To map the **`enum`** attribute to a database, we can use the **`@Enumerated`** annotation. We can provide different values to this **`enum`**, which decides in what way the **`enum`** element is stored in the database. If we use **`@Enumerated(EnumType.ORDINAL)`**, then the index number of the **`enum`** is persisted in the database. However, if we use **`@Enumerated(EnumType.STRING),`** then the string value of **`enum`** is persisted in the database.

What is a transaction? How to manage a transaction in Hibernate?

A **transaction** simply represents a unit of work. It means that if one step fails, the whole unit fails. A transaction can be described by **Atomicity, Consistency, Isolation, and Durability** (**ACID**) properties. In *Hibernate*, the **Transaction** interface defines the unit of work. It has JTA and JDBC as the implementations of the transaction. The transaction is always associated with **`Session`**. The method **`session.beginTransaction()`** enables the start of a new session.

The **`Transaction`** interface has methods as follows:

- begin(): starts a new transaction.
- commit(): ends the unit of work unless FlushMode.NEVER is set up.
- rollback(): forces the transaction to rollback.
- setTimeout(): sets a transaction for a certain timeout for any transaction started by a subsequent invocation to begin on the instance.

Hibernate Query Language

Hibernate Query Language (**HQL**) is very similar to **Structured Query Language** (**SQL**), with one important difference. HQL uses the class name in the query; on the other hand, SQL uses the table name. It means HQL is independent of any database.

What are the advantages of HQL?

Some of the key advantages of HQL are:

- HQL is database-independent.
- HQL always supports polymorphic queries.
- HQL supports object-oriented features like inheritance, polymorphism, and associations as well.
- HQL is easy to learn for a Java programmer.

Could you explain the disadvantages of HQL?

Some of the key disadvantages of HQL are:

- DDL operations cannot be performed by HQL.
- As compared to SQL, the HQL query gives negligible performance degradation because of conversions.
- PL/SQL program cannot be invoked by HQL.

What is caching? Why is caching used?

In *Hibernate*, when more data is fetched from a database, due to the size of the data, the performance of an application is impacted. In case of finding data every time, we need to hit the database. This process takes more time to load the data over the network. Instead of hitting the database every time, it is a good approach to hit temporary local storage. This storage is a buffer memory, which lies between the application and the database, is termed as **cache**. The cache memory stores recently used data to reduce the number of database hits as much as possible.

Could you explain caching in Hibernate?

This question can be reframed as:

- *Can you explain caching architecture in Hibernate?*
- *Explain first-level and second-level caching.*
- *Explain second-level caching.*

The following figure explains the architecture of caching in *Hibernate*:

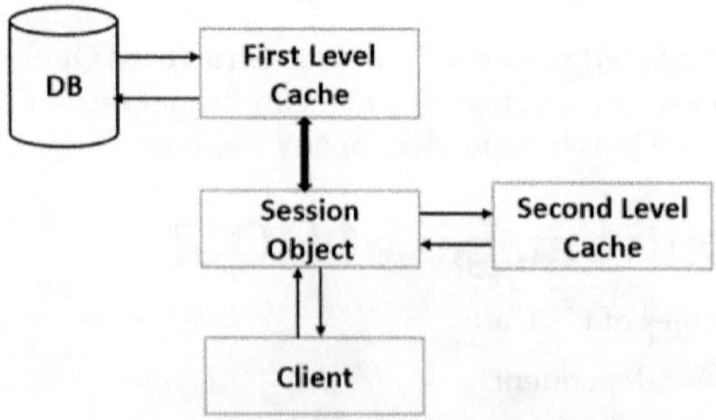

Figure 13.3: Caching architecture

To understand first-level and second-level cache:

- **First-level cache**: Whenever the data is loaded from a database, we are unknowingly using *first-level* cache. The *first-level* cache is nothing but the *Session* cache. It is a mandatory cache through which all requests are passed. The *Session* object keeps an object with itself before committing it to the database. We can use the *first-level* cache to store the data locally or the data that is needed by the *Session*. The *first-level* cache is enabled by default.

- **Second-level cache**: The *first-level* cache is enabled by default. However, the *second-level* cache is optional. The *first-level* cache will always be consulted before any attempt is made by the *second-Level* cache to locate an object. We can configure the second-level cache on a per-class and per-collection basis, which is responsible for caching objects across sessions. The *second-level* cache is maintained at the **`SessionFactory`** level and is available to all sessions.

  The *second-level* cache is disabled by default. *Hibernate* also does not provide any caching implementation for that. *EHCache, OSCache, warmCache,* and *JBossCache* are some third-party caches that can be used with *Hibernate*. To handle cache implementation, we must implement **`org.hibernate.cache.CacheProvider`**.

Could you explain the difference between the first-level and second-level cache, or the first-level cache versus the second-level cache in Hibernate?

Some of the differences between *first-level* and *second-level* cache are as follows:

- The very basic difference is that the *first-level* cache is maintained at the *Session* level, and the *second-level* cache is maintained at the **`SessionFactory`** level.

- The *first-level* cache is accessible only to the `Session` that maintains it. However, the *second-level* cache is accessible to all.
- The *first-level* cache is by default enabled, but the *second-level* cache is by default disabled.

What is the similarity between cache and lazy loading?

Both caching and lazy loading help in improving application performance. However, the mechanism and the concept are very different. Caching is used to store the data either in `Session` or using the *second-level* cache locally. Lazy loading loads the data only when requested. Lazy loading is more of a concern when dealing with a one-to-many association.

What is an immutable class in Hibernate? How to make an immutable class in Hibernate?

In *Hibernate*, classes or objects are by default mutable, which allows the class or collection to add, update, and delete. Whenever this mutability is set to false, the class and its related collection cannot be changed. We can use `@Immutable` to annotate an entity as immutable.

`@Immutable` marks an entity as immutable. We can use it when the lists, maps, or collections rarely mutate. The updates for the class will be ignored, without any exception being thrown. Only the `add` and `delete` operations are allowed on this class.

Immutability specifies the object cannot be mutated, but sometimes, the object needs to be updated in the database. How to change the data of such an object?

We can annotate the class to stop mutation. It means the states tend to be rarely changed. It is because of this that once we make any object immutable, there is no way such an object can be modified at runtime using the *Hibernate* API. In case the change of data has to be made, it can be done manually, via *SQL*, or via an administration application.

Note: **Hibernate cache must be taken into consideration while we talk about mutability. When the reference data changes, arrangements have to be made to make sure that the applications using that data are notified. This is done by the `refresh()` method or by restarting the application.**

What is Automatic Dirty checking in Hibernate?

Hibernate provides **Automatic Dirty checking** as one of its very powerful features. In this concept, the changes made to a persistent object are automatically saved to the database when the session is flushed or the transaction is committed. It enables implicit updates of the object, and the code does not need to invoke an explicit save or update.

What is an inspection strategy in Hibernate?

When an object is loaded from the database, a snapshot of it is kept in memory. Now, when the session is flushed, *Hibernate* compares the stored snapshot with the current state. In case these differ, the object is marked as dirty, and to update the state, a suitable SQL command is enqueued. This strategy of *Hibernate* is termed **inspection strategy**.

What is the use of the @NamedQuery annotation?

In an application, in many scenarios, we need to find a similar query, probably with different parameters. Thus, the developer would always insist on pulling this query from some centralized repository instead of writing it repetitively. The **`@NamedQuery`** annotation is used to declare such types of queries. This annotation takes two parameters: name, which is the identification of the query, and query, which is the actual query that you would like to execute.

Conclusion

In this chapter, we discussed the architecture of *Hibernate* through different interview questions. We talked about how *Hibernate* simplifies the usage of heavyweight JDBC code by providing an automotive persistency mechanism. We also discussed how to implement different strategies of *Hibernate* for association and inheritance. Along with it, we also covered different concepts like the *first-level* and *second-level* cache and what role they play in the persistency mechanism. Most importantly, we discussed most of the questions with answers that could be asked in a *Hibernate* interview.

Building on this foundation, it is equally important to understand how these persistence concepts fit into modern application architectures. In the next chapter, we will explore Spring Boot Microservices, one of the most in-demand topics in Java interviews today, and learn how to design scalable, distributed systems using industry-standard practices.

CHAPTER 14
Microservices Architecture

Introduction

Modern software systems are expected to be scalable, resilient, and capable of evolving rapidly to meet changing business requirements. The traditional monolithic architectures often become difficult to maintain and scale up as applications grow in size and complexity. Now we need to address these challenges, and that is where the software architects began adopting architectural styles that will promote modularity and faster and independent development. The microservices architecture emerged as a practical approach in designing complex enterprise applications. It encourages building applications as a set of loosely coupled services that align closely with business domains. This architectural style has been widely adopted by large technology organizations to support continuous delivery and rapid innovation. As a result, the microservices have become an important topic in modern Java-based enterprise development and technical interviews.

Structure

We will be covering interview questions based on the following topics in this chapter:

- Overview of microservices architecture
- Cloud Config Server
- Inter-service communication
- Discovery Server
- Load Balancers
- Gateway API Server
- Resiliency
- Distributed request tracing

Objectives

The primary objective of this chapter is to prepare job seekers for technical interview questions related to the microservices architecture. It presents a collection of commonly asked interview questions along with clear and concise explanations to help candidates understand the underlying concepts. The chapter aims to strengthen the reader's ability to explain architectural principles, design considerations, and practical aspects of microservices. By studying these questions, readers will gain confidence in discussing microservices-related topics during interviews. This chapter also helps candidates articulate their understanding in a structured and professional manner, which is essential for succeeding in technical discussions.

Overview of microservices architecture

Microservices are a collection of many smaller, independent services designed to perform specific tasks. Each service focuses on a single business capability and can be developed, deployed, and scaled independently. These services can communicate with each other using lightweight protocols such as REST APIs or messaging systems. The microservices architecture improves the flexibility, maintainability, and scalability of the applications. It also allows different teams to work on different services simultaneously, enabling faster development and deployment. The beauty is that each of these services can be developed using different languages and even different databases.

What exactly makes microservices architecture different from monolithic architecture?

Both monolithic and microservices architectures are approaches to designing software applications. In earlier years, developers commonly developed applications after collecting the requirements with the help of the waterfall model approach. This model consists of several sequential stages, such as requirements, design, implementation, testing, deployment, and maintenance.

The developers were developing applications for the customers or clients, but they would have glimpses of it only after the actual development was done. Usually, this process used to take a long time, so there were high chances of changes in the initial requirement, or changes in some business logic, etc. However, by the time the developer team became aware of this, it was often too late. Now, the only way to accommodate this updated requirement would be to go back to the application development step and rewrite the code, followed by all the further processes. Obviously, this would be painful and, more importantly, time-consuming.

Instead, we are now developing applications in smaller chunks. In this way, whenever a piece is ready, we can test and deploy it independently. In the future, if any changes are required, we do not need to change everything; we can only change the concerned service or a piece of code.

Moreover, when a monolithic application fails, everything fails, and then, due to its size, even spinning up a new instance is a time-consuming task. In microservices, we do have smaller services. Thus, when a particular service fails, only the requests made to that specific service will fail. The rest of the services work well. Due to the smaller code, the deployment will not be as difficult, and it will be less time-consuming than monolithic applications.

As microservices have their own responsibility, the codebase is smaller and simpler than that of monolithic applications, where all the required modules and their code are present in a single package.

However, attention must be given to the database layer as well. We all know that one database is not a fit for all the requirements in the enterprise applications. However, we did not have the freedom to choose different databases or to use SQL sometimes and NoSQL other times. Microservices change this entirely. As we do have multiple services, each one of them can use different databases or different types of databases if required.

Do we really need microservices? Why do we need microservices?

Yes, we need them. We need the microservices due to the nature of modern applications and frequent changes in the requirements. We need them to cope with the rapidly changing technologies. The following are multiple reasons to use microservices:

- The applications can now be developed as a collection of smaller services, and as each service is developed, it can be made available to end users independently.
- The testing of these developed units can be performed simultaneously as they are being developed.
- When it comes to deployment, each of the services can be deployed and redeployed independently.
- When there is a requirement to handle the increasing load, some services can be vertically or horizontally scaled.
- Any new piece of the logic can be easily plugged into the application without disturbing the existing ecosystem.
- The best part of microservice architecture is that if any of the services fail, only that specific service and the requests directed to that service are affected. The other services continue to function as they were and are capable of handling the request and generating the response as well.

When do we need a microservices architecture? Why is monolith architecture not sufficient? Could you list the drawbacks of monolith architecture?

We need microservices if:

- We already have an application up and running that needs to be updated for a new requirement altogether. Yes, we can change the existing, but that is a lot of work. It needs changes in the actual codebase; maybe there is a need to change the database as well. Then there is the testing. Instead, we can develop the microservice application separately, test it separately, and then plug it into the existing application, which may or may not be a microservice.
- We want to develop a new big, complex application altogether. It is going to take a long time for development, testing, and then its release. Instead, it is easier to develop the application into smaller parts, test, deploy, and release them independently. This is how microservices architecture helps.
- Few endpoints will be overused, and others will not be used so much. We need such frequently used endpoints to be deployed separately and then horizontally scaled as well.
- The monolith application has a huge amount of code, which makes it difficult to understand; instead, microservices has clear and concise syntaxial code, reducing the cognitive load on the developer.

Is it possible to implement microservices architecture using any programming language?

Microservices is an architectural style. So, it is not a feature that only certain frameworks, platforms, or languages can provide. Many modern frameworks provide tools and libraries that simplify the development of microservices. For example, **Spring Boot** is a popular framework in the Java ecosystem, and **Spring Cloud** extends it by providing features that help in building and managing microservices-based applications. Additionally, Python and Node also support the development of microservices.

Can you tell us about the different components of the microservices?

The following are the key components of microservices architecture:

- **Independent microservices**: The microservices architecture consists of multiple small and independent services. Each service is responsible for performing a specific business function and can be developed, deployed, and maintained independently.

- **Inter-service communication**: Microservices often need to communicate with other services to complete a task or retrieve required data. This communication is usually achieved through REST APIs, messaging systems, or declarative tools such as FeignClient.
- **Horizontal scaling**: Some services may experience higher demand than others. In such cases, multiple instances of those services can be created to distribute the workload, which improves system performance and availability.
- **Discovery Server**: In a microservices environment, the service instances may dynamically scale up or down. A Discovery Server helps services automatically register themselves and enables other services to discover them without hardcoding their locations.
- **Load Balancers**: When multiple instances of a service are available, a Load Balancer distributes incoming requests among them. This ensures efficient utilization of the resources and prevents any single instance from being overloaded. And as we are having more than one instance, it enables us to guarantee high availability.
- **Cloud Config Server**: Microservices require configuration parameters such as database URLs, credentials, and sometimes environment-specific values. A Cloud Config Server centralizes these configurations and allows them to be stored in external repositories, making configuration management easier without duplicating them in each individual service configuration. As the configuration is centrally placed whenever there is a need for a change, we only need to do it at one place and not at the individual service level.
- **Distributed tracing tool**: In a microservices architecture, a single request may pass through multiple services, as each service will be responsible for a dedicated task to perform. The distributed tracing tools, such as **Zipkin** or **Jaeger**, help to track these requests across the services, making it easier to monitor, debug, and analyze system behavior, including potential bottlenecks.

What is Spring Cloud?

Spring Cloud is an extension of the Spring Framework. This extension provides various tools and patterns for building and managing distributed systems such as microservices. The Spring Cloud module allows the development of the Config Management Server, Discovery Servers, and services. It also provides load balancing as well as resiliency mechanisms. It enables microservice developers to focus on business logic by offering pre-built solutions to build enterprise applications that are smaller, manageable, scalable, and resilient. As the services are independent. Whenever required, the services from other platforms or languages can also make requests to one another.

Cloud Config Server

A *Cloud Config Server* is used in the microservices architecture to provide centralized configuration management for all the services. Instead of storing configuration files separately within each microservice, the configurations that are common in multiple services are maintained in a central repository. Each service retrieves its configuration from the config server at runtime. This approach ensures consistency across the services and simplifies configuration updates. It also allows the configuration changes to be applied without re-deploying the microservices. The *Spring Cloud Config* is one such module commonly used to implement this concept.

Why do we need to use Cloud Config Server?

We are talking about an ecosystem that contains various microservices. We are developing these services so that they can be reusable rather than implementing the repeated code for the same business logic. Of course, duplication is not only considered for the code implementation, but it is also considered for the configuration. Consider, we have more than 3 to 4 services communicating with the same database. Obviously, in this case, we need to configure the database communication parameters in each of the services.

There are two complications in this scenario. First, we need to write the same configuration in all of the services, and second, when we intend to reconfigure the database configuration, then such changes need to be made in each of the services. For any reason, if we fail to configure a single service configuration, then the entire ecosystem may not function as expected.

So, we have to properly document everything in the documentation about repeating the configuration for all the services where it is needed. Instead of rewriting it repetitively, it is better to place it in a centralized location from which all the services can refer to it. In this way, we are externalizing the configuration in the repository so that the services can use it.

Inter-service communication

In a microservices architecture, an application is composed of multiple independent services, each responsible for a specific business capability. However, these services rarely operate in isolation. To complete a business operation, they often need to interact with other services. This interaction between different microservices is inter-service communication.

Inter-service communication enables services to exchange data, coordinate actions, and maintain overall system functionality. It can be implemented using different approaches such as synchronous communication (for example, *REST APIs* or *gRPC*) and asynchronous communication (for example, message queues or event streaming). Choosing the right communication mechanism is important to ensure scalability, resilience, and loose coupling between services.

Have you done microservices inter-communication? Why do we use it?

Be honest when answering such questions. You can answer this in *Yes* or *No* based on your working experience with the concept.

In a microservices ecosystem, we develop multiple services that are dedicated to a specific task. As each service has a specific task to complete the entire business logic, the service may need to communicate with other services. This is termed inter-service communication. In this way, we can develop smaller services that are easy to develop, test, deploy, and manage. Most importantly, the service becomes reusable.

Why is inter-service communication so important in microservices architecture?

The whole point of using microservice architecture is to develop an enterprise application or part of it as a swarm of microservices. So that, instead of waiting for all the modules of the application, the developers can keep on releasing smaller modules of it as they get developed. And as per the customer feedback, they can be modified as and when required without disturbing the other services. When the services need similar logic, there is no point in rewriting it in multiple places. By writing the logic in one place, we can save time in development, testing, and maintaining it, and then by communicating the logic to such a service, it can be reused.

What are the different ways of inter-service communication?

There are various ways of synchronous inter-service communication. Let us look into them one by one, starting from the most micromanaged approach and moving towards the declarative way:

- **Using RestTemplate**: **`RestTemplate`** is a legacy, synchronous, blocking HTTP client that is used for inter-service communication. As of now, it is officially in maintenance mode and deprecated. The WebClient is preferred as a non-blocking HTTP client.

  Key benefits of using **`RestTemplate`** are:

  - **`RestTemplate`** is a synchronous way of communication between the services. It means when the developers use the RestTemplate to invoke the downstream service, the upstream invoking service waits until it receives the response. Obviously, this has an impact on the performance.
  - It is a simple, straightforward templated style for invoking the APIs.
  - It also offers a flexible way for custom HTTP request and response configurations, which provides a robust exception handling approach.

- **Using WebClient**: **`RestTemplate`** was a legacy approach for inter-service communications. Nowadays, **`WebClient`** is the modern, recommended approach for inter-service communication. It has a non-blocking, reactive nature, which provides higher scalability and performance as compared to the **`RestTemplate`**. Additionally, it supports both synchronous and asynchronous operations.

Key benefits of using **`WebClient`** are:

- **`WebClient`** utilizes Mono and Flux reactive types provided by the reactive streams. This allows the services to handle concurrent requests efficiently, as it does not block the requests while waiting for a response.
- It is built for asynchronous communications, which is very crucial in microservice architectures, considering the performance and resiliency.

- **Using FeignClient**: **`FeignClient`**, provided by OpenFeign, is a declarative HTTP client that simplifies inter-service communication. Usually, while using the **`WebClient`** or **`RestTemplate`** for communication, we need to write a lot of boilerplate code. So, instead of writing such a repetitive boilerplate code to build HTTP requests, we can use **`FeignClient`** as a declarative approach where the proxy implementation will be provided by the framework at runtime.

  Key benefits of using **`FeignClient`** are:

  - **`FeignClient`** reduces the need to write the code for HTTP communication as compared to **`RestTemplate`** or **`WebClient`**.
  - This is a cleaner, easier, and more maintainable way, as it has a declarative and interface-based approach.
  - The **`FeignClient`** allows seamless integration with Discovery Services and Load Balancers so as to dynamically locate and distribute the requests across all the available service instances.
  - The **`FeignClient`** works well when it comes to resiliency to handle downstream service failures gracefully.

Could you elaborate on the workings of FeignClient?

As we know in a microservices ecosystem, we have many smaller, independent, reusable services dedicated to performing a certain task. To respond to a request, a service may need data or logic that may not be its responsibility. Here, the service makes API calls to other services. Such API calls can be done by using legacy **`RestTemplate`**, modern **`WebClient`**, or declarative **`FeignClient`** as a client.

The earlier two allow developers to micro-manage the way the call is going to proceed. However, it is just a process of making an HTTP request to another endpoint. The aspects that are going to change are the endpoint, the HTTP methods supported by endpoints, the inputs, and the expected output. However, the process will remain the same even if each one of these parameters changes. The whole responsibility of a developer is to focus on logic building instead of managing the calls and generating the response. This is where **FeignClient** plays a crucial role.

FeignClient allows developers to make API calls to the downstream services without writing any piece of communication call as well as the response. The developer just needs to declaratively specify in the interface where to make the call, what the inputs are, and what the response is going to be. The rest will be handled by the framework at runtime.

Using **FeignClient** not only saves the developer's time but is also a cleaner approach as it takes away repetitive boilerplate code and enables the developer to focus on building the logic.

Can you explain the implementation of FeignClient using some code snippet?

Let us take an example where the upstream service intends to make a call to the downstream service, which is exposing a *GET* endpoint at **/values/{category}**. The endpoint accepts the name of a category as an input path variable and returns the list of products from the specified category. The following will be the *FeignClient* code, which allows us to initiate the communication with the downstream endpoint:

```
@FeignClient(name="demo-downstream-service")
public interface Demo_Feign_Client {
    @GetMapping("/values/{category}")
     ResponseEntity<Prduct> searchProductByCategory(@
PathVariable("category")String
category);
}
```

Now, instead of writing any code, we simply have to auto-wire this interface and make the call to its method to initiate the downStream API call. As we have declared the method signature in the interface and not implemented it, it is a totally declarative approach. At runtime, the framework will provide the communication code by reading the interface declaration with the help of a proxy implementation. In this way, the developer will get the response from the downstream service without getting involved in the communication process directly. And all the developer has to do is use the response to perform business logic.

Can we declare more than one method in the interface used as FeignClient?

The **FeignClient** is all about defining an interface that has the contract to communicate with the downstream endpoint and receive the response. As the interface does not impose any restriction on the number of method declarations, we can declare as many methods as we wish. The declaration of the method will comprise the information about the endpoint to invoke, which is exposed on a certain HTTP method, the input values for the endpoint, and the response from it. The `@FeignClient` annotation has the name or URL attribute, which provides the information for identifying the downstream service or instances of the downstream service.

Can we use the same FeignClient to communicate with more than one service?

No, we cannot communicate with more than one service from the same `FeignClient`.

The definition of `FeignClient` has an interface annotated with the `@FeignClient` annotation. It has various attributes; typically, `name` and `url`. These attributes provide the information on the whereabouts of the downstream service. Here we are dealing with a single service that may have multiple instances. When the downstream service has been horizontally scaled and has multiple instances. In this scenario, the `name` attribute provides a way to discover all the instances of the downstream with the help of the Discovery Server. Then the internal Load Balancer comes into play to choose one of the available instances of the downstream service.

As for each `FeignClient`, we can specify only one URL or a single name of the service attributes. It is not possible to use it to communicate with more than one downstream service. However, in the application, we can have more than one FeignClient definition, allowing developers to communicate with more than one downstream service.

Discovery Server

In a microservices architecture, for high availability, services are often deployed dynamically and may run on different machines or containers. Since their network locations (IP address and port) can change frequently, as the instances may be scaled up or scaled down. In these circumstances, it becomes difficult for services to locate and communicate with each other directly.

A Discovery Server solves the problem by acting as a central registry where all microservice instances register themselves when they come up. Other services can then query the Discovery Server to find the location of the required service instance. This enables dynamic service discovery, reduces hard-coded dependencies, and improves the scalability and flexibility of the entire system.

The common tools used for implementing a Discovery Server include *Netflix Eureka, Consul,* and *Apache Zookeeper*.

Have you heard of Naming Server, Eureka Server, or Discovery Server?

Yes, we have used the *Naming Server* in our code. The *Naming Server, Eureka Server,* and *Discovery Server* are all the same. It acts as a dynamic approach that manages the map, having all available instances of the services in the ecosystem and their current locations. We can consider this as a simple phone directory that comprises the name of people and their phone numbers. The difference here is that for one service, we can have multiple URLs, as each URL represents the path where the instance of a service is deployed.

In short, the *Naming Server* allows us to keep track of available instances and indirectly eases the use of horizontal scaling without worrying about their discovery.

Why do we need Discovery Server?

In a normal scenario, we will have some of the services that can cope even if the request load on them increases, but as the scenario gets complex, we might need to use multiple services. Some of these services may need to handle more request load than others. It means we may need to go with horizontal scaling for such services.

Now, consider a situation where one upstream service intends to make a call to another service that has more than one instance deployed. There is a possibility of getting up more instances or taking down some of them if not required. Sometimes, even the instances may not be working and need to be redeployed. So, when we write the code for communication and rely on the hard-coded value for URL, it will be very likely to fail for all the obvious reasons of reallocation of the instances. Obviously, we need a system to keep track of all the *UP* and *DOWN* instances associated with a service dynamically. This is where *Naming Service* plays a crucial role. It keeps track of all the instances with the name of a service.

When one service intends to communicate with another service, instead of directly using its URL, it talks to the *Naming Server*, which takes the name of the service for the lookup and then returns all the available instance lists matching the service name. Now, the internal Load Balancer comes into play to choose one of the available instances. And this chosen instance is where the client service communicates.

Load Balancer

A Load Balancer is an important component in microservice architecture that distributes incoming client requests across multiple instances of a service. This distribution helps prevent any single instance from becoming overloaded and ensures better system performance. By routing traffic to healthy service instances, a Load Balancer also improves fault tolerance and high availability. Unlike the monolithic applications, the load balancing is implemented at the client side. The tools such as Spring Cloud Load Balancer and NGINX are commonly used to implement load balancing in microservices.

Can you explain how load balancing is achieved in the microservices architecture?

Load balancing always comes into play when we have more than one instance of a service. When the request is received for such a multi-instance service, the Load Balancer helps in choosing the instance to handle the request.

When we include the Load Balancer dependency in the application, it provides a Load Balancer within the application. This Load Balancer uses round robin as a default strategy to choose an instance from the available list of service instances.

In monolithic applications, the client requests an API from the service, which has multiple instances. Once the request is received at the server side, the server-side Load Balancer comes into action and forwards the request to one of the healthy available instances. Totally opposite to the monolith, in microservices, the Load Balancer is on the client side. In microservices architecture, the client Load Balancer provides an instance to which the request will be made by RestTemplate, WebClient, or using the **FeignClient**.

What strategies are used for selecting a service instance in a microservices environment? What is the default strategy, and can it be customized?

The *Round Robin* is a default strategy provided by the Round Robin Load Balancer to choose the instance. However, we can switch to a different strategy by implementing a custom Load Balancer.

We have *Weighted Load balancing, Zone Based Load balancing, Instance Health Check* for Load Balancer, and some instance-preferred request-based sticky session for Load Balancer.

We have two ways that help to choose from the available strategies. One approach is to configure the strategy by setting the property in the configuration file. Another approach is to provide our own **ServiceInstanceListSupplier** bean.

We can use the following configuration to provide this bean as shown by the code:

```
@Configuration
public class CustomZonePreferredLoadBalancerConfiguration {
    @Bean
    public ServiceInstanceListSupplier instanceListSupplier(
            ConfigurableApplicationContext context) {
        return ServiceInstanceListSupplier.builder()
                    .withDiscoveryClient()
```

```
                    .withCaching()
                    .withZonePreference()
                    .build(context);
    }
}
```

Similarly, we can provide the beans for other strategies, and instead of using round robin as the default way, these beans will be used for the customization of the strategy.

Gateway API Server

A Gateway API Server, simply referred to as a service, acts as a server, which is a single, centralized entry point for all client requests to the application in a microservices architecture. The API Server operates between the client applications and the actual backend services. The primary purpose of the Gateway API Server is to decouple the clients from the underlying system. It also handles common tasks that all the services need instead of repeating them in each individual service.

Why is the Gateway API Server used? What are the core functions of the Gateway API Server?

The main purpose of the Gateway API Server is to help the services avoid repeating the same task implementation in every service. Sometimes multiple microservices intend to perform the same task, which may not be business logic or a core concern. However, it is a cross-cutting concern. The Gateway API helps in taking out such repetitive cross-cutting tasks from all the services and places them in a single service. Then it executes such a task depending upon the configuration.

The Gateway API Server manages the following functionalities as well:

- **Routing the requests**: The Gateway API Server inspects the incoming request and then routes it to the appropriate downstream service. We can configure the routing configuration via taking the declarative approach in the configuration file or programmatically.
- **Pre or post-processing of the requests and responses**: The Gateway API provides a centralized location where the preprocessing of the incoming request can be achieved by performing encryption, decryption, adding headers, or other data to it. Similarly, after receiving the response, some post-processing, updating the headers or data. This is known as *pre* or *post*-processing of the requests.
- **Security by adding authentication or authorization**: We can add security policies, rules, permissions to access certain resources, and ways of verifying the clients via tokens, API keys, etc.

- **Response aggregation**: As we know, many times one upstream service needs to communicate with one or many downstream services to perform a task or to obtain data from them. Now, when we consider the inter-service communication, it is one service communicating to another, as without this communication, the response cannot be generated. In Gateway Server, the situation is a bit different. Here, data or logic to perform the task is not a requirement, but the data from multiple services needs to be formatted or aggregated before sending it to the client.
- **Limiting the requests:** The service may not be able to handle the request when it receives more requests than normal. The Gateway API Server limits the requests a client can make within a specified time to the downstream service and protects the service from being over-requested or encountering any malicious attack.
- **Monitoring the services:** It can have a mechanism to collect the logs and metrics to understand and analyze the performance and other insights about the services.

Resiliency

Resiliency is the ability to anticipate, withstand, adapt, and then quickly recover from a failing situation. A service can fail due to multiple reasons, the outages, cyberattacks, or high traffic are some of them. The resiliency enables the system to continue with minimal impact on users and provides maximum availability. In a microservices architecture, resiliency is achieved by implementing patterns such as circuit breakers, retries, timeouts, and fallbacks. These mechanisms prevent cascading failures and ensure that a problem in one service does not bring down the entire system.

How are microservices useful in handling the increasing load? How to handle massive, unpredictable traffic using concepts like high availability and fault tolerance?

Now there are two possibilities for how the interaction with the interviewer will start. If you are a fresher, the interviewer may start with some simple questions to know your level of understanding about the conceptual knowledge of scaling, and then, one by one, the interviewer will move to more complex questions if required. However, if you are an experienced developer, then they might want to understand how the scaling is implemented in the code. Let us explore this one by one, as we really do not know how the interview will shape up.

Scaling means adding more resources or adding more instances. The services are meant to handle the request and generate the response. On a normal day, the service can handle the usual request load, but when the load increases, the service may not be able to achieve this. Also, sometimes the service needs more resources, such as computing resources, CPU, to execute certain tasks. If such resources are not available, then either the performance will be hampered or, in the worst case, the service will fail to respond and will become unhealthy. As we are developing microservices for high availability, the scaling helps to enhance availability, performance, and handle increasing load. The scaling can be either horizontal or vertical depending on different requirements.

What is vertical scaling?

Consider that on normal days, the service is able to handle X requests. However, on other days when the load becomes 2X, it is really difficult to handle it. So, to handle the increasing load, the easiest way is to make more resources available to it. It is also known as scaling up. The scaling up is increasing the power of a single system or the server by adding more resources such as RAM, CPU, and storage to handle more load. The vertical scaling makes the system stronger for the same application by adding more resources, such as increasing the hardware capacity. We need to know well in advance, before application deployment, about how many resources to allocate, as often the upgrades require downtime.

We need to understand that resource allocation includes analyzing the performance and resource needs of the service under minimal and maximum load. We also have to consider service interdependencies and their communication patterns. Then, by balancing cost optimization with performance, we can calculate the initial hardware requirement to ensure that we do not allocate resources unnecessarily.

What are the drawbacks of vertical scaling?

The following are some of the drawbacks of vertical scaling:

- It is difficult to know exactly how many resources are required, as the load that the service is going to handle is uncertain.
- When it needs to update the resources by adding more hardware, the application will face downtime.
- It is not cost-effective to handle the increasing load. The system cannot keep on adding resources every now and then.
- Having a single system where service is deployed leads to a single point of failure, and we may not be able to stand by the promise of high availability.
- There is always a limitation on how much CPU, storage, and RAM can be physically added.

What is horizontal scaling?

The horizontal scaling, or scaling out, is to add more systems where the service instances are deployed. So, when there is a high load, the incoming requests can be distributed between the available resources. As the load is going to be distributed, the performance will improve, and more requests can be handled efficiently without leaving everything to a single system. One system can fail; however, when we have similar instances deployed on some other systems as well, we have a better fault-tolerance system. One thing we need to keep in mind is to have a Load Balancer to distribute the load.

What are the advantages of horizontal scaling?

The following are some of the key advantages of horizontal scaling:

- **High availability**: As we have more than one instance, even though one system fails, others will continue to serve. This enables better fault tolerance and high availability.
- **Cost-effective**: As we are having microservices, we need smaller, much cheaper systems. So even in the case of scaling out, it will be cheaper.
- **Performance**: As we have more instances, more load can be handled efficiently by distributing the incoming requests among all available instances.

How is the horizontal scaling achieved?

For any service, we can achieve horizontal scaling either manually or by using a tool like **Docker** or **Kubernetes (k8s)**. Once the instances are up and ready to take requests, whenever a request is received, the Load Balancer will choose one of the instances. Then, either by using one of the clients, such as the `WebClient`, `RestTemplate`, or `FeignClient`, the request can be made to this chosen instance.

Whenever scaling up or down happens, the registration and de-registration of the instances with the Discovery Server are done dynamically. This helps in effectively managing the needs of instances with cost efficiency.

What is the role of Kubernetes in horizontal scaling?

Any developer can launch any number of instances in the development or testing phase. How do we achieve the same in the production phase? It is not practically feasible to launch new instances or take down available ones as and when required manually. The reason is simple: we do not have just one or two services. We are dealing with multiple microservices and their multiple instances. The best way to dynamically handle it, depending upon the requirement or condition, is with the help of K8S, i.e., **Kubernetes**. In the **Kubernetes** configuration file, we can specify how many minimum instances are required all the time. Also, we can mention the conditions for launching new instances.

Have you heard of Fail-safe and Fail-fast? What does resiliency mean? Why do we need resiliency? What are the patterns of resiliency?

The microservices promise high availability. However, due to a number of reasons, the service may fail to respond. Let us take into consideration a situation. We have a service that is requesting another downstream service. The upstream service is healthy and up and running. However, the requested downstream service is taking more time to respond or is totally unavailable to respond to the request. Obviously, it will impact how the upstream service responds to the client. It is because of this that the client's requests for such services also face the same impact. Now, the upstream service is failing to respond because of the downstream service. Here, the resiliency mechanism helps the upstream service to recover by providing a partial or alternative response rather than just failing.

There are various patterns supporting resiliency:

- **Circuit breaker**: The Circuit breaker prevents the service from calling the failing service repeatedly. This is also known as a failing fast to avoid cascading failures. If there is proper communication between both the calling and called services, we term it as a *Closed* circuit. When this communication cannot be established, it is an open circuit. When the circuit is in the *Open* state, and the failure rate exceeds a threshold value, it attempts test calls periodically to check if the called service has recovered and is ready to accept the requests before sending the request to the downstream service
- **Retry**: One way is to try to communicate with the service, and if the communication fails, just give up further attempts to communicate with that service. However, it may be possible that initially the service was unavailable when it was invoked, but now it is available to take up the calls. So instead of backing off, the calling service can reattempt the requests. The developers can decide how many times to do re-attempts and what the waiting period between the next re-attempt will be.
- **Fallback**: When the service requests are failing or if the circuit is in the *Open* state, instead of just failing, an alternative method can be invoked implicitly to handle the situation. This alternative method is known as a *fallback* method, and it is executed in order to provide a default response or an alternate response to handle the failure gracefully. The response can be a partial response as the data or response from the called service is unavailable.
- **Bulkhead**: The bulkhead isolates the service calls to an external service by separating them into separate, limited resource pools. So that in the event of failure, one will not exhaust the resources for the entire service.
- **Time limiter**: Sometimes, in inter-service communication, the failure is not because the downstream service is unavailable. It is due to the time taken by it to execute the request. The time limiter enforces a maximum duration for the request call. When the

called service exceeds the threshold value, it will be aborted and prevent long-running requests from occupying up the resources for an indefinite time.

- **Rate limiter**: Sometimes the service gets more traffic, and then it will fail to serve the requests, and in the worst case, it becomes unhealthy to respond at all. The rate limiter controls the rate at which requests are allowed to a service. This prevents excessive traffic and protects the service from getting overloaded.

Distributed request tracing

In a microservices architecture, a single client request often travels through multiple services before producing a final response. The request tracing is a technique used to track and monitor the path of that request as it flows across different microservices. It helps developers to understand how services interact with each other and identify performance bottlenecks or failures in the system. We use the Spring **Cloud Sleuth** library to trace the requests. It automatically generates *TraceId-per-request* and attaches *SpanID-per-operation*. Using these unique trace identifiers, all related service calls can be correlated and analyzed. This improves observability, simplifies debugging, and helps maintain the reliability of distributed systems.

What is the need for request tracing?

In microservices architecture, when the request is fulfilled by a single service, tracing the request to understand execution time and tracking all the intermediate steps taken by it becomes easier. However, in a more complex situation, one request cannot be handled from the business logic perspective by a single service. Under such scenarios, more than one service endpoint needs to be executed one after the other or sometimes in parallel. In simple words, one request will span across multiple services, which might be deployed at a different location than that of the invoking service.

Here, just by observing the logs, we cannot determine which service is responsible for the bottleneck, which service is responsible for the latency issues, or which service is failing, or the reasons for its failure. We need a dedicated system that, irrespective of the span of services, can find individual execution time, performance, and failures. This is termed request tracing.

Zipkin and **Jaeger are the tools that enable tracing the request** spans across the services by adding a specific ID to each one of them. It has a simple UI to observe individual service requests, execution time, or other things, such as resiliency in case of failures.

Why can we not directly use a simple logging mechanism to trace our request?

In microservices architecture, each service can implement its own way to log the requests. However, these logs are for individual services, and under normal situations, the log files will be available on each of the servers. We can log messages to a single file instead of managing multiple files. When multiple services write the messages to the same file, there is a possibility of mixing the lines, or partial logs will be written in the file. The request handling will be slower, which increases the latency, resulting in a bottleneck in the logging. There is a high possibility of having multiple logs from the same service, as it may face some challenges in acting smoothly. Unless we have a set mechanism to know which service has written which message, the tracing for some specific service log will be quite challenging.

For all these reasons, instead of using a simple logging mechanism as that of a monolithic application for request tracing or debugging a request, we need a separate tracing mechanism in place. That is why we use **Spring Cloud Sleuth** instead of the **ELK** stack.

How is the database handling different in microservice architecture as compared to monolith? What are different patterns to use in database handling?

In monolithic applications, we have one single application performing all the functionalities to provide the required business logic as well as a single database integration for the persistency. This database has the most complex design with all the required data normalization. However, this database consists of lots of tables with *one-to-one* or *one-to-many, uni-directional* or *bi-directional* relations for normalization. When any failure occurs in the database server that impacts all the users, it is a single point of failure. Due to the amount of data, even the recovery is slow. When the data request is made to perform a fetch operation, due to the number of records, the performance will be impacted.

In contrast, the microservice architecture uses different database servers for the same database. Instead of going with *one-to-many* or *many-to-many* relations, we go with a simple individual table having a way to relate the data in different ways. Here, we can also use more than one database altogether. As the data is distributed to various servers, even if any of the servers fail, it will not impact 100% of users. The recovery and the fetch operations are also faster due to the amount of data. We have multiple design patterns to use the database in the microservice architecture.

Can you list different ways of using a database in a microservice architecture?

As we have multiple services, we can use more than one database of SQL or NoSQL type. We have multiple patterns to handle the database as per the requirements. Here are the patterns that help us in database integration in the service:

- Database-per-service
- Shared database

- Saga
- Command side replica
- API composition
- CQRS
- Event sourcing
- Domain event

Why have we heard a lot about DevOps inclusion in microservices architecture? Why do we use Docker or K8s in microservices architecture so frequently compared to a monolith?

In a monolithic application, we have a single application that has all the required functionalities. Thus, when it comes to deploying the application, we will just need to deal with one application. However, in microservices architecture, we have more than one application for deployment. We also may need to deploy them in more than one instance, depending upon the traffic load on each one of them. Along with the services performing the business logic, we also have more than one instance of Config Server, Discovery Server, and *Gateway API* services. Manually handling all these service instances for their high availability is very complex and time-consuming.

Instead, we can use tools such as **Docker** and **Kubernetes(K8s)** to configure how many service instances we need. Even if some of the instances failed, started feeling unhealthy or unresponsive for any reason, the tool will launch new instances on its own and ensure that the configured number of instances is always available for use. Even the configuration can launch new instances dynamically depending upon the condition we have configured. The tool enables configuring the number of instances, updating the instances with a newer version, and strategies to upgrade the application to a newer version with less or no human interference.

Microservices architecture promises to provide high availability. How is this high availability achieved in the microservices environment?

The microservices are light in code and easy to deploy. They promise high availability. However, when the service is running only on a single server, there is a chance of failure. This chance may be around 0.0001%, but still, there is a chance of failure. It might not always be due to the code, but the environmental parameters also play a role in such failures. So, in reality, achieving 100% availability is a myth. We can avoid the failure situation by taking some measures. It is always good to start by understanding how much traffic load the service is going to handle at peak. This information is useful to determine the hardware requirements for where the service is going to be deployed. This also lays the foundation for implementing horizontal scaling. The horizontal scaling provides more than one instance of the same service available to serve the client's request. Even if one of the instances is down, we will have an alternate instance that can be chosen by the Load Balancer to serve the client's request. We will make sure these instances of the application run on multiple servers that are physically separated from each other. Now, as the instances are from different regions, it is highly unlikely that all of them will fail at the same time.

Now, instead of managing this complex ecosystem manually, the developers usually use tools such as Docker and **K8S** to manage the instances.

Conclusion

This chapter provided an overview of microservice architecture and the key components commonly discussed in technical interviews. We explored concepts such as centralized configuration using Cloud Config Server, inter-service communication using RestTemplate and Feign Client, service discovery using Discovery Server, and mechanisms for maintaining high availability. The chapter also covered essential infrastructure elements like Load Balancers, API Gateway, resiliency patterns, and distributed request tracing, which help to build scalable and reliable distributed systems. Understanding these concepts not only helps in answering interview questions confidently but also provides a strong foundation for designing modern enterprise applications.

With this chapter, you now have a comprehensive overview of important Java and microservice topics typically expected in interviews. Best wishes for your journey towards successfully cracking Java developer interviews.

Index

C

D

T

U

www.ingramcontent.com/pod-product-compliance
Lightning Source LLC
Chambersburg PA
CBHW061352240926
51846CB00007B/1382
* 9 7 8 8 1 6 7 0 8 0 9 2 9 *